The New Garden Apartment

Current Market Realities of an American Housing Form

Carl F. Horowitz

Printed in the United States of America

Published by the Center for Urban Policy Research
Building 4051, Kilmer Campus
New Brunswick, New Jersey 08903

Library of Congress Cataloging in Publication Data

Horowitz, Carl F.
The new garden apartment.

Bibliography: p.
Includes index.
1. Garden apartments—United States. 2. Rental housing—United States. I. Rutgers University. Center for Urban Policy Research. II. Title.
HD7287.6.U5H67 1983 333.33'8 83-7364
ISBN 0-88285-093-8

To My Parents

CONTENTS

LIST OF EXHIBITS

Acknowledgments

This book would not have been possible without the generous assistance of many current and past associates. A large measure of credit must go to Dr. Robert Burchell of the Center for Urban Policy Research. He initially suggested the topic of garden apartments as being ripe for research, and devoted considerable time and effort in guiding the work toward valid results and lucid interpretations. I must also gratefully acknowledge the role of Dr. George Sternlieb, Director of the Center, who provided both intellectual patience and financial support that enabled the work to be completed. The helpful comments of Dr. David Listokin and Dr. Patrick Beaton, also of the Center, steered the author away from potential pitfalls. William Dolphin must be cited for his effort, skill, and, above all, good humor in conducting the computer programming. Deborah Brenner assisted with the keypunching. James Nemeth, Melinda Artman, Michael Pawlik, Mark Solof, and Steven Barker each contributed to the time-consuming telephone callbacks to residents.

The efforts of persons outside the Center cannot go unnoticed. Samuel Herzog, President, Village Associates, a prominent building firm in New Jersey, provided wry and valuable insight into the current state-of-the-art of garden apartment development. Betty Treadwell, Executive Secretary, Transaction Publishers and Linda Ryan, Virginia Polytechnic Institute, College of Architecture and Urban Studies, skillfully typed much of the final manuscript, despite considerable time constraints. Mary E. Curtis assisted with the proofreading of the initial draft.

Finally, I wish to express deep gratitude toward my father, Irving Louis

Horowitz, who rendered financial and emotional support in seeing the project (and myself) through to its completion. The time-tested phrase "he was there when it counted" would be an underestimation of his role.

Any errors of omission or commission, of course, are the responsibility of the author. Writing this work was itself an experience. Yet the final product will hopefully be judged not by the sheer amount of labor, but by its usefulness to others.

Introduction

There was a time in America's not-too-distant past when "apartments" were considered by many to be virtually interchangeable with "tenements," bearing with them connotations of noise, dirt, overcrowding, and other assorted ills. The scabrous condition of much of the existing apartment stock in large cities played no small part in engendering this view.[1] County and local governments in outlying, developable areas viewed apartments as uncomfortably close to a world documented by Jacob Riis, Lawrence Veiller, and other early housing reformers. They gradually recognized the potential leverage of the zoning ordinance in barring their construction—and usually found ample support in the courts.[2]

By mid-20th century, however, this attitude lay out of step with reality. Technological innovations (both in the homebuilding process and the housing it created) and rising real incomes had made a profound impact on the design of the low-rise apartment as they had done on the design of other forms of housing. The garden apartment was a principal manifestation. Originating in the 1920s, garden apartments—low-rise rental multifamily dwellings in complexes with a substantial degree of open space—had become by the beginning of the 1960s familiar sights on the suburban landscape. Today, they are the bulwark of American rental housing production. Only 0.9 percent of the nation's total housing stock in 1960 consisted of garden apartments. By 1978, the figure had risen to 7.1 percent. The respective proportions of the rental stock for these years were 2.5 and 21.0 percent. Still more extraordinary is the fact that by 1978 (excluding mobile home shipments), 48.8 percent of all existing rental units built since 1960 were of this type.[3]

In numerous ways, the garden apartment represents a break with prior methods of housing production.[4] Yet like other forms of rental dwellings, it has housed a largely young, married adult population (i.e. "marrieds") whose intent is more frequently than not to become homeowners in the near future. Developers and other proponents of expanded multifamily rental production have often rested their case upon the need for garden apartments to house the upwardly mobile. These apartments must be available as a pleasant, habitable conduit or "way station" to homeownership.

The central purpose of this book is to investigate the likelihood, extent, and implications of the pivotal shift in garden apartment tenant composition during 1970–80: fewer nuclear families (with and without children) and more "nontraditional" households (singles, single mothers, empty nesters, and the elderly). Published Annual Housing Survey data suggest the magnitude of potential change. During 1970–80, married couples headed by an adult under 35 (the traditional core of garden apartment demand), as a proportion of all renters, declined from 26.4 to 19.0 percent. By contrast, this demographic bracket, as a proportion of all homeowners, increased from 15.0 to 16.3 percent.[5] As a proportion of all American households, these combined figures signify a loss. Therefore, the young nuclear family's declining share of the population, together with its apparently continued ability to afford homes,[6] have left a vacuum in the demand for rental housing readily filled by other types of households. A corollary issue is the extent to which garden apartment complexes opened for occupancy after the early-70s, because of their higher development costs[7] (and subsequently higher rents), contain a higher proportion of marrieds (who are more affluent, given their greater potential for dual income) than those built prior to that time. Given the importance of this type of housing in the current rental market, the usefulness of identifying the shifts in demographic composition needs little amplification.

There are several additional concerns. First, marrieds in garden apartments may have decreased their length of occupancy in their present apartments (i.e. increased their mobility), while, conversely, other types of households may have increased it. The demand for homeownership within the former group by the 1960s and 70s, prior to the interest rate surges of the 80s, became so pervasive that the period during which they remained in their apartments, as brief as it may have been in the past, became even briefer. For elderly households, whose moves are generally permanent or near-permanent, any increase in the length of tenure has probably not been sizeable.[8] For other nontraditional households, however, an increase may have been quite substantial. The comparatively low level of rental starts since 1974, accompanied by the recent wave of condominium conversions, has left vacancy rates unusually low and subsequently, has made the moderate-income garden apartment renter increasingly reluctant to move, even if only to another similar unit. This shift will not be as pronounced in newer complexes, with their higher proportion of marrieds.

Second, dwelling unit satisfaction may have lessened. Incomes in the rental sector as a whole have not risen as rapidly as operating costs. The owners of garden complexes may not be able to provide maintenance and other services commensurate with tenants' expectations. This causes displeasure with the condition of the unit itself. In newer complexes, satisfaction levels will be higher, due to the more traditional composition of the tenantry.

Why should the results be of potential significance for planners and policymakers, aside from the sheer growth of the garden apartment stock in recent years? Consider the fact that the non-economic rewards of renting continue to lag behind those of owning. Upward mobility has traditionally been a canon of the American character, and the desire to own a home, preferably detached, is one of its most tangible and deeply-rooted expressions.[9] That is why homeownership is so frequently typecast as "the American Dream" in recent popular and even academic literature on the subject. The privacy, security, and prestige that a home provides its occupants cannot generally be matched by rental accommodations, with the exception of the better luxury apartments. This holds true even for condominiums, for although they lack a private plot of land, they still provide an opportunity for private ownership.

Consider also that owning a home has usually proven for well over a decade to be a greater lure to the private investor than, for example, stocks, savings accounts, and bonds, with their fixed-dollar returns and redemption values.[10] Rapid appreciation in home values leaves an increasing portion of the rental stock to households whose gains in income are not keeping pace with those of rents.[11] Upwardly mobile renters view homeownership as a long-term boon, despite the initial sacrifices inherent in any homebuying decision.

What, then, becomes of rental housing? The revenue base necessary to sustain the operation of existing rental housing and, by extension, of rental housing-to-be, becomes increasingly difficult to attract when marrieds, given their ability to draw upon two paychecks, are a declining force in rental demand. Their likely attrition from the garden apartment market may be a product of their declining willingness to rent as well as of their shrinking proportion of all American households. Those who have taken their place are less likely to be married and, consequently, less likely to afford a home. To be sure, some people of economic means choose to rent because they have fewer interior space needs or are adverse to performing routine housing maintenance. However, such households are in a minority, and even these two advantages of renting can be acquired by way of condominium ownership.

In this likely scenario, garden apartments are the recipients of households who live in their units for longer periods of time, but do so out of a lack of available alternatives. Perceiving themselves to be "squeezed," they guard whatever turf they have managed to gain, often pressuring their management to better maintain the premises and lobbying their local government to enact a rent control ordinance.[11] Though they may eventually seek to buy a home, they would rather wait until mortgage interest rates come down to manageable levels or until they have accumulated enough savings to make a sizeable down payment. If homeownership is symbolic evidence of one's attainment of the good life, then increasing numbers of garden apartment residents are likely to be on the outside looking in for a long time. Though the structural condition of the rental housing stock continues to improve, maintaining it in accordance with current expectations has become an expensive venture, one made all the more difficult by the emerging tenantry.

The cost burden has prompted some observers to conclude that the overall rental market faces a potentially ominous crisis. The recent President's Commission on Housing reports that only a minority of privately operated rental properties provides its owners with a return comparable to that of a thirty-year Treasury Bond.[12] Former HUD Secretary Robert C. Weaver has labelled rental housing "an endangered species."[13] The General Accounting Office states that "the rental housing problem is so severe that it requires the immediate attention of and action by Congress and Administration."[14] Left to their own devices, apartment owners frequently face the unpalatable choice of cutting some building services or selling their investment. This is a major explanation behind the expanded role of government in the private rental market over the past decade—and why builders have become hesitant about engaging in rental ventures in the absence of a mortgage insurance and/or a subsidy commitment.[15] The role of government may be reduced as a result of the recommendations of the above-mentioned Commission Report and the cutbacks indicated in the 1983 HUD Budget. Yet pressures for intervention may remain as potent as ever, in light of the Census Bureau's projected proportionate decline in nuclear families in the nation during the 1980s from 61.6 to 56.6 percent.[16] While perhaps not yet meriting that amorphous term "crisis proportions," the rental problem is accentuated by this demographic shift. At the very least, vacancy rates may remain at near-zero levels in some metropolitan areas.

This book examines the garden apartment in precisely this larger context. Thus, it begins and concludes with a discussion of the rental market as a whole. Chapter One discusses the sources of demand and supply of rental housing and why they differ from those of owner-occupied housing. The fundamental concept here is "family life-cycle," which compresses a household head's age, marital status, and number and age of children present into a single variable assuming a roughly chronological progression. Chapter Two focuses upon the garden apartment as a generic housing form—its design characteristics, historical origins, magnitude of growth, and factors accelerating and limiting growth. Chapters Three and Four contain the results of the survey data, indicating the extent of demographic change and other trends and conditions pertinent to the garden apartment market. Chapter Three contains an analysis of U.S. Census and Annual Housing Survey data that compares changes in the garden apartment market with those in other markets, renter- and owner-occupied. Chapter Four contains the results of a questionnaire survey administered to garden apartment residents in suburban New Jersey communities. Finally, Chapter Five discusses the implications of the findings of the previous two chapters and suggests feasible government strategies for new production and conservation of the garden apartment stock.

NOTES

1. See, for example, Anthony Jackson, *A Place Called Home: A History of Low-Cost Housing in Manhattan*, Cambridge, Mass.: MIT Press, 1976, pp. 9-50.

2. Richard F. Babcock and Fred P. Bosselman, "Suburban Zoning and the Apartment Boom," *University of Pennsylvania Law Review*, Vol. 111, 1963, pp. 1040–91.

3. See Exhibit 2-2 in this book.

4. Chapter Two summarizes these ways.

5. U.S. Bureau of the Census, *Current Housing Reports*, Series H-150-80, "Annual Housing Survey: 1980," Part A, General Housing Characteristics, Washington, D.C.: U.S. Government Printing Office, February 1982.

6. The debate over homeownership affordability is far from having been resolved. Those who maintain that a crisis has existed since the mid-70s and those who maintain that one has not have marshalled an impressive array of statistics to bolster their cases. For reasons described in Chapter Five, this book leans toward the second position; that even despite frequently double-digit interest rates, homeownership remains within the reach of a great many Americans. For supporting evidence, see the following: Anthony Downs, "Public Policy and the Rising Cost of Housing," *Real Estate Review*, Vol. 8, No. 1, Spring 1978, pp. 27–38; John C. Weicher, "The Affordability of New Homes," *Journal of the American Real Estate and Urban Economics Association*, Vol. 5, No. 2, Summer 1977, pp. 209–26; Weicher, *Housing: Federal Policies and Programs*, Washington, D.C.: American Enterprise Institute, 1980; Douglas B. Diamond, Jr., "The Next Housing Crisis," *Real Estate Review*, Vol. 10, No. 3, Fall 1980, pp. 65–71; James Follain and Raymond Struyk, "Is the American Dream Really Threatened?" *Real Estate Review*, Vol. 9, No. 4, Winter 1979; Donald M. Kaplan, "Homeownership Affordability: A Summary of the Issues and a Point of View," in *The Cost of Housing*, Proceedings of the Third Annual Con-

ference of the Federal Home Loan Bank of San Francisco, San Francisco: Federal Home Loan Bank of San Francisco, 1978, pp. 346–66.

7. This is borne out by data in an ongoing study of construction costs of various types of apartments (including garden) by the National Association of Home Builders. In a number of reporting counties in Western states, for example, it was not uncommon for the average cost per square foot to more than double during 1977–80. See Michael Sumichrast, Gopal Ahliwalia, and Paul Rappoport, *Multifamily Component Cost Data*, Vol. VII, Washington, D.C.: National Association of Home Builders, and Philadelphia: Applied Business Research Institute, 1981.

8. See Elizabeth A. Roistacher, "Residential Mobility," in *Five Thousand American Families: Patterns of Economic Progress*, Vol. 2, J. N. Morgan, ed., Ann Arbor: University of Michigan, Institute for Social Research, 1974, pp. 41–78; C. Goldschneider, "Differential Residential Mobility of the Older Population," *Journal of Gerontology*, Vol. 21, 1966, pp. 103–08.

9. Such a conclusion is plausible in light of numerous surveys confirming the overwhelming housing preference of American adults to be owners of detached homes. See studies cited in Earl W. Morris and Mary Winter, *Housing, Family and Society*, New York: John Wiley & Sons, 1978, pp. 105–23.

10. See John Tucillo, *Housing and Investment in an Inflationary World: Theory and Evidence*, Washington, D.C.: Urban Institute, 1980; Thomas P. Boehm and Joseph McKenzie, "Inflation, Taxes, and the Demand for Housing," *Journal of the American Real Estate and Urban Economics Association*, Vol. 10, No. 1, Spring 1982, pp. 25–38; James Follain, "Does Inflation Affect Real Estate Behavior: The Case of Housing," *Southern Economic Journal*, Vol. 48, January 1982, pp. 570–82.

11. See Ira S. Lowry, *Rental Housing in the 1970s: Searching for the Crisis*, Santa Monica, Cal.: Rand Corporation, January 1982.

12. Office of the White House, *Report of the President's Commission on Housing*, Advance Edition, Washington, D.C.: Office of the White House, April 1982, p. xxxvi.

13. Robert C. Weaver, "Rental Housing: An Endangered Species?", *Journal of Property Management*, September/October 1979, pp. 271–74.

14. U.S. General Accounting Office, *Rental Housing: A National Problem that Needs Immediate Attention*, Washington, D.C.: U.S. General Accounting Office, November 8, 1979, p. 1.

15. Rents in over 50 percent of all rental units constructed in 1980 were directly subsidized. If HUD-insured (but not subsidized) projects were to be included in the total, the figure would be over 75 percent. See Lowry, *Rental Housing in the 1970s*, p. 9.

16. U.S. Bureau of the Census, *Current Population Reports*, Series P-25, No. 805, "Projections of the Numbers of Households and Families: 1979–1995," Washington, D.C.: U.S. Government Printing Office, 1979.

1

Rental Housing and the Household Life-Cycle: A Conceptual Overview

---

Introduction

Since garden apartments are rental dwellings, they cannot be divorced from the factors that affect the character of the rental market as a whole. The influences on the demand for garden units are to a large extent identical to those on all rental housing. The purpose of this chapter is to link the various motives behind renting to the components (or stages) of the household life-cycle. As will be explained later in the chapter, understanding the household life-cycle is crucial to analyzing housing demand.

The Demand for Rental Housing

Overview

Why do some people rent their dwellings? That renting is for many (even renters) a less attractive form of tenure than owning is supported by a number of rather long-standing realities. First, the "bundle" of physical attributes is considerably smaller. Accommodations for rent have less to offer to the consumer than those for sale, whether measured in terms of number of rooms, number of bedrooms, presence of yard space, or structural quality.[1]

Second, renting cannot provide the occupant with a capital gain, once the unit is resold.[2] Third, the availability of tax deductions and credits is almost nil in comparison to owner-occupied units. Fourth, a tenant's autonomy is greatly restricted by a lease agreement. Finally, renting usually does not provide the self-esteem of owning.[3] Given all this, why would a household choose to rent? What are the facets of the rental stock that make it something more than merely housing of the last resort?

Advantages of Renting

Lower Cost

Renting has been and remains substantially less expensive than owning. Moreover, its cost increases have been less pronounced, as the Consumer Price Index figures in Exhibit 1-1 indicate. In 1965, the cost of renting lay slightly above the figures for homeownership and the composite index. Over the next five years, however, it had crept up by only 13.6 percent, while the cost of ownership climbed by almost three times that amount. The difference existing at the beginning of the 1970s had grown even greater by the early-1980s. While renting did rise by an appreciably greater rate than it had during the 60s, especially in the wake of soaring heating and electricity costs, homeownership rose even faster. From 1970 through May 1982, the homeownership index rose by 193.7 percent; the index for rent and all items rose by 101.5 and 146.9 percent, respectively.

EXHIBIT 1-1

Consumer Price Index for All Items,
Homeownership, and Rent: 1960–82

Year	*All Items*	*Homeownership*	*Rent*
1960	88.7	86.3	91.7
1965	94.5	92.7	96.9
1970	116.3	128.5	110.1
1971	121.3	133.7	115.2
1972	125.3	140.1	119.2
1973	133.1	146.7	124.3
1974	147.7	163.2	130.6
1975	161.2	181.7	137.3
1976	170.5	191.7	144.7
1977	181.5	204.9	153.5
1978	195.4	227.2	164.0
1979	217.7	263.6	175.9
1980	248.8	317.9	191.8
1981	281.5	367.8	216.5
1982 (May)	287.1	377.4	221.8

Source: U.S. Department of Labor, Bureau of Labor Statistics, *CPI Detailed Report*, Washington, D.C.: U.S. Government Printing Office, monthly.

Recent Annual Housing Survey data support the CPI figures. In 1980, the median monthly cost of owning a home with a mortgage was $367; the median gross monthly nonsubsidized rent (i.e. including utilities) was only $253. The relative cost to the potential buyer has become even more disadvantageous, since the $367 figure reflects home purchases made almost exclusively during periods of single-digit interest rates.[4]

More obviously, renting requires of a tenant only a small front-end investment. Prior to moving into a dwelling, a tenant must typically pay the first month's rent plus a security deposit of at least that amount. While these payments may present a burden, they are in no way comparable to the funds required for a downpayment on a home mortgage. With the price of an average conventionally-financed home reaching $78,200 during the second half of 1981,[5] the necessary initial outlay (including fees) is now usually a minimum of $10,000 no matter how favorable the terms of the mortgage.

Renting is therefore a genuine bargain for the young household that seeks to minimize housing-related, as opposed to non-housing-related expenditures. For many adults, the choice of rental tenure is a quite rational one. Not all households need nor necessarily desire lavish, spacious accommodations. This is especially true for childless households (often consisting of a single person) who rarely require more than four or five rooms to house their personal belongings. Additionally, a household may wish to buy only when it feels that it can afford a structurally sound, attractive home in a good neighborhood, one which is likely to appreciate in value. This household may view renting as an opportunity to accumulate the down payment necessary to subsequently secure a home mortgage.

Lower Moving Expenses

Housing stands unique in relation to other goods in the marketplace because substituting consumption of one item for another is expensive. The monetary and opportunity costs of selling a piece of furniture and buying a more desirable equivalent piece (e.g. a coffee table) are far less pronounced than those of moving out of one dwelling unit and into another.[6] The cost of moving is such that families may be unwilling to respond rapidly to changes in their desired housing consumption, remaining instead in their present dwelling until the cost of relocating becomes less burdensome. According to Muth, ". . . consumers view moving costs as arbitrarily high relative to the gain from balancing housing against other consumption."[7]

As high as search and moving costs are for housing in general, they are lower for prospective renters than owners.[8] The reason is twofold. First, renting requires fewer and less complex legal and financial activities to complete a "purchase." A prospective renter applies for a lease and, if fortunate enough to find an apartment, signs it. A prospective buyer, on the other hand, must apply for a mortgage (and, therefore, undergo a lengthy interview process), acquire title and property insurance, and pay fees related to these and other hurdles. For households with limited incomes, the rewards of the process may not be worth the costs, all borne prior to the actual move. Second, a renter is not an investor; he does not bear the burden of falling or stagnating property values. The owner, however, is concerned with the value of the dwelling and is therefore more predisposed to incur additional costs to protect and enhance the value of the newly-acquired investment.

Less Maintenance and Other Operating Tasks

In addition to opportunity costs incurred during a housing search, there are likewise such costs involving legally retaining and physically maintaining the property. Here, too, a renter is less burdened than an owner. In leasing the property, the landlord makes payments on the mortgage, property taxes, property insurance, and (quite often) utilities. The landlord must call a contractor if certain repairs must be made. He must continually evaluate the financial attractiveness of the investment and seek out potential buyers if he wishes to sell. The tenant is merely obligated to pay the contract rent on schedule and live up to other conditions of the lease that usually require a minimum of time and effort. The homeowner is faced with the same tasks as the landlord and, in addition, conducts various types of structural and yard maintenance, from mowing lawns to painting rooms. These may not only be time-consuming, but in the cases of the elderly and the handicapped, physically arduous as well.

An Overview of the Household Life-Cycle

The Introduction suggested that certain changes have taken place in the demographic composition of a particular type of rental housing, the linchpin of which is a concept known as "household (or family) life-cycle." This refers to a series of chronological shifts in a person's family attachments. One of these shifts—the aging process—is involuntary; the others—the decision to marry, divorce, or raise children (and how many) are voluntary. Here, the focus is upon the linkage between actual and anticipated changes in the life-cycle and corresponding changes in housing needs, aspirations, and mobility. A household's life-cycle position affects its likelihood of renting; similarly, a society's distribution of households in various life-cycle stages affects the aggregate demand for rental housing. Therefore, a proportional redistribution of the types of households associated with renting will affect the demand for rental housing, unless patterns of demand within various stages change themselves. This is the central concern of this book. Due to the attrition of one set of life-cycle stages—marrieds—from the American population and given their lessening propensity to rent, the garden apartment may have been the recipient of other households whose collective ranks have expanded and whose propensity to rent has possibly even increased.

The household life-cycle is a powerful research tool that has gained increasing acceptance among planners and social scientists over the past several years. Though not expressed as any single uniform manner, it does contain certain elements common to virtually all of its definitions.

First, the life-cycle begins at the time when a person, usually a young adult, establishes his or her own household. In other words, a household becomes so defined when a former dependent, for whatever reason (college, marriage, employment, etc.), moves out of his or her previous dwelling unit and into a separate one. Though some researchers have distinguished between family and non-family stages of the life-cycle, arguing that the latter are actually not stages,[9] none exclude even these from consideration as separate households.

Second, life-cycle refers to a sequence of events, and, therefore, to one's chronological age. As the head of the household moves from one stage in the cycle to the next, he or she often moves into an older age bracket as well.

Third, life-cycle typically revolves around the conjugal family and, more specifically, widespread participation in it as an institution. Given the importance of marriage in shifting household structure and its necessary adjustments of personal objectives and needs, it must be viewed as a key determinant of life-cycle stage.[10] Marriage remains a strong institution in the United States, reports of its demise notwithstanding, and continues to serve as a point of demarcation between stages.[11]

Fourth, there is the consideration of the presence or absence of children. Childrearing forces added responsibilities upon adults. Moreover, it is an activity in which parents are engaged for almost two decades, and even longer if the household raises more than one child.[12]

Finally, for households having children, the life-cycle can be further demarcated by the age of the youngest or oldest child. In moving behavior, for example, the quality of a local school system takes on an importance for parents with school-age children that did not exist when the children were younger.[13]

Thus, household life-cycle is a function (within the context of one or more persons under a separate roof) of chronological age, marital status, and childrearing patterns. Though somewhat more complex a concept than age, it is a superior predictive tool for economic analysis. Lansing & Kish, for example, conducted a survey of consumption patterns among 3,000 metropolitan households and found that for six dependent variables, life-cycle brought out more statistical variation than did age.[14] Glick & Parke demonstrated that identical Census birth cohorts over several decades exhibited markedly different life-cycle experiences.[15]

Categories in Life-Cycle

There is no commonly recognized set of boundaries that define the life-cycle; various analyses have assigned to it anywhere from six to twenty-two stages. Much is at the discretion of the researcher. This book uses ten stages (see Exhibit 3-9). However, because certain stages are largely similar in character, the discussion, until Chapter Three, will be limited to six major categories.

Singles

A "single" household can denote a person or persons of any age range. For practical use, however, the ranks of this particular stage are restricted to young singles, persons for whom marriage and childrearing are likely eventualities. Included here are not only unmarried heads of household living alone, but also unrelated roommates among whom there is no definitive head, and a small, growing number of young divorced and separated persons without children for whom remarriage can be considered likely.

Marrieds without Children

The term "marrieds" refers in this context to relatively young, legally married couples; the term "without children" means none present under the same roof. The age bracket that denotes the life-cycle stage for these and all other married couples (both spouses present) is designated not by the term "head" (which, until recently, the Census Bureau assumed to be the male), but by the principal wage earner.[16]

Young and Mature Marrieds with Children

Because the childrearing function lasts for a minimum of nearly two decades, the age restriction on adults is loosened here to include early middle-aged couples. Children in these households are full-time dependents.

Young and Mature Female Heads with Children, No Husband Present

These households consist of all separated, divorced, widowed, and married (spouse not present) women with dependent children. They are a diverse lot, and, as revealed in research by Bane & Weiss, differ markedly in income, housing choice, and moving behavior.[17] The financial situation of the single mother (unlike the single father) is often precarious and unstable; thus, she must be considered as part of a separate type of household with children.[18] Included in this category are "palimony" relationships, in which an unrelated male adult lives with the mother and children, and may be the principal wage earner.[19]

Empty Nesters

The conception of an empty nester household is usually that of a middle-aged husband-wife couple whose children have "flown the coop." For research purposes, this category can be broadened to include adults of any marital status between early middle-age and senior citizenhood, whether or not they have reared children at any particular time in the past.

Elderly

The elderly consist of all persons of any marital status whose principal wage earner (or Social Security recipient) is at least 65 years old. In conducting specialized studies of this group, the younger are considered separately from older households, as the younger frequently share more in common with empty nesters than they do with the latter.[20]

Qualifying Remarks

Several comments must qualify this typology. First, these stages do not always (even excluding female heads with children or persons experiencing untimely death) assume a chronological pattern for each household. Several examples illustrate this point. Some young adults remain with their parents for their entire single lives, marry (and remain married) and therefore never constitute a "single" household. Many young adults establish separate households and do not marry until late in life, if at all. Many married couples never raise children. Second, these stages need not be experienced only once. For example, a husband-wife couple with a child may divorce, with the mother receiving custody, and several years later, remarries. A single person may marry and divorce or separate at a young age, thus reverting back to single status.

In summary, the household life-cycle, unlike age, does not progress along a straight, smooth line. While there is a general chronological pattern, for individual families the pattern often experiences reversals, skips, and other irregularities. Its great advantage as a research tool is that it combines several demographic variables into one. Its relationship to housing is a task for the next section.

Household Life-Cycle and Housing Choice

Several empirical studies have uncovered the weighty influence of family life-cycle upon housing needs and choices. This is especially true for moving behavior. Rossi, in his classic research on residential mobility in several Philadelphia neighborhoods, concluded, ". . . the major function of mobility (is) the process by which families adjust their housing to the needs that are generated by the shifts in family composition that accompany life-cycle changes."[21] Almost two decades later, Goodman remarked, "... households experiencing a life-cycle change have a higher probability of moving than households remaining in the same stage."[22]

A nuclear family that remains intact (until one spouse dies) goes through a maze of housing changes based upon need (given the prevailing social criteria of need) and the ability to fulfill such a need (given budgetary constraints). The following is an ideal-type of the progression of an American household's housing choices from its formation to its end. It does not necessarily correspond to any one particular household. This is not the purpose of an ideal-type.[23] The purpose is rather to describe, allowing for a reasonable amount of leeway, a prevailing pattern that a majority of Americans experience or can expect to experience during their lifetimes. Though written two decades ago, this description, allowing for the decline in birth rates since then, remains richly applicable today:

> The life-cycle of the "normal" housing consumer takes him through some, but rarely all, of those other classes of a household. Thus, the "typical" housing consumer may occupy a small apartment as a single person from an age of 20 to 22. He may move to an apartment with a friend for two years. At age 24, he marries and moves to a larger apartment which they occupy for the next three years. At the age of 29, a second child arrives, the first one is now three years old and needs outdoor play space; the second child needs a bedroom.
>
> The family would like to buy a home, but still lacks the downpayment or income. They rent an older home near the edge of the city for two years. In their early thirties, with the third child on the way, they purchase a small new suburban house with three bedrooms. It is too small, but it is the best they can afford, and the family occupies it usually until the husband is in his mid-forties. Then, if the husband's income has increased substantially, they sell their house for enough to get the downpayment on a larger house, one with four bedrooms and a den-guest room to accommodate visiting parents and friends.
>
> Here the "typical" family plans to stay "for the rest of their lives." But in fact, if their income goes up, they may move again to a still better home or neighborhood. The likelihood is that the family will remain in

the second owned home for twelve to fifteen years. Then all of the children will be graduated from high school and will be employed, away at college, or possibly married and living in their own homes. Some families at this stage of the family cycle move to the greater convenience of an apartment or a smaller house. Others may move to a more pretentious home. But most will continue to occupy their "permanent" home.

After the death of one partner, usually the husband in his mid-sixties, the remaining partner may move to a smaller apartment or into the home of a married child.

The "typical" family has occupied six apartments, one rented house, and two or three owned houses during its life-cycle, a total of ten dwellings. Its longest period of tenure was between ten and fifteen years, in later middle-age. A change of job to another city, a war, a depression, a divorce, an early death—any of these contingencies of life might have produced a larger total number of dwellings and other types of locations.[24]

There are several salient characteristics of this fairly representative working family:

a) The principal wage earner is assumed, in economic terms, to be upwardly mobile for at least several decades.

b) In the single and childless married stages, the person/household is likely to rent.

c) Once the household acquires a higher income and new children (and, as a consequence of the latter, a greater need for interior and yard space), it buys a home.

d) With income and household size continuing to expand, the household sells its home and moves into a larger, more expensive one.

e) Even after all children have established their own separate households, a reversion back to renter status on the part of the parents occurs only occasionally.

f) Moving is far less frequent in the later years.

Encapsulated further, the earlier the household's stage in the life-cycle: 1) the more likely it will be to rent than to own; and 2) the more frequently it will move until it can afford to own.[25] Alternately stated, a young household views renting as a relatively brief transitory phase between new formation and anticipated home purchase and it occupies each dwelling during this phase for a short period of time. This is the crux of the "way-station" analogy described in the Introduction. Much of the research conducted during the 1950s and 60s supports both tendencies.

With respect to the first, Rossi found that renters accounted for a greater proportion of households under 35 than did owners, although in the household consisting of four or five members (usually including more than one child), the proportion of owners was higher.[26] Duncan & Hauser's study of households in Chicago revealed that the rate of homeownership sharply climbed from 15 percent for young couples with children to 53 percent for somewhat older families with at least one child, and showed a slight decline to 44 percent among older couples without children.[27] Lansing & Kish found that the homeownership ratios for singles, marrieds with children, and older married couples were 20, 71, and 49 percent, respectively.[28] Fredland found that among households in the Penn-Jersey Transportation Study Area, the probability of a couple with one child purchasing a home, given a move, was three times greater than that of a single person of the same age and income bracket.[29]

With respect to the second tendency, Foote, Abu-Lughod, Foley, and Winnick's survey of central city apartment dwellers classified the following proportions of life-cycle stages as "mobile": premarriage, 59 percent; childless, married, 64 percent; young children, married, 48 percent; and older children, married, 23 percent.[30] Rossi found that 81 percent of renter families with children and 57 percent of those without children desired to move from their present dwelling. For equivalent owner households, the figures were 34 and 33 percent, respectively.[31] Fredland compared the probability of a move over the next five years by 25-year-old owners and renters, both with a child under five, and estimated that the renters were ten times more likely to move.[32] Speare's sample of Rhode Island residents revealed that of all persons who had married within the past year, 81 percent had moved since that time, a figure far greater than the 17 percent of other married couples under 45 who had no children five or older.[33]

A household's predominant chronological pattern of tenure over its lifetime is primarily rent-own and secondarily rent-own-rent; its predominant pattern of mobility forms a downward sloping curve after an early peak. While households below the poverty line, especially if female-headed, are not marked by these tendencies, the bulk of middle- and working-class households are.[34] Young married couples without children or with very young ones (the traditional source of demand for garden apartments) rent more out of financial necessity than out of choice, as they seek to minimize current housing expenditures in order to hasten their probable status as owners.

The conception of homeownership as a "deeply-rooted," quintessentially American trait is quite prevalent, despite the fact that the ratio of owners to renters did not surpass 50 percent until the years immediately following World War II.[35] Abrams, for example, commented during that time:

> Home ownership is America's tradition. American poets have sung its praises. Our chief executives have proclaimed it as a vital link in democracy. Any Congressman can deliver a homily on the subject without a minute's preparation and often does.[36]

How is it, then, that although the proportion of nuclear families has been declining since the mid-1950s, the ratio of owner-occupancy has continued to climb to a level now exceeding 65 percent? Alternately, why has renting had such a limited capacity to attract its "natural" constituency? There are two principal reasons. First, real income has grown with each decade following the Great Depression. As a result, more households have acquired the benefits of homeownership, together with the rise in quality of new dwellings.[37] Second, various types of households not traditionally associated with homeownership have begun to flex their muscle in the homebuying market. This has been especially true of condominium developments, which are often designed and advertised to attract affluent unmarried adults.[38] Indeed, given the unprecedented rates of new household formation during the 70s and 80s, the most remarkable aspect of the rise in the homeownership ratio by a few percentage points during that time was not that it was modest, but rather that it had occurred at all! Had singles and other "nontraditionals" been represented in the same proportions in the 70s as they were in the 50s, the homeownership ratio might very well currently be over 70 percent.

Conclusion

Rental housing has both disadvantages and advantages in competing with for-sale housing for the consumer dollar. As a bundle of physical attributes, as a source of capital gain, as a tax shelter for the resident, as a source of legal autonomy, and as a source of self-esteem for the upwardly mobile, the rental stock is the less attractive of the two. As a source of cost-savings in occupancy, search, and moving and as a refuge from operating tasks, it is the more attractive. The weight that each factor exerts on a household's tenure decision is deeply intertwined with the progression of the family life-cycle. Each partially explains why the shift from renter to homebuyer is felt most during the early years of a household's existence and why, once experienced, it is only very occasionally reversed.

As a result, rental housing represents a short-term accommodation, both as a fairly brief phase within the household life-cycle and as a briefly occupied individual unit within this phase. Any recent divergence from this dual pattern will be not so much due to a greater long-term attachment of married couples to renting, as it will be to a large-scale entry into the housing market by certain households who: 1) do not have an income of a size and stability matching that of married couples; and 2) until recently, did not comprise a sizeable share of all American households.

Despite several slumps, the decades following World War II have been ones of rising real incomes. Facilitated by the use of fully-amortizing, long-term mortgages, the nation's unprecedented prosperity altered the concept of homeownership-as-American dream from homily to statistical reality. Yet there remains a large renter population who, whatever its plans with respect to moving, childrearing, employment, and other activities, requires housing that meets acceptable contemporary standards and accommodates the trend of suburbanization. The next chapter addresses the housing industry's foremost response to this challenge: the garden apartment.

NOTES

1. See U.S. Bureau of the Census, *Current Housing Reports*, Series H-150-80, "Annual Housing Survey: 1980," Part A, General Housing Characteristics, Table A-1, Washington, D.C.: U.S. Government Printing Office, February 1982.

2. The advantages of buying and selling during the 1970s are clearly evident in Leo Grebler and Frank G. Mittlebach, *The Inflation of House Prices*, Lexington, Mass.: Lexington Books, 1979.

3. As Foote, et al. argue:

> . . .owning a home, even more than suburban living per se, is a basic part of the American Dream of the good life. The fact that economists regard it as a questionable course of action on the part of the marginal buyer is more or less beside the point. Homeownership is not a purely rational utilitarian choice. It is overcrusted with sentiment, symbolic value, and considerations of status and prestige.

See Nelson N. Foote, Janet Abu-Lughod, Mary Mix Foley, and Louis Winnick, *Housing Choices and Housing Constraints*, New York: McGraw-Hill, 1960.

4. U.S. Bureau of the Census, *Current Housing Reports*.

5. Advance Mortgage Corporation, *U.S. Housing Markets*, Special Subscribers' Report, Detroit: Advance Mortgage Corporation, February 5, 1982.

6. Jerome Rothenberg, *Urban Housing Markets and Housing Policy: Selected Readings in Urban Policy Analysis*, Cambridge, Mass.: Massachusetts Institute of Technology, Department of Economics, Working Paper No. 150, 1975, pp. 1–13.

7. Richard Muth, "Moving Costs and Housing Expenditures," *Journal of Urban Economics*, Vol. 1, No. 1, January 1974, pp. 108–25.

8. Keith Ray Ihlanfeldt, "An Empirical Investigation of Alternative Approaches to Estimating Demand for Housing," *Journal of Urban Economics*, Vol. 9, No. 1, January 1981, pp. 97–105.

9. Paul C. Glick, "The Family Cycle," *American Sociological Review*, Vol. 12, No. 2, 1947, pp. 164–74; Daniel R. Fredland, *Residential Mobility and Home Purchase*, Lexington, Mass.: Lexington Books, 1974, p. 73.

10. See T. H. Holmes and R. H. Rahe, "The Social Readjustment Rating Scale," *Journal of Psychosomatic Research*, Vol. 11, 1967, pp. 213–18.

11. Over 1960–79, the percentage of women 65 and over who had never previously married declined from 8.5 to 6.1 percent. U.S. Bureau of the Census, *Current Population Reports*, Series P-20, No. 349, "Percent Single (Never Married) for Women, by Age: 1979, 1970 and 1960," Washington, D.C.: U.S. Government Printing Office, May 1980.

12. This assumes, of course, that a child will remain within the parents' dwelling unit until at least roughly the age of 18.

13. Albert Chevan, "Family Growth, Household Density, and Moving," *Demography*, Vol. 8, 1971, pp. 45–58.

14. John B. Lansing and Leslie Kish, "Family Life-Cycle as an Independent Variable," *American Sociological Review*, Vol. 22, No. 1, February 1957, pp. 512–19. These variables were "Own home," "Have debts," "Wife working," "Income over $4,000," "Bought new car," and "Bought TV."

15. Paul C. Glick and Robert Parke, Jr., "New Approaches in Studying the Life-Cycle of the Family," *Demography*, Vol. 2, 1965, pp. 187-202.

16. The Census Bureau no longer uses the term "household head," but rather "person on line 1," "person on line 2," etc. In survey research of whatever nature, it is now fairly common to encounter resentment on the part of women in cases where the enumerator considers the husband automatically to be the "household head," especially where both spouses share decisonmaking. The Institute for Social Research uses a term closely related to "principal wage earner": "economic dominant." The term refers to the spouse who financially contributes most to the support of the household. If both spouses are employed and make relatively equal sums of money, the term refers to the owner of the house (if owner-occupied) or the person whose name appears on the least (if renter-occupied). If both names appear, then the person whose age is closest to 45 is designated the economic dominant. If both spouses are 45 or over (or, in any case, of equal age), the decision at this point is arbitrary. This system is used in the survey described in Chapter Four. Telephone interview with John Scott, Director of Field Operations, Institute for Social Research, University of Michigan, Ann Arbor, Michigan, June 12, 1980.

17. Mary Jo Bane and Robert S. Weiss, "Alone Together: The World of Single-Parent Families," *American Demographics*, May 1980, pp. 11-15, 48.

18. Bane & Weiss; see also Robert W. Weiss, "Housing for Single Parents," *Policy Studies Journal*, Vol. 8, No. 2, 1979, pp. 241–48.

19. The justification for this assignment is that here the relationship between the male and female is very often one of temporary (and economic) convenience. The male is, hence, an "outsider" and does not have decision-making autonomy, at least not over the mother's child(ren).

20. See Bernice L. Neugarten, "Age Groups in American Society and the Rise of the Young-Old," *Annals of the American Academy of Political and Social Science*, Vol. 415, September 1974, pp. 187–89.

21. Peter H. Rossi, *Why Families Move: A Study in the Social Psychology of Urban Residential Mobility*, Glencoe, Ill.: Free Press, 1955.

22. John Goodman, "Local Residential Mobility and Family Housing Adjustment," in *Five Thousand American Families: Patterns of Economic Progress*, Vol. 2, James N. Morgan, ed., Ann Arbor: University of Michigan, Institute for Social Research, 1974, pp. 79–106.

23. An ideal-type is a "freely created mental construct. . .by means of which an attempt is made to order reality by isolating, accentuating, and anticipating the elements of recurring social phenomenon. . .into an internally consistent system of relationships." See Julius Gould and William L. Kolb, *UNESCO Dictionary of the Social Sciences*, New York: Free Press, 1964, p. 312.

24. Martin Meyerson, Barbara Terrett, and William L. C. Wheaton, *Housing, People, and Cities*, New York: McGraw-Hill, 1962, pp. 93–94. See similar discussions in Foote, et al. "Housing Choices and Housing Constraints."

25. An excellent summary of these traits is provided in G. C. Pickvance, "Life-Cycle, Housing Tenure, and Intraurban Residential Mobility: A Causal Model," *Sociological Review*, Vol. 21, No. 2, May 1973, pp. 279–97.

26. Rossi, *Why Families Move*, p. 73.

27. Beverly Duncan and Philip M. Hauser, *Housing a Metropolis: Chicago*, Glencoe, Ill.: Free Press, 1960, p. 241.

28. Lansing & Kish, "Family Life-Cycle," p. 514. "Older married couples" here refers to both empty nesters and the elderly.

29. Daniel Fredland, *Residential Mobility and Home Purchase*, Lexington, Mass.: Lexington Books, 1974, p. 94.

30. Foote, et al., *Housing Choices*, p. 420.

31. Rossi, *Why Families Move*, p. 72. While a desire to move did not necessarily result in an actual move, the author found that in most cases, it did (pp. 107–12).

32. Fredland, *Residential Mobility*, p. 59.

33. Alden Speare, "Home Ownership, Life Cycle Stage and Residential Mobility," *Demography*, Vol. 7, No. 4, November 1970, pp. 449–65.

34. U.S. Bureau of the Census, "Annual Housing Survey: 1979," Part C; *Current Population Reports*, Series P-20, No. 353, "Geographic Mobility: March 1975 to March 1979," Washington, D.C.: U.S. Government Printing Office, August 1980.

35. See John P. Dean, *Home Ownership: Is It Sound?* New York: Harper Brothers, 1945; Theodore Caplow, "Home Ownership and Locational Preferences in a Minneapolis Sample," *American Sociological Review*, Vol. 13, 1948, pp. 725–30; Charles Abrams, *The Future of Housing*, New York: Harper Brothers, 1946; W. W. Jennings, "The Value of Home Owning as Exemplified in American History," *Social Science*, Vol. 13, 1938, pp. 5–15. Each argued the case for home-ownership as integral to the American character and each article or book had been written during or even prior to the ascendance of owner-occupancy as the prevailing mode of tenure.

36. Abrams, *The Future of Housing*, p. 36.

37. John C. Weicher, *Housing: Federal Policies and Programs*, Washington, D.C.: American Enterprise Institute, 1980, pp. 92–109.

38. See Thomas J. Parliment, James S. Kaden, Carroll R. Melton, and Kenneth Thygerson, *Homeownership: Coping with Inflation*, Washington, D.C.: U.S. League of Savings Associations, 1980, pp. 3–5.

2

The Garden Apartment: An American Housing Form

Introduction

The present discussion narrows its focus from rental housing in general to the garden apartment in particular. The tasks at hand are to define the garden apartment's structural and site characteristics, trace its historical origins and development, identify the magnitude of its growth, discuss the factors accelerating and limiting its growth, and assess its impact thus far on the American housing market.

To a large extent, the same consumption and production activities that comprise the rental market also comprise the garden apartment market. Some renter households base their decision to move to a particular dwelling solely on the basis of cost and will not be overly concerned about the appearance of the structure. Yet many others will be at least partially concerned about appearance. That the garden apartment now comprises almost one-half of all post-1960 rental construction (see Exhibits 2-2 and 2-3) and is sufficiently unique in its design justifies its treatment as a distinct phenomenon.

What is a Garden Apartment?

A garden apartment is a low-rise rental dwelling, but unlike its high-rise counterpart, its characteristics encompass more than merely structural height. Not unexpectedly, existing definitions of this housing type have varied.[1] Several elements, however, recur as universal attributes. A garden apartment always contains the first four of the following six characteristics and usually the latter two as well.

Rental Tenure—Ownership of a unit falls under the landlord-tenant relationship. Although a cooperative, condominium, or fee simple dwelling may assume the physical attributes of a garden apartment, because the occupants of each are owner-investors and not tenants, neither qualifies as a garden apartment.

Low-Rise Structure—Garden apartments are uniformly housed in walk-up buildings, usually of one, two and one-half, or three stories.[2] One- and four-story structures are rarely encountered, the latter, in fact, having fallen into disuse long ago.

Floor plan on the same story level—A garden apartment is a "flat"; the entire floor plan is located on one level. A townhouse, by contrast, whether owned or not, is a single-family, attached dwelling whose floor plan encompasses at least two and often three levels. The distinction is more than cosmetic. First, garden units are not only vertically-stacked atop one another, they usually have less interior square footage than townhouses, even though the structures of the latter may be narrower. Second, garden units do not provide their residents with as much a feeling of ownership as do townhouses, even if the residents are owners in both cases.[3] These differences largely explain why the townhouse, rather than the garden unit, is the preferred design alternative in condomimium developments.

Open space—Inherent in the term "garden apartment" is the existence of clustered open space taken up by walkways, lawns, trees, shrubbery, and recreation areas available for use by the occupants of each unit. Besides density, the amount and concentration of open space is one of the major differences between garden apartment complexes and the classic "apartment houses" of older, grid pattern neighborhoods. In principle, the maximum ratio of building to land (including parking space) is 25 percent, and often closer to 15 percent.[4]

Location in a complex—Garden apartments are typically included in a complex, an arrangement of structures of similar appearance on the same large tract of land. Each structure almost invariably contains a minimum of eight units—four units each on the first and second floor. Often, zoning ordinances specify maximum structural lengths of 150 to 200 feet. Only occasionally are entire developments contained within a single structure—and most of these have not been recently built.

Semi-private exterior doorways—A two-story garden apartment building usually contains an exterior door that leads to a small interior alcove and stairway. These, in turn, lead to one or two dwelling units on both the ground and top floors. As a variation, an individual exterior door, often requiring a key to open, leads to a common lobby on each floor. This door serves a sizeable cluster of units within the garden structure, but not the entire structure itself. In each case, the limited access is designed to foster privacy and security among residents.

Any dwelling that has the first four of these characteristics is a garden apartment. Moreover, if it does contain the first four, it usually contains the latter two as well. Other features associated with this type of housing include balconies, gabled roofs, standardized floor plans, and outdoor recreational amenities. Although they are not essential characteristics of garden units, they are frequently included in the overall design, especially in newer complexes.

Garden Apartments: A Historical Perspective

To understand how garden apartments came to be a distinct form of rental housing, it is useful to examine the origin of the word "garden" in that term. Garden apartment developments are scaled-down variants of the garden communities envisioned by Ebenezer Howard at the turn of the century.[5] These garden cities were to have their own employment base, and were simultaneously to offer the economic opportunities of the city and the spaciousness of the countryside, with the disadvantages of neither. These settlements would not exceed a population of 30,000, and their residential density would not exceed fifteen dwelling units per acre. Of concern here is how, particularly in the United States, the idea of the garden community became incorporated into the idea of rental housing developments.

The prototype garden apartment complex in America is generally considered to be the privately-financed, 1,202-unit Sunnyside Gardens in Queens, New York City, built during 1924–28 (though it does contain some owner-occupied units). Though intended as a scaled-down version of early British garden cities, this complex was itself intended to be a springboard for the planning of a larger garden community (Radburn, New Jersey) shortly thereafter. As Clarence Stein, one of the project's principal architects noted, "The ultimate aim. . .was to build a garden city. Knowledge and experience gained at Sunnyside was intended to serve that objective."[6] Unlike the earlier and much larger Forest Hills (also located in Queens),

Sunnyside Gardens' apartments would be of modest cost and would principally serve a working-class population.[7] Although the sponsor was unable to secure a single superblock with which to work, the apartment houses in the development pioneered several practices in the design of multifamily housing, such as the clustering of buildings into patterns that create open courtyard greens accessible to the rear of each building, the clustering of buildings of differing height and bulk, the standardization of interior floor plans, and the construction of off-street parking facilities (in this case, carports).

The concepts embodied in this development would also come to fruition over the next several years in complexes such as Phipps Gardens (New York City) and Chatham Village (Pittsburgh) and in communities such as Radburn (Fair Lawn, New Jersey), Baldwin Hills (Los Angeles), and the three Greenbelt Towns built under the Roosevelt-era Resettlement Administration.

The garden apartment gradually gained acceptance among builders over the course of the next several decades. By the 1950s, it had clearly superseded the apartment house as the leading form of rental housing construction, although it would not constitute a large percentage of total new construction until the sharp resurgence of rental demand arising near the end of that decade.

During this time, developers began to equip their garden apartment complexes with amenities such as wall-to-wall carpeting, central air conditioning, swimming pools, and patios.[8] This represented a clear break with the past. Previously, however immaculately a development had been maintained, those with luxuries were the exception. The growing ability and desire on the part of some renters to acquire the luxuries of a private home without necessarily owning one, the development and refinement of previously nonexistent technologies (e.g. central air conditioning), and the rising standards of what constituted "good housing," all combined to catalyze this new trend. By 1960, certain amenities had become almost *de rigeur*. One builder remarked at the time, "No one I know of is building apartments without pools or air conditioning. They're just as important as bathrooms and telephones."[9] Another remarked, "Our vacancies were running close to 30 percent at the start of this year. So we put in a swimming pool (it opened about June 1) and now we have a waiting list."[10]

During the mid-60s, the "total environment" apartment complex came into being. Woodlake and The Meadows in Southern California and Willow Creek in Dallas were the prototypes of this spare-no-expense approach, with several dozen others to follow. These garden developments contained dwelling amenities such as sunken bathtubs, fireplaces, and panelled dens, and site amenities such as golf courses, artificial lakes, gymnasiums, and tennis courts.[11] The number of these developments remains limited due to the relatively low willingness of households to remain tenants, given their high monthly rent, and to the necessity of including hundreds of apartments in a single complex to make these amenities cost-efficient. Yet when carefully targeted toward the upper reaches of the leisure-oriented market for multi-family housing, they have proven successful in attracting tenants.

What are some of the distinguishing physical and geographic features of current garden apartment production?[12] First, some of the less lavish facets of the amenity-laden complex—swimming pools, dishwashers, carpeting, and (especially) balconies and patios—have become fairly institutionalized, even in less expensive, cheaply-built developments. Second, builders have moved away from the use of brick in exterior facing and toward "cleaner" materials, such as stucco and vertical wood panelling. Third, complexes are no longer built on a traditional grid street. As late as the 1960s, these sites were not uncommon. New construction is now almost exclusively situated along the fringes of suburban and metropolitan development, a testament, in part, to the loosening of many once-exclusionary zoning ordinances. Finally, over the past fifteen years, new complexes have increasingly come to exist as part of Planned Unit Developments or cluster projects, in which they are but one of several types of housing built on the same tract.

Despite the dissenting voices of Jane Jacobs and others who argue that the concepts behind the garden apartment are symptomatic of a malaise of 20th century design,[13] the acceptance of this housing by the American population has become firmly established. However, with the exception of Canada, the design of low-rise rental housing developments outside the United States is fairly different.[14] Only a minute portion of the housing stock in other nations consists of dwellings that could be called garden apartments. There are several reasons for this. First, nations such as Great Britain, West Germany, and France have limited supplies of raw land and cannot absorb rapid suburban growth as easily as the United States. This is why these countries, among others, adopted relatively centralized systems of land use control that by American standards might be considered Draconian. The result is a greater emphasis on more compact, mid- and high-rise developments. Second, (and related to the preceding point), while mid- and high-rise structures are frequent development alternatives in America, they are generally restricted to locations near the urban core, whereas in Europe, they have been quite common as suburban housing, underscoring the major influence of Le Corbusier. Projects such as Park Hill and Hyde Park in Sheffield, England, for example, would be difficult to envision in any American suburb. Finally, if the definition of a garden apartment is limited to rental tenure, a large portion of low-rise developments in both industrialized and developing nations would be excluded from consideration by virtue of their cooperative ownership.

The Magnitude of Garden Apartment Growth

The garden apartment was an innovation of the early-1920s, but did not become a major force in the American homebuilding industry until over thirty years later. The multifamily component of annual housing starts, indicated in Exhibit 2-1, suggests the growth cycles of garden apartments over the past half-century. Until the Depression, apartment construction during this century occurred at a relatively brisk pace, usually averaging approximately 20 percent of total residential starts; during the 1925–29 boom years, it averaged 30 percent. Schafer points out that most large-scale employment opportunities for urban immigrants tended to be clustered around metropolitan centers, often adjacent to key transportation lines. Employees were frequently constrained by commuting costs to live close to work and in areas where the high cost of land necessitated dense (i.e. multifamily) construction.[15] The overwhelming majority of these structures, however, were not garden apartments.

The fortunes of the homebuilding industry plummeted during the Depression; multifamily starts during 1930–34 averaged less than one-seventh of the level of the previous five-year period. During 1935–39, the situation had only marginally improved. Still, these starts comprised over 15 percent of the total because a large fraction of former homeowners were temporarily consigned to renting. The early-40s, like the early-30s, were deep trough years for multifamily construction, as the nation mobilized its resources for World War II. Conversions of existing into separate units and doubling of separate households into the same unit often took place during this period. The immediate aftermath of the war witnessed a restoration of prosperity, high rates of new household formations and births, and a strong promotion of homeownership opportunities by FHA and VA mortgage insurance programs. The result was an extraordinary boom in single-family construction for owner-occupancy.[16] In both absolute and relative terms, new SFU (single-family unit)-detached starts from 1946 through 1956 outstripped production levels of any other eleven-year period preceding or following it. The sharp, if brief, flurry of multifamily construction during 1948–50 was almost entirely due to the short-lived Section 608 Program. By the middle-50s, Grebler, Blank, & Winnick argued that the trend toward private dwelling construction was a powerful, almost irreversible outgrowth of growing incomes and a high demand for dwelling and yard space.[17]

Abruptly, however, multifamily construction began an upswing in 1957 to the point where in 1963, it accounted for one-third of all starts. After ex-

EXHIBIT 2-1

New Privately Owned Housing Starts, By Number of Units in Structure: 1930–81 (in thousands)

Year	TOTAL Number	TOTAL Percent	1-2 Units Number	1-2 Units Percent	3 or More Units Number	3 or More Units Percent
1930-34	937	100.0	785	83.8	152	16.2
1934-39	1,709	100.0	1,449	84.8	260	15.2
1940	530	100.0	474	89.4	56	10.6
1941	620	100.0	562	80.6	58	9.4
1942	301	100.0	270	89.7	31	10.3
1943	184	100.0	154	83.7	30	16.3
1944	139	100.0	126	89.9	14	10.1
1945	325	100.0	310	95.4	15	4.6
1946	1,015	100.0	968	95.3	48	4.7
1947	1,265	100.0	1,193	94.3	72	5.7
1948	1,344	100.0	1,240	92.3	104	11.3
1949	1,430	100.0	1,268	88.7	162	11.2
1950	1,408	100.0	1,249	88.8	159	6.2
1951	1,420	100.0	1,332	93.8	88	5.7
1952	1,446	100.0	1,363	94.3	83	6.7
1953	1,402	100.0	1,308	93.3	94	5.9
1954	1,532	100.0	1,442	94.1	90	5.3
1955	1,627	100.0	1,540	94.7	87	6.2
1956	1,325	100.0	1,243	93.8	82	10.2
1957	1,175	100.0	1,055	89.8	120	12.9
1958	1,314	100.0	1,144	87.1	170	15.2
1959	1,495	100.0	1,468	84.8	227	15.2
1960	1,230	100.0	1,017	82.7	213	17.3
1961	1,285	100.0	990	77.0	295	23.0
1962	1,439	100.0	1,017	70.7	422	29.3
1963	1,683	100.0	1,046	66.1	537	33.9

Year	TOTAL Number	TOTAL Percent	1 Unit Number	1 Unit Percent	2-4 Units Number	2-4 Units Percent	5 Units or More Number	5 Units or More Percent
1964	1,529	100.0	971	63.5	108	7.1	450	29.4
1965	1,473	100.0	964	65.4	87	5.9	422	28.6
1966	1,165	100.0	779	66.9	61	5.2	325	27.9
1967	1,292	100.0	844	65.3	72	5.6	376	29.1
1968	1,508	100.0	899	59.6	82	5.4	527	34.9
1969	1,467	100.0	811	55.3	85	5.8	571	38.9
1970	1,434	100.0	813	56.7	85	5.9	536	37.4
1971	2,052	100.0	1,151	56.1	120	5.8	781	38.1
1972	2,356	100.0	1,309	55.6	141	6.0	906	38.5
1973	2,045	100.0	1,132	55.4	118	5.8	795	38.9
1974	1,338	100.0	888	66.4	68	5.1	382	28.6
1975	1,160	100.0	892	76.9	64	5.5	204	17.6
1976	1,538	100.0	1,162	75.5	87	5.7	289	18.8
1977	1,987	100.0	1,451	73.0	122	6.1	414	20.8
1978	2,020	100.0	1,433	70.9	125	6.3	462	22.9
1979	1,745	100.0	1,194	68.4	122	7.0	429	24.6
1980	1,292	100.0	852	65.9	110	8.5	381	25.6
1981	1,084	100.0	705	65.0	91	8.4	288	26.6

Source: U.S. Bureau of the Census Construction Reports, "Housing Starts," Series C-20, Washington, D.C.: U.S. Government Printing Office, May 1982; Housing Construction Statistics: 1889-1964, Washington, D.C.: U.S. Government Printing Office, 1966 (for all pre-1964 data).

periencing a slight decline during the mid-60s, it again rose, this time to an almost 40 percent average during 1969–73, spurred by the Section 236 rent subsidy program and by the rapid emergence of real estate investment trusts. After a sharp downturn during the mid-70s recession, multifamily starts have since climbed back to roughly 25 percent of the total; in absolute numbers, however, they have been declining since 1979.

Exhibit 2-1 provides data on an annual basis over several decades, but does not differentiate between garden apartments and other multifamily dwellings, nor does it exclude condominium and cooperative starts. Exhibits 2-2 and 2-3, however, indicate the size of the housing stock by Census region and SMSA location, respectively, delineating garden apartments through the use of a Census-derived definition (see Exhibit 3-1 and supporting discussion). The tabulations by SMSA location are for 1978 only. In both cases, the exhibit compares the entire existing stock with that portion built since March 1960.

Exhibit 2-2 reveals the sheer magnitude of garden apartment growth relative to that of other housing types. In 1970, there were 3,520,000 garden units extant, approximately 15 percent of the total rental stock. Eight years later, the number of garden units grew to 5,915,000, or approximately 21.0 percent of the rental stock, a proportionate increase of about 40 percent, with the sharpest growth occurring in the Southern and North Central regions. Outside of mobile homes, no other form of housing, renter- or owner-occupied, grew so quickly.

The trendline is accentuated by examining the total 1978 stock constructed after the 1960 Census of Housing. Of the 10.5 million rental units constructed from April 1960 through 1978, 4,843,000 or 45.9 percent were garden apartments. If mobile homes were excluded from consideration here, the figure would rise to 48.8 percent. If the predominant pattern of 1960–78 were extrapolated to the present (1982), even allowing for conversion of garden rentals to condominiums and other forms of ownership, the figure would likely be even higher. *Thus, since March 1960, garden apartments have accounted for roughly half of all conventional rental starts. Moreover, 81.9 percent of all garden apartment units existing in 1978 had been constructed during those previous eighteen years.* Among non-mobile units, not even high-rises have approached these figures, even with the high scrappage rate of the latter quite evident in the 70s.

At the same time, these findings must be placed in the context of total production. The owner-occupied, single-family home, as a portion of the 1970 and 1978 stock, stands as the homebuilding industry's leading link to the consumer. Its total for each of these years exceeds the combined total of all other types of housing. With homeownership rates continuing to rise, and with the townhouse (SFU attached) structure experiencing substantial growth, the garden apartment, as a percentage of all dwellings, has a limited capacity for further impact.

Exhibit 2-3 breaks down 1978 data by SMSA location, revealing the garden apartment to be slightly more prevalent in suburbs than in cities. Of the 4,164,000 metropolitan garden apartments of known SMSA location, 2,111,000 or 50.7 percent were located outside the central city. This share increases to 53.5 percent for the post-1960 stock, a figure identical to the cumulative total for other forms of rental housing. This may be surprising in light of the tendency of this book to intertwine the discussion of suburban and garden apartment growth. It is important to realize, however, that the central city figures include small cities as well as large ones, and that they include cities (principally in the South and West) that have incorporated "suburban" growth into their boundaries via annexation. Moreover, the data suggest that in 1960, American cities as a whole, still had sizeable vacant tracts of land on which to build. The overall suburban trend is shown to greater effect by examining owner-occupied units; 76.6 percent of all owner-occupied SMSA units built since 1960 were located outside the central city.

The Garden Apartment Boom: Accelerating and Limiting Factors

The recent growth of the garden apartment having been established, it is now necessary to document the reasons for that growth. Both the demand- and supply-side discussions center around two questions: What have been the factors responsible for the garden apartment's rapid growth in the housing market? And what are the existing or imminent countertrends, if any?

Demand-Side Factors

Changing Demographic Structure

This book emphasizes family life-cycle as a predictor of dwelling preference and moving behavior. It is thus the focal point in examining the effect of demographic shifts on the garden apartment market. The analysis will center upon the six general groupings discussed in Chapter One: singles, marrieds without children, marrieds with children, female-headed households with children, empty nesters, and the elderly.

Singles. The young American adults who established their own households during the late-60s and early-70s are an aggregation whose ranks have been the content of countless books, articles, and memoirs: the post-World War II baby boom generation. In 1945, there were 20.4 live births per 1,000 population; in 1946, the ratio leaped to 24.1 per 1,000.[18] This was the largest

EXHIBIT 2-2

Size of Total Housing Stock, By Region: 1960, 1970, and 1978

	RENTER OCCUPIED						
LOCATION AND YEAR	Garden Apt.	2-3-4 Unit Structure	SFU Detached	SFU Attached	Mobile Home	High-Rise	Other Rental
1970							
Total Units (000s)	3,520	6,920	7,720	830	280	1,230	3,660
Northeast	640	2,290	780	220	50	740	1,940
North Central	750	1,730	1,810	110	50	210	980
South	1,030	1,350	3,490	350	130	180	280
West	1,100	920	1,640	150	50	100	460
1978							
Total Units (000s)	5,915	7,853	7,739	1,116	729	1,283	3,545
Northeast	902	2,576	771	289	100	750	1,824
North Central	1,223	1,976	1,695	283	125	227	774
South	2,163	1,816	3,420	318	373	233	360
West	1,627	1,485	1,852	226	130	73	586
% Change: 1970-78							
Total Units	+68.0%	+24.8%	+ 2.4%	+34.4%	+160.3%	+1.4%	-3.1%
Northeast	+40.9	+12.5	- 1.2	+31.4	+100.0	+1.4	-6.0
North Central	+63.1	+14.2	- 6.4	+157.2	+150.0	+8.1	-21.0
South	+110.0	+34.5	- 2.0	-9.1	+186.9	+29.4	+28.6
West	+47.9	+61.4	+12.9	+50.7	+160.0	-27.0	+27.4
1978 (Built Since March 1960 only)							
Total Units (000s)	4,843	2,054	1,467	388	628	709	461
Northeast	701	253	109	53	85	353	170
North Central	1,095	417	199	112	108	149	85
South	1,775	726	716	137	351	154	93
West	1,273	658	443	85	83	54	113
1978 (Built Since March 1960 only) as a Percentage of (total)							
Total Proportion	81.9%	26.1%	19.0%	34.8%	86.1%	55.3%	13.0%
Northeast	77.7	9.8	14.1	18.7	85.0	47.1	9.3
North Central	89.5	21.1	11.7	39.6	86.4	65.6	11.0
South	82.1	40.0	20.9	43.1	94.1	66.1	25.8
West	78.2	46.1	23.9	37.6	63.8	73.9	19.3

EXHIBIT 2-2 (Continued)

Size of Total Housing Stock, By Region: 1960, 1970, and 1978

	OWNER OCCUPIED			
LOCATION AND YEAR	*SFU Detached*	*SFU Attached*	*Mobile Home*	*Other Owned*
1970				
Total Units (000s)	38,150	1,220	1,520	9,910
Northeast	7,400	740	140	3,180
North Central	12,000	60	360	2,360
South	12,370	250	610	1,650
West	6,380	170	410	
1978				
Total Units (000s)	46,031	1,896	3,476	3,426
Northeast	8,514	897	340	1,331
North Central	13,580	206	731	920
South	15,864	518	1,433	609
West	8,073	276	972	387
% Change: 1970-78				
Total Units	+20.7%	+ 55.4%	+128.7%	-27.2%
Northeast	+15.1	+ 21.2	+142.8	-43.6
North Central	+13.2	+243.3	+103.1	-61.0
South	+28.2	+107.2	+134.9	-77.6
West	+26.5	+ 72.5	+137.0	-76.5
1978 (Built Since March 1960 only)				
Total Units (000s)	19,422	712	3,921	1,174
Northeast	2,785	132	325	281
North Central	4,078	133	701	254
South	7,983	256	1,375	387
West	3,945	190	890	253
1978 (Built Since March 1960 only) as a Percentage of (total)				
Total Proportion	42.1%	37.6%	97.4%	36.2%
Northeast	32.7	14.7	95.6	21.1
North Central	34.7	64.6	95.9	27.6
South	50.3	49.4	96.0	63.5
West	48.9	68.8	91.6	65.4

Source: U.S. Bureau of the Census, 1970 Census of Housing and 1978 Annual Housing Survey, Public Use Tapes.

EXHIBIT 2-3

Size of Total Housing Stock, By SMSA Location: 1978[1]

	RENTER-OCCUPIED							OWNER-OCCUPIED			
LOCATION AND YEAR	Garden Apt.	2-3-4 Unit Structure	SFU Detached	SFU Attached	Mobile Home	High-Rise	Other Rental	SFU Detached	SFU Attached	Mobile Home	Other Owned
1978											
Total Units (000s)	5,915	7,853	7,739	1,116	729	1,283	3,545	46,030	1,896	3,476	3,246
Inside SMSAs	5,285	6,312	4,393	914	305	1,253	3,155	30,359	1,698	1,732	2,835
Inside central city	2,053	3,090	1,169	381	19	922	2,258	6,315	757	130	1,324
Outside central city	2,111	1,882	1,702	302	111	222	587	14,015	606	767	905
SMSA unknown	1,211	1,340	1,522	231	175	109	310	10,029	355	865	606
Outside SMSAs	630	1,541	3,346	202	424	30	390	15,671	198	1,714	411
1978 (Built Since March 1960)											
Total Units (000s)	4,843	2,054	1,467	388	628	709	461	19,421	712	3,291	1,174
Inside SMSAs	4,352	1,604	896	327	266	679	434	12,975	620	1,655	1,074
Inside central city	1,545	520	150	103	11	450	197	1,821	113	116	309
Outside central city	1,781	647	382	159	102	167	191	6,208	326	730	440
SMSA unknown	1,026	437	364	65	153	62	46	4,946	181	809	325
Outside SMSAs	491	450	571	61	362	30	27	6,446	92	1,636	100
1978 (Built Since March 1960) as a percentage of total											
TOTAL	89.1%	25.2%	19.0%	34.8%	86.1%	55.3%	13.0%	42.1%	37.6%	94.7%	36.2%
% Inside SMSAs	82.3	25.4	20.4	35.8	87.2	54.2	13.8	42.7	36.5	93.9	37.9
%Inside central city	75.2	16.8	12.8	27.0	57.9	48.8	8.7	28.8	14.9	89.2	23.3
%Outside central city	84.4	34.4	22.4	52.6	91.9	75.2	32.5	44.3	53.8	95.2	48.6
%SMSA unknown	84.7	32.6	23.9	28.1	87.4	56.9	14.8	49.3	54.0	93.5	53.6
%Outside SMSAs	77.9	29.2	17.1	30.2	85.3	100.0	8.4	41.1	46.5	95.4	24.3

[1]Figures for 1970 are not included here because in the Public Use Sample in that Census, there was a large number of dwellings in each structural category for which no geographic destination was given (unlike for the 1978 Annual Housing Survey, where at least the "unknowns" were part of an SMSA). Thus, for the sake of historical comparability, the 1970 and 1978 stock constructed since 1960 is a far more telling indicator of long-run growth (or lack of it).

Source: U.S. Bureau of the Census, 1978 Annual Housing Survey, Public Use Tapes.

increase in the birth rate for any single year in the nation's history. The rate would remain within the 24.0–25.5 range through 1959 before beginning a slide that would reach 17.5 per 1,000 in 1968. Singles have traditionally been renters; the children born during the 1946–59 period thus began to make their mark on the garden apartment market during the late-60s, which was, in fact, the beginning of the last boom in multifamily production. This factor obviously does not account for the sudden growth in apartment construction ten years before, but its impact has been weighty, and is almost inevitably cited by builders in their efforts to gain local approval of multifamily rental proposals.

Beyond shifts in the birth rate are other, deeper-seated explanations for the boost in the size of the unmarried renter population. First, the median age of a first marriage rose from 22.5 to 23.2 over 1959–70, a reversal of the fifteen-year period immediately preceding it.[19] Though on the surface this appears to be a fairly insignificant change, it actually accounts for an additional several million singles in the total population, affecting females, in particular. In 1969, the percentage of never-married women 20–24 years old stood at only 28.4 percent; in 1981, it climbed to 50.2 percent. For women 25–29, the figure rose from 10.5 to 20.8 percent over this period.[20]

An additional factor is the rise of opposite sex couples cohabitating out of wedlock. In 1970, there were 523,000 "living together relationships"; in 1981, there were 1,560,000.[21] While in the cases of many couples, this arrangement precedes marriage, in many others, it precludes it—at least with that particular partner.

Furthermore, adults are leaving their parents' homes and establishing separate households earlier in life. Much of this, no doubt, is tied to the availability of housing; the very existence of an abundant supply of apartments has made the search easier for the young renter. Much of it is also due to the large increase in college students under 25 years of age who leave home, and in so doing, add to the total number of household formations. It was hardly an accident that beginning in the latter half of the 60s, there was a burst of garden apartment construction in various "college towns" from Gainesville, Florida to Lawrence, Kansas. Additionally, young adults tend to assert a degree of independence that makes them the envy of many of their European brethren.[22]

Finally, the rise in divorce rates (see discussion under "Young and Mature Female-Headed Households with Children, No Husband Present") has created a sizeable number of once-married adults who temporarily or permanently revert to singlehood, if often only temporarily.

While the growth of the singles population, both as a whole and as garden apartment renters, has been large, and while some of the trends responsible for their growth will probably continue through the end of the century, several countertrends are already at work that will lessen their force in the rental marketplace.

First, young adults born during the baby boom will have almost entirely advanced into the 35–44 age cohort by the end of the decade, and in doing so, will consist far more of owners than of renters. The Census Bureau projects that between 1979 and 1990 while persons in the 18–34 bracket will increase by only 3.0 percent, the total population will increase by 10.4 percent.[23] When segmented by age, this bracket all too accurately mirrors the declining birth rates of the 1960s. Those 25–34 will increase by 17.3 percent, while those 18–24 will *decrease* by 16.4 percent.[24] And since the older portion of this spectrum, in large number, will have already married and acquired their first home, the pool of young single renters (especially first-time single renters who comprise the low end of the market) will inevitably shrink.

Second, as marked as the rise in divorce rates has been, it has begun to show signs of approaching a ceiling or at least a prolonged plateau. The dramatic increase during the 1960s continued into the first half of the 70s, but since then, has levelled off; the rates per 1,000 persons for 1975 and 1980, respectively, were 4.9 and 5.3.[25] Corresponding to this shift, therefore, has been a levelling off of married persons who revert to single status.

Finally, young unmarried persons are one of the fastest growing components of the homebuying market. Not long ago, homeownership was considered forbidden fruit for young, childless singles. Over the course of the 70s, with the mushrooming of condominium construction and conversion and the passage of the Equal Credit Opportunity Act of 1975,[26] unmarried persons have discovered the rewards of homeownership. The United States League of Savings Associations, for example, conducted a survey in 1979 revealing that 22.4 percent of all homebuyers were either unmarried individuals or couples, a figure up from 17.0 percent in a survey that it had conducted only two years before.[27]

Marrieds without Children. There have been expanding and contracting forces affecting the childless married portion of the garden apartment market. On the positive side of the ledger, the childless proportion of all nuclear families (of all ages) at a trough level of 43.1 percent in 1960, had steadily risen to 47.5 percent in 1979.[28] The average household size during 1960–80 declined from 3.33 to 2.76,[29] a decline in the number of children per household being the leading cause.[30] Since the decision to buy a home is often precipitated by the actual or anticipated addition of children, garden apartments have probably added more couples than would have been the case had childrearing patterns remained constant.

Further, these families' space needs make them ideal candidates for garden apartments. Since garden units rarely contain more than five rooms and very often contain as few as three, many childless marrieds who have sought out this housing may not have been as willing to do so had they been raising children, given other rental alternatives (e.g. single-family detached units).

Finally, childless couples are further away from reaching their peak earning power than are those with children. In 1978, nuclear families with at least one child under 18 had a median income of $15,410, whereas childless families had a median income of $13,432.[31]

There are also countervailing forces at work. In 1960, 1970, and 1981, husband-wife couples of all ages accounted for 74.4, 70.6, and 59.8 percent, respectively, of all households.[32] The Census Bureau projects this figure to further decrease to 56.6 percent by 1990.[33]

In addition to their declining share of total households, marrieds, both with and without children, are increasingly entering the ranks of homeowners. The often-repeated assertion that the young, first-time homebuyer "can no longer afford a home" must be reconsidered in light of Annual Housing Survey data. In 1974, 55.6 percent of all married couples in the 25–34 age bracket were homeowners; by 1980, this figure had reached 67.9 percent, a 22.1 percent increase.[34] The time horizon of an anticipated home purchase inevitably varies from family to family. Those households whose incomes are well below the national median, whose wives do not work (or if they do, only sporadically), whose principal wage earner has yet to settle into a long-term employment position, or who are childless and plan to remain so (and who therefore do not require the additional rooms that single-family dwellings usually provide) will tend to push back their home search. The eventuality of homeownership, however, remains a generally common denominator, despite both the cumulative percentage increase in the Consumer Price Index for homeownership of 193.7 over 1970–82 (May) and the continuing gradual decrease in the mean number of children per household.

The purchasing power (and, thus, homebuying capacity) of nuclear families is bolstered by the rise of the working wife. In 1970, 40.8 percent of all married females with husband present participated in the paid labor force; in 1979, this figure had risen to 49.4 percent. Among those 20–44, this figure now approaches 60 percent.[35] Further, 46.7 percent of wives of childless couples were employed, compared to 43.2 percent of those with at least one child under 6.[36] Where the wife was employed, the median rose from $9,304 to $17,791 (91.2 percent). Particularly striking is the fact that only 17 percent of all husband-wife households have both members working full-time year-round.[37] The reservoir for further increases in the effective demand for homeownership is vast because of the recent large-scale entry of women into careers whose high incomes had hitherto demarcated them as "men's work" (e.g. law, corporate management, medicine).[38] While the twin functions of childbearing and childrearing place inherent limits on the capacity of young married women to work full-time, even these factors are partially offset by the growing acceptance and use of day care centers for pre-school children, flexible work scheduling, and paid maternity leaves.

There will continue to be a sizeable demand for garden apartments by childless marrieds. The preference for a suburban environment[39] and perhaps more importantly, the lesser expense of renting[40] insure a residual demand for garden apartments. When weighed against the latter trendlines, however, it is one whose limits are apparent.

Young and Mature Marrieds with Children. The reversal of the baby boom has been extensive. Married couples with children actually declined in absolute numbers during 1970–81 (from 25.5 to 24.9 million) as well as a proportion of the aggregate (from 40.3 to 30.3 percent).[41] However, this figure means little in itself because married couples with children represent a significantly smaller source of demand for garden dwellings than those without children. Moreover, there is a distinction to be made within the former category. The younger and the fewer in number that the family's children are, the greater the likelihood will be that the family will rent, since its bedroom and yard space needs are less. In this respect, declining birth and fertility rates have *accelerated* the demand for garden apartments among young marrieds. In 1970, for example, 14.7 percent of all nuclear families had three or more children under 18 present in the household; by 1981, this figure had dipped to 6.9 percent. Even the ratios for those with one and two children declined slightly during this period.[42]

Oddly enough, this factor contains its own built-in inhibitor. In 1960, 1970, and 1978, the percentages of married women under 25 who had previously given birth were 47.6, 56.6, and 50.9, respectively.[43] The trend of the 1970s added to the ranks of singles and/or childless couples. Thus, more couples raised their first child at an older age, when they were better able to afford a home. Delayed childrearing, itself partly a response to inflation, improves one's homebuying capacity, enabling a greater shift of funds from child-related expenses (clothing, cribs, food, etc.) to housing. Economist Thomas Espanshade estimated that when controlling for the effects of certain variables, such as medical care, race, and region, the cost of raising a child from the time of birth, assuming eighteen years under the parental roof and four years at a public university, increased during 1977–80 from $44,000 to $58,000 for families with after-tax incomes in the $14,000–18,000 range.[44]

Young and Mature Female-Headed Households with Children, No Husband Present. Once an anomaly, the single mother has come to head a sizeable portion of households in this country. In 1960, 1970, and 1981, respectively, female-headed families with children under 18 stood at 4.7, 5.7, and 9.3 percent of all family households.[45] Indeed, former Census Bureau Director Paul Glick projects that given recent trendlines, 45 percent of all children born in 1977 will have at some point lived in a single-parent family, usually with the mother, before the age of 18.[46]

Since single mothers have incomes far below those of husband-wife couples,[47] their expanding numbers has created a new source of demand for garden apartments. With the exception of instances where mothers are widowed (and, therefore, can collect life insurance and social security payments), female-headed families usually cannot afford more than modest accommodations and are subject to frequent moves. If they live in a home owned by their former husband (if having married at all), in all likelihood, they will move either immediately after the termination of the marriage or within a year after.[48]

Another precipitating factor in the rise of single mother renters is the growing tendency among divorced women not to remarry. In 1965, the remarriage rates among females 14–24 and 25–44 were 471.0 and 139.9, respectively, per 1,000 widowed and divorced women. By 1979, these figures had declined to 312.6 and 127.5.[49]

Finally, the illegitimacy rate has increased. In 1970, 10.7 percent of all births were out of wedlock; by 1979, this figure had climbed to 17.1 percent.[50] Though it is true that many unmarried women with newborn children do marry shortly thereafter,[51] a gain of this magnitude has probably boosted the demand for rental housing.

There are also dampening forces. First, as discussed previously, the divorce rate has levelled off over the last several years. During 1965–75, the number of divorces per 1,000 population increased from 2.5 to 4.9, a gain of 96.0 percent. By 1980, however, the rate stood at 5.3 per 1,000 population, a subsequent gain of only 8.1 percent.[52]

Second, although fewer divorced women remarry now than during the 1960s, of those who do, the time elapse between divorce and second marriage has narrowed. In 1970, the median age of divorce for women after their first marriage was 27.9 and the median age at remarriage stood at 33.3. By 1979, these respective totals stood at 28.7 and 31.9.[53] Thus, the median period in which divorced women remain unmarried has narrowed from 5.4 to 3.2 years. Such a trend underscores Kingsley Davis's observation that rising divorce rates in and of themselves do not suggest the incipient collapse of the nuclear family.[54] Given that remarriage brings these women back to a level of (inflation adjusted) income much closer to that of the original marriage,[55] it simultaneously propels them into the homebuying market.

Third, there is evidence that owners and managers of rental properties are becoming more restrictive in leasing to families with children.[56] As long as garden apartments are represented in this off-limits sector of the rental market, single mothers must frequently find other alternatives, such as moving back in with their parents.[57]

Finally, as with childless mothers, rising participation in the labor force and the continuing enforcement of the Equal Credit Opportunity Act will, if only gradually, enable single mothers to enter the homebuying market. This will be particularly true for women whose youngest child is of school age or older. The orientation of parental supervision around work (rather than vice versa) will enable working mothers to assume employment positions of sizeable responsibilities and incomes.

Empty Nesters. Empty nesters have never been a major force in the garden apartment market. Yet despite consisting more of homeowners than of renters, they have contributed a noticeable share to the demand for garden units, particularly in luxury and semi-luxury complexes because: 1) they have no need for the interior space that they did during their childrearing years; 2) they do not wish to perform maintenance tasks; and 3) they desire access to community recreational amenities, such as a swimming pool, a club house, or a golf course. Garden complexes frequently satisfy these objectives.

A less obvious reason for their contribution to garden apartment demand has been the rise in divorce rates. In 1980, only 12.1 percent of all nuclear families in the 45–64 age range were renters; for other households in this bracket, the figure was 41.2 percent.[58] This disparity should not be surprising, since the incomes of the former are twice those of the latter. Especially telling is the fact that among non-nuclear family households in the 45–54 age bracket, over two-thirds are headed by women.[59] Since among divorcées women have lower remarriage rates then men,[60] there has likely been a large influx of middle-aged women seeking modest-priced garden apartments.

Finally, the aging of the young adults of the baby boom will be felt in the older brackets by the end of the century. Between 1990 and 2000, for example, the number of households in the 45–54 age range is expected to increase by over 40 percent.[61]

All of this said, the capacity of garden apartments to attract empty nesters is limited by the reality of an exceptionally high homeownership ratio for those in their age brackets. Furthermore, each of the advantages of garden apartments stated previously can be acquired through condominium ownership.

Elderly. Almost nonexistent in the garden apartment market a quarter century ago, several reasons exist why the elderly have also made an impact. First, the ratio of elderly to all households has been climbing steadily upward. From 1950 to 1979, it increased from 8.1 to 11.2 percent. Nor is the ratio likely to level off soon. Quite the contrary, by the year 2000, it is expected to rise to 12.2 percent, and by 2025, to 18.2 percent.[62] Part of the explanation for this is the attainment of senior citizenhood by surviving baby boom adults. Part of it can also be attributed to continuing increases in the human life span. In 1950, the average life expectancies for a male and a female were 60.8 and 65.2, respectively. By 1970, these figures rose to 67.1 and 74.8, and by 1979, they had reached 69.9 and 77.8.[63]

Second, the economic fortunes of the elderly have improved. Expanded coverage of OASDHI Social Security benefits and increasing participation in pension and deferred profit sharing plans have been primary explanations, with the Age Discrimination in Employment Act of 1978 likely to have a further beneficial effect.[64] With the improvement in purchasing power has come the expansion of residential choice. There was a time earlier this century when the elderly lived out their remaining years with offspring or other relatives. Their large-scale release from this condition has been one of the remarkable changes shaping our recent history. "Throughout European history and in the United States up to the Second World War," Tom Wolfe writes, "old age was a time when you had to cling to your children or other kinfolk, and to their sufference and mercy, if any. The Old Folks at Home happily mingling in the old manse with the generations that followed? The little ones learning at Grandpa's and Grandma's bony knees? These are largely the myths of nostalgia."[65]

The forces that limit the elderly's share of the garden apartment market, however, are also potent. First, the majority of the elderly consist of homeowners and prefer to remain that way. In an analysis of 1977 Annual Housing Survey data, Gleeson found that 72 percent of all families with an elderly head owned their home and that 86 percent of these owners held a free and clear title to the property.[66] This latter finding is crucial to understanding the elderly homeowner's reluctance to move, even if his or her present dwelling contains an interior square footage well in excess of need. Debt service currently represents about two-thirds of the total cost of an owner-occupied home with a mortgage and probably substantially higher for a recently purchased home.[67] With all fifty states providing property tax relief for the elderly in the form of exemptions, circuit breakers, or freezes,[68] the median monthly cost for free and clear ownership to the elderly was probably only a little above $100 in 1980. Gleeson further demonstrated that during 1972–80, elderly homeowners consistently devoted a smaller share of expenditures for housing than did elderly renters.[69] The Congressional Budget Office concluded that during 1970–75, senior citizens were the least disadvantaged of all first-time and repeat homebuyers.[70] The economic incentive for an elderly homeowner to remain in his or her dwelling is quite evident.

There are also noneconomic motives for renting. The process of searching for and moving into a different unit is often time-consuming and even physically strenuous for these people. Additionally, the fact that they have lived in the same unit for so long (given their retirement of mortgage debt) suggests strong emotional ties to neighborhood and community, attachments that only a traumatic downturn in life situation, such as a crippling illness or the death of a spouse, can break.[71]

Second, the purchasing power of the elderly, while increasing over the long run, has demonstrated recent signs of stagnation. Since 1976, for example, the number of OASDHI reduced benefit claims has exceeded the number of full benefit claims, the latter category having declined in absolute numbers since 1965.[72] The respective labor force participation rates for males and females 65 and over were 19.1 and 8.1 percent, down from 26.8 and 9.7 percent in 1970.[73] A recent Congressional report indicates that in 1979, 15.1 percent of all Americans 65 and over were living below the poverty line ($5,700), up from 14.1 percent in 1978.[74] Increases in the required Social Security contribution and the taxable wage base can offset these problems, but there are limits beyond which further proposed increases become politically unfeasible.[75] The majority of senior citizen homeowners could realize full equity from the sale of their homes, but as explained earlier, they are usually hesitant to do this.

Finally, although a certain portion of the elderly does make the transition from owner to renter, the garden apartment is not necessarily the destination. High- and mid-rise elevator structures have become the most common forms of new construction for the elderly, especially in federally-insured or subsidized projects. In these structures, security and social services can be provided on a centralized basis, an advantage for those whose physical condition often restricts their freedom of movement.[76]

Employment Opportunities in the Suburbs

While mass automobile ownership has enabled people to commute to work over distances previously considered insurmountable except through rail lines, the degree of proximity to the workplace continues to be a major determinant of residential choice.[77] The more economic activity is dispersed, the more housing construction will likewise be dispersed. Much of the demand for garden apartments has emanated from the need for housing suburban employees in basic and non-basic industries, many of whom could not afford to own a home.

Apartment construction is especially likely to occur in metropolitan fringe areas. Both Schafer[78] and Neutze,[79] using data from the Detroit and Chicago Area Transportation Studies,[80] calculated that renters in outer suburbs had a significantly greater tendency to work in these communities than did homeowners. This was to be expected since: 1) renters have lower incomes than owners and therefore spend less on commuting; and 2) the excess of good, low-cost apartments in central cities had gradually been eliminated by the end of the 1950s. Prior to the 50s, in fact, there had been much *reverse* commuting (i.e. from city to suburb). Why was this so? As Schafer explains:

> As the decade of the 1950s progressed, the quality and volume of the central city's multifamily housing stock depreciated due to: 1) decreased maintenance necessary to rent at below equilibrium prices; 2) demolitions for highways and urban renewal; 3) declines in the level of public services; and 4) declining neighborhood quality (including elements of discrimination in the choice of neighbors). Furthermore, the costs of rehabilitating the low quality stock exceeded the rents that could be demanded given the level of neighborhood quality and public services in the central city. . .A major consequence of this shift was an increase in the price of good quality central city housing. . .As households became better off, they demanded a higher quality environment (neighborhood and public services).[81]

A later study by Straszheim of the San Francisco area supported this finding.[82] The growth of the suburban work force has thus led to the growth of suburban rental construction. In seeking to minimize commuting costs, the younger employees proved to be a fertile source of demand.

Tastes and Preferences

Many of the qualities that people desire in a residence—open space, tranquility, privacy, security, recreation—are to be found in suburbs in greater abundance than elsewhere. Renters want these features as much as owners. Their rising real incomes have brought them more within reach. As one observer remarked over a decade ago about the growth of the luxury garden apartment market, "People are anxious for recreation, space, escape, and privacy. And significantly, people are more willing than ever to find these things in apartment living."[83] Schafer's analysis of new apartment complexes in Boston area suburbs revealed that according to a hedonic price index, the three features most demanded by households were adult recreation facilities, personal security, and child-oriented outdoor recreational facilities.[84]

Garden apartment developers, in responding to this preference, bestow rustic names upon their developments, such as "Wedgewood Green," "Parkview Terrace," and "Birchwood Gardens." Apartments in suburbs must compete with private dwellings for the middle-class dollar. This image salesmanship is necessary, from the developer's view, to prevent at least some existing and potential tenants from hastening their decision to become homeowners.

Supply-Side Factors

The Changing Homebuilding Industry:
Economies of Scale

Garden apartments may be heterogenous in design, but placed within the context of their complexes, comparably-sized units are almost always similar, if not identical, in floor plan and building materials.[85] As a form of mass housing, their emergence has been largely predicated upon industrialization and other means of incorporating economies of scale into the building process. To a certain extent, the growth of the garden apartment was made possible by the introduction of off-site operations into homebuilding. Industrialization, once almost exclusively the province of Europe, captured the interest of American builders to the degree that by the early-70s, about 90 percent of all housing starts in this country partially or wholly consisted of off-site, mass-produced and assembled material.[86] Where doors once took several hours to hang, they now usually come pre-hung from the factory, requiring only a few minutes to install. Windows, roof trusses, and stairs are also cut and assembled off-site. The extensive use of ready-mixed concrete has greatly cut down the time necessary for on-site preparation. Material and labor costs, as a proportion of the finished product, have declined as a result.[87] The increased capital-intensity of residential building has engendered greater standardization of the dwelling—and the garden apartment, more than its predecessors, is a creature of standardization.

Ease of Land Assembly

The movement of firms from city to suburb and the expanded network of highways and roads improved the feasibility of residential construction on previously remote tracts of land. Even more than the narrow grid layout, these tracts provided homebuilders with opportunities to take advantage of economies of scale in land acquisition. It was and remains easier for developers to assemble large tracts of land in the suburbs than in the city. Suburban property owners are more willing than urban owners to sell at a less inflated price. Moreover, outlying vacant land has much less of the fragmentation of ownership that accompanies the acquisition process in a city or a developed suburb. Finally, the sheer abundance of vacant land allowed developers to provide clustered open space on the project site.

Though these factors have been significant, the availability of vacant parcels for development does have limitations. The ability of a builder to assemble property for development, apartment or not, hinges not so much on the supply of vacant land per se, but on the supply of buildable land. Zoning, environmental controls, transfer of development rights, and unearned increment taxes on vacant land all reduce a developer's options. While the grip of zoning has been loosened over the past several years, other development controls (e.g. environmental) continue to tighten.

Cost of Vacant Land

The cost of vacant land has been the most rapidly rising component of overall residential construction cost over the past several decades, particularly as it applies to the private home. A National Association of Home Builders survey indicated that in 1949, land acquisition and site preparation comprised 11.0 percent of the total cost of new single-family units, a figure rising to 21.4 percent in 1969 and to 25.0 percent in 1977.[88] Several reasons underlie this trend: a finite supply of buildable land within local housing markets, local land use restrictions, creation and/or expansion of transportation arteries to previously inaccessible areas, speculation in vacant land, and competition between nonresidential and residential uses. Garden apartment projects benefitted from this trend because more so than elevator projects, their land value-to-improvement value ratios are lower, thus providing a greater basis for depreciation write-off.

Federal Programs and Policies

The early-1930s witnessed an atrophy of the United States's productive capacity that affected the homebuilding industry with particular severity. In 1933, total housing starts were a meager 93,000. One of the Roosevelt Administration's measures to restore potency to the industry was the creation of the Federal Housing Administration (FHA) as part of the National Housing Act. The agency's primary function was to insure fully-amortizing mortgage loans in return for a monthly premium paid by the lender. The multifamily facet of its operation began in 1938 with the enactment of the Section 207 Program and was expanded in 1942 with the enactment of the Section 608 Program. Both offered insurance on long-term (usually forty years), high loan-to-value ratio (90 to 100 percent) mortgage loans at low interest rates, making various allowances for builder profit and overhead. Under Section 207, the loan-to-value ratio was based upon FHA's estimate of the value of the project upon completion; under Section 608, the sponsor was allowed to specify all costs prior to construction and retain the remaining insured money subsequently not needed. It was not until after the war, however, with the influx of returning servicemen, that either program significantly contributed to new additions to the garden apartment stock.

During its brief heyday, Section 608 stimulated a remarkably high level of production (in its peak year, 1950, almost 150,000 units, most of them stripped-down garden apartments), but, in the process, invited massive abuses, and was subsequently discontinued in the early 1950s.[89] Section 207 played a notable role in fostering the rental construction boom of 1957–64; although still in effect, the growth of private mortgage insurors has diminished its role. Congress gave a boost to the rental sector in 1961 by incorporating below-market interest rate subsidies into the Section 221(d) (3) FHA mortgage insurance program, giving first priority to proposals located on cleared Urban Renewal sites. Section 236, enacted under the 1968 Omnibus Housing Act, proved to be an enormous boon to rental construction, permitting HUD to subsidize virtually the entire interest rate. It financed the construction of over 450,000 units by the end of Fiscal Year 1973 until then-President Nixon impounded further appropriations in January of that year, amid revelations of an unduly high per unit cost.[90] The program was supplanted in August, 1974 by the New Construction component of the Section 8 Rental Housing Assistance Payments Program, Title II of the Housing and Community Development Act. Though within two years, the annual commitment for production had reached 125,000 units, currently (Fiscal 1983) it is only a few thousand units for the elderly.

Subsidized garden apartment construction received an additional impetus from a provision in the 1968 Housing Act prohibiting high-rise construction for any federally-subsidized rental housing project, save for those intended exclusively for the elderly or those for whom the sponsor could adequately demonstrate a lack of feasible alternatives. This stipulation was inspired, in the main, by a sizeable and growing body of research suggesting that some of the growing social disarray in high-rise public housing projects, such as Pruitt-Igoe and the Robert Taylor Homes, were due to their very high-rise design.[91]

The Federal government contributed to the growth of the market in other ways. In 1962, for example, Congress permitted savings & loan associations to devote a larger portion of their investment portfolios to multifamily construction.[92] This action stimulated the financing of much suburban (and, thus, garden) apartment development. As Babcock and Bosselman explained at the time:

> The typical S & L is not large enough to participate in the big multiple family housing projects in the central city, nor does it feel comfortable outside the local neighborhood in which it grew up. Suburban apartments are, therefore, the common and easy answer to the S & L's need for diversification.[93]

The effect on the garden apartment supply by various IRS tax code provisions allowing accelerated depreciation for apartment construction can hardly be overstated. The impact of the first provisions in 1954 was marked, but even more pronounced was the impact of those contained in the 1969 Tax Reform Act, which helped to trigger the unprecedented (and since unequalled) apartment construction boom that lasted until the 1974–75 recession.[94] In the 1976 Tax Reform Act, Congress reversed some of the ground charted by the 1969 legislation, deciding that the massive outflow from the Treasury was unjustified. The Economic Recovery Tax Act of 1981 liberalized the depreciation write-off period to a mere fifteen years. Whether or not this provision will have the salutary effect on the housing industry that its backers believe it will remains to be seen.

Even in somewhat muted form, however, generous depreciation provisions stimulate apartment construction. In some cases, they allow the write-off to exceed the project's market value. Furthermore, investors can take advantage of new schedules on the full value of the property regardless of prior accumulated equity. Given that improvements rather than land are depreciable, high-density garden-type developments become especially attractive. As Seldin and Swesnik note, ". . .the tax shelter is normally greater in garden apartments than in other types of income-producing property."[95]

Suburban Zoning Ordinances

The gradual tilt in the content and judicial interpretations of suburban zoning ordinances toward the promotion of multifamily construction has been one of the most significant factors in unleashing the floodgates of garden apartment production. The pressures toward removal of prohibitions against and the alleviation of restrictions on such housing grew noticeably during the late-60s and even more so during the 70s. Clearly, this is not a context in which to recite a litany of sins of presumably myopic suburban officials. The reasons often given for the exclusion of apartment provisions on zoning maps—the inability of apartments to generate a favorable cost-revenue balance, the straining of local street and road capacities, the attraction of transients and lower-class persons, the destruction of the character of the community—are frequently misleading, if not false.[96] Yet it is worth remembering that when localities adopt restrictive zoning ordinances, they are responding primarily to the wishes of their respective electorates. If in a metropolitan area, most suburban juridictions establish their ordinances on the basis of such arguments, regionalism is the logical remedy. This has been the argument underlying the shift of judicial attitudes on apartment zoning by nearly 180 degrees from the 1940s to the 80s; from the belief that "apartment" is interchangeable with "tenement," to the belief that localities should promote housing opportunities for low- and moderate-income households in the region.[97]

The anti-exclusionary zoning movement has induced many outer ring suburban jurisdictions to allow a greater number of low-rise apartments to be built than they otherwise would have allowed. Yet this does not necessarily translate into watershed years ahead for garden apartments. The criteria for evaluating remedies invariably differ from community to community. The very vagueness in defining terms such as "fair share" and "developing municipality" enables local jurisdictions to employ delay tactics, even after being brought to court. Moreover, the zeal underlying the *Oakwood at Madison*[98] and *Mount Laurel*[99] decisions by the state courts is tempered by the *Valtierra*[100] and *Arlington Heights*[101] decisions by the U.S. Supreme Court.

The zoning variance has been an even more potent weapon in the apartment developer's arsenal. This method of gaining approval is powerful because it is based on informal, short-term negotiation as well as on the letter of the law. Developers learned to use the device to appeal initial rejections and by the close of the 1960s, they had apparently become quite successful at it.[102] Oddly enough, however, the variance has a built-in defect that can inhibit the very garden apartment growth that it had set in motion only a few years before. As the New Jersey County and Municipal Government Study Commission states:

> One result of this (variance) process is a proliferation of poorly planned and conceived developments, which in turn have generated the following "boom-bust"cycle of multifamily development in many municipalities. Communities that have welcomed multifamily development. . .have done so with few effective planning controls. As a result, given the massive demand for rental housing, thousands of multifamily units have been constructed in short periods of time, to the accompaniment of widespread profit for individuals involved and often questionable practices by local officials. Given the lack of planning and design controls and the ensuing results, the community sooner or later almost invariably pulls back and may subsequently ban multifamily development altogether. This cycle, in turn, often has a chilling effect on plans on proposals for multifamily development in other municipalities not presently engaged in large-scale apartment construction.[103]

Thus, the ability of the zoning ordinance to serve as a mechanism for promoting garden apartment growth has limits, and cannot supplant market decisionmaking.

Conclusion

As with any form of housing, garden apartments offer both advantages and disadvantages. If there has been a crowning achievement of the garden apartment, it has been the housing of large numbers of people whose mobility would otherwise have been substantially inhibited. The sheer quantity of its delivery to the American public, even as the overall homeownership rate continues to rise, testifies to its importance in the current housing industry and to its role in reducing the overall person per household ratio over the past quarter-century. Representing a moderate-cost solution to the imperatives of mass housing production, the garden apartment has created housing opportunities. A common observation about the housing market is that suppliers readily respond to shifts in demand. What may not be so apparent, yet no less a reality, is that this process also works in reverse: household decisions concerning whether and where to move are responses to the existing supply. The garden unit has sufficed best for persons whose ability to bid for good housing would ordinarily be so low as to restrict them to household and/or locational arrangements that, from their view, would be unacceptable.

Second, their fiscal impact is favorable. Very few cost-revenue studies have revealed a negative impact by garden apartment complexes on their respective communities, either in and of themselves or in comparison to single-family developments.[104]

Finally, they constitute an approach, though admittedly not the only one, to addressing the problems related to residential sprawl. If made part of an infill development strategy, garden apartments can mitigate energy overconsumption, overloading of traffic arteries, and excessive layout of utility lines, among other problems of modern suburban growth.[105]

On the negative side, garden apartments have often been examples of a quantity-over-quality ethic in the homebuilding industry. Their low front-end investment and low operating costs (in comparison with mid- and high-rises)[106] have attracted certain developers who seem to crave the application of Lewis Mumford's term "prefabricated blight" to their creations. For these complexes, short-term pecuniary gain appears to be the central motive for their having been built, a sharp reversal of the *zeitgeist* of Sunnyside Gardens. More than one interviewee in the resident survey (see Chapter Four) energetically described his surroundings as "plastic," "cheap," or "synthetic." This was especially true of the larger developments. Poorly constructed and sometimes balkanized from existing residential areas, these complexes were perceived to be in communities, yet not really of them.

Moreover, expanding residential mobility bears risks as well as rewards.

Garden apartment residents are often young and financially insecure. Many seek rental accommodations as quickly as possible and anticipate their following move to be in the same spirit—as quickly as possible. While they eventually seek durable attachments to home, neighborhood, and community, they are willing to temporarily forego them in favor of acquiring moderately-priced shelter and little else. The resultant high rate of turnover carries with it a price tag not only to the landlord, but also to the surrounding community. If many of these complexes are built within a short time in a single locality, as they often have been, if they contain hundreds of units each, and if they are advertised in such a way as to attract the highly mobile (e.g., billboards), the end product is likely to be an aggregation of dwellings only incidentally related to the fabric of the surrounding neighborhood or community.

Despite these reservations, the total evidence suggests a more favorable overall view. Egregious characteristics can be found in all modern forms of housing development, and the garden apartment does not necessarily contain a higher quota than others. Quite frequently, the garden apartment complex reflects a high degree of quality in architecture, site planning, and construction. It provides numerous advantages of medium-density development, such as energy and land conservation. It affords a reasonable degree of space and privacy for its residents, given the confines of a multifamily structure. It provides access to a host of recreational amenities previously unavailable to apartment dwellers. Finally, it can and has accomplished these ends at manageable rents.

NOTES

1. See Maury Seldin and Richard H. Swesnik, *Real Estate Investment Strategy*, New York: John Wiley & Sons, 1970, p. 153; Mary Alice Hines, *Principles and Practices of Real Estate*, Homewood, Ill.: Richard D. Irwin, 1976, p. 360; Carl Norcross and John Hysom, *Apartment Communities: The Next Big Market*, Washington, D.C.: Urban Land Institute, 1968, p. 7; Woodbridge Department of Planning and Development, *Garden Apartment Evaluation*, Woodbridge, N.J.: Township of Woodbridge, Department of Planning and Development, August 1968, p. 1; Westchester County Department of Planning, *School Taxes and Residential Development*, White Plains, N.Y.: Westchester County, Department of Planning, November 1971, p. 28; Urban Land Institute, *Residential Development Handbook*, Washington, D.C.: Urban Land Institute, 1978, p. 126.

2. Two and one-half story structures refer to those whose first floor is constructed partially below the surface of the ground.

3. Carl Norcross, *Townhouses & Condominiums: Residents' Likes and Dislikes*, Washington, D.C.: Urban Land Institute, 1973.

4. Urban Land Institute, *Residential Development Handbook*, p. 128.

5. Ebenezer Howard, *Garden Cities of To-Morrow*, London: Faber, 1965 (originally published in 1902).

6. Clarence S. Stein, *Toward New Towns for America*, New York: Reinhold, 1957.

7. Sponsored by the Russell Sage Foundation and designed by Fredrick Law Olmstead and Grosnevor Atterbury, Forest Hills had predated Sunnyside Gardens by almost a decade.

8. An amenity, according to Webster's Dictionary, is "something that conduces to material comfort or convenience." In a housing development, an amenity is a feature of the dwelling unit or site that goes beyond housing code requirements, enhancing the development's attractiveness to those who are willing and able to pay for it. Heating, water, and electrical systems do not apply here. Swimming pools, garages, and carpeting do.

9. "The Demand for Good New Apartments," *House and Home*, October 1960, p. 93.

10. "The Demand for Good New Apartments."

11. "Much More than Garden-Type Apartments," *Business Week*, March 14, 1970, pp. 146–47.

12. See *Residential Development Handbook*, pp. 124–28; *Housing* (formerly *House and Home*), various issues over the past fifteen years.

13. Jane Jacobs, *The Death and Life of Great American Cities*, New York: Random House, 1961. The author roundly attacks architects, developers, planners, and public officials for favoring certain forms of housing development—the garden apartment among them—that emasculate the *joie de vivre* of urban life. Those planning or supporting garden apartments and other outgrowths of garden city principles, in confusing density with overcrowding, age with decay, and heterogeneity with chaos, inhibit neighboring, sensory stimulation, and entrepreneurship—the very things that enabled cities to grow and flourish in the first place. "The myth that plentiful cities are 'wasteful'. . ." Jacobs writes, "comes of course from the Garden City and Radiant City theorists who decried the use of land for streets because they wanted land consolidated instead into project prairies. . .Superblock projects that are apt to have all the disabilities of long blocks, frequently in exaggerated form, and this is true even when they are laced with promenades and malls. . .These streets are meaningless because there is seldom any active reason for a good cross-section of people to use them." (pp. 185–86). For arguments along a similar line, see Nathan Glazer, "Slum Dwellings Do Not Make a Slum," *New York Times Magazine*, November 21, 1965; Richard Sennett, *The Uses of Disorder*, New York: Alfred A. Knopf, 1971.

A detailed response to this position lies outside the scope of this book, which no more seeks to venerate the garden apartment than to discredit it. Yet, in examining this position, certain factors must be taken into consideration, most notably, the highly impressionistic nature of this critique, the glossing over of the importance that households place on privacy in their residential environment, and the extreme difficulties, economies of scale aside, in creating urban environments anew on vacant suburban tracts. The garden apartment remains a popular rental housing choice, much as its residents may enjoy shopping or strolling in downtown areas of the city.

14. See Martin Pawley, *Architecture Versus Housing*, New York: Praeger, 1971.

15. Robert Schafer, *The Suburbanization of Multifamily Housing*, Lexington, Mass.: Lexington Books, 1974, p. 7.

16. Although figures prior to 1964 do not distinguish between one- and two-unit structures, it is more than evident that the former comprise the vast majority of starts. Note that for 1964 and after, the sum total of two-, three-, and four-unit structures, hovered around the six percent mark. It is inconceivable that prior to this

period, two-family structures alone could have surpassed this figure—or even matched it.

17. Leo Grebler, David M. Blank, and Louis Winnick, *Capital Formation in Residential Real Estate: Trends and Prospects*, Princeton, N.J.: Princeton University Press, 1956.

18. U.S. Public Health Service, *Vital Statistics of the United States*, Vol. I, Part A, Washington, D.C.: U.S. Government Printing Office, 1900–70 (reprinted in U.S. Bureau of the Census, *Historical Statistics of the United States: Colonial Times to 1970*, Part 1, Series B5-10, Washington, D.C.: U.S. Government Printing Office, 1975, p. 49).

19. U.S. Bureau of the Census, *Current Population Reports*, Series P-20, No. 242, "Marital Status and Living Arrangements: March 1972," Washington, D.C.: U.S. Government Printing Office, 1972.

20. U.S. Bureau of the Census, *Current Population Reports*, "Single (Never-Married) Persons 18 Years Old and Over as Percent of Total Population by Age and Sex," Series P-20, No. 365, Washington, D.C.: U.S. Government Printing Office, 1981.

21. U.S. Bureau of the Census, *Census of Population, 1970* and *Current Population Reports*, Series P-20, No. 365, 1981.

22. Tom Wolfe, *Mauve Gloves & Madmen, Clutter and Vine*, New York: Farrar, Straus, and Giroux, 1976, p. 122. See also Sylvia Lewis, "More and More People Are Saying, 'I Want to be Alone'," *Planning*, September 1978, pp. 28–32.

23. U.S. Bureau of the Census, *Current Population Reports*, Series P-25, Nos. 310 and 311, "Estimated and Projected Population by Age and Sex, 1950 to 2010," Washington, D.C.: U.S. Government Printing Office, 1980. All projections are Series II, unless otherwise noted.

24. *Current Population Reports*, Series P-25, Nos. 310 and 311.

25. U.S. National Center for Health Statistics, *Vital Statistics of the United States*, annually.

26. See Elizabeth A. Roistacher and Janet Spratlin Young, "Two Earner Families in the Housing Market," *Policy Studies Journal*, Vol. 8, No. 2, Fall 1979, p. 228.

27. Thomas J. Parliment, James S. Kaden, Carroll R. Melton, and Kenneth Thygerson, *Homeownership: Coping with Inflation*, Washington, D.C.: U.S. League of Savings Associations, 1980, pp. 3–5.

28. U.S. Bureau of the Census, *Current Population Reports*, Series P-20, No. 371, "Percent Distribution of Families by Number of Own Children Under 18 Years Old: 1950 to 1981," Washington, D.C.: U.S. Government Printing Office, May 1982.

29. U.S. Bureau of the Census, *Current Housing Reports*, Series H-150-80, "Annual Housing Survey: 1980," Part A: General Housing Characteristics, Washington, D.C.: U.S. Government Printing Office, March 1982.

30. For example, between 1960 and 1979, the percentage of households without children increased from 43.1 to 47.5 percent, while those with three or more children decreased from 20.5 to 13.0 percent. See U.S. Bureau of the Census, *Census of Population, 1960* and Current Population Reports, Series P-20, No. 353, Washington, D.C.: U.S. Government Printing Office, 1960 and 1980.

31. U.S. Bureau of Labor Statistics, *Marital and Family Characteristics of the Labor Force, March 1979*, Special Labor Report, No. 237, Washington, D.C.: U.S. Government Printing Office, January 1981.

32. U.S. Bureau of the Census, *Current Population Reports*, Series P-20, No. 371.

33. *Current Population Reports*, Series P-20, No. 349.

34. *Annual Housing Survey, 1980*, Part A.

35. Marital and Family Characteristics of the Labor Force, No. 237.

36. Marital and Family Characteristics of the Labor Force, No. 237.

37. Stephen Rawlings, "Perspectives on American Husbands and Wives," *Current Population Reports*, Special Series P-23, No. 77, Washington, D.C.: U.S. Government Printing Office, December 1978.

38. U.S. Bureau of the Census, *Current Population Reports*, Special Series P-50, No. 62, Washington, D.C.: U.S. Government Printing Office, 1980. It is important to bear in mind that with the acquisition of a stable, well-paying job, a woman who feels trapped in an unsatisfactory marriage will be more predisposed toward dissolving the marriage. Thus, the entry of wives into the paid labor force indirectly reduces the share of young and mature married couples. See Heather L. Ross and Isabell Sawhill, *Time of Transition: The Growth of Families Headed by Women*, Washington, D.C.: Urban Institute, 1975.

39. See James Zuiches, *Residential Preferences and Population Mobility*, Washington, D.C.: National Institute of Mental Health, November 1974; David Birch, et al., "Residential Mobility," in *The Behavioral Foundations of Neighborhood Change*, Vol. IV, Cambridge, Mass.: Harvard-MIT Joint Center for Urban Studies, 1977; New York Times, "The Many Faces of Suburban Life," November 12, 1978.

40. *Current Population Reports*, Annual Housing Survey, 1979.

41. *Current Population Reports*, Series P-20, No. 371.

42. *Current Population Reports*, Series P-20, No. 371.

43. U.S. Public Health Service, *Vital Statistics of the United States*, annually.

44. "The $85,000 Baby," Urban Institute, *Policy and Research Report*, Vol. 10, No. 4, Winter 1980, pp. 21–22.

45. *Current Population Reports*, Series P-20, No. 371.

46. Cited in U.S. Department of Housing and Urban Development, *The Housing Needs of Non-Traditional Households*, Washington, D.C.: U.S. Government Printing Office, March 1980, p. 10.

47. U.S. Bureau of the Census, *Current Population Reports*, Series P-60, Nos. 80, 118, and 123, "Total Money Income of Families, by Type of Family and Race and Spanish Origin of Householder: 1978, 1977, and 1970," Washington, D.C.: U.S. Government Printing Office, 1980.

48. Single mothers, generally, are reluctant to move into substandard housing in unsafe neighborhoods and, furthermore, desire to remain close to friends and to keep their children in the same schools. See Susan Anderson-Khleif, *Strategies, Problems and Policy Issues for Single-Parent Housing*, Washington, D.C.: U.S. Department of Housing and Urban Development, July 1979.

49. U.S. Public Health Service, *Vital Statistics*.

50. *Vital Statistics*.

51. James McCarthy and Jane Menken, "Marriage, Remarriage, Marital Disruption, and Age at First Birth," *Family Planning Perspectives*, Vol. 2, No. 1, January/February 1979, pp. 21–30. The authors also found that 71 percent of the women who had out-of-wedlock conceptions leading to live birth had married by the time the baby was born.

52. *Vital Statistics*.

53. *Vital Statistics*.

54. Kingsley Davis, "The American Family in Relation to Demographic Change," in *Demographic and Social Aspects of Population Growth*, Vol. I, Report of the Commission on Population Growth and the American Future, Charles Westoff &

Robert E. Parke, Jr., eds., Washington, D.C.: U.S. Government Printing Office, 1972. As Davis argues, "Americans expect a great deal out of the state of wedlock, and when a particular marriage proves unsatisfactory, they seek to dissolve it and try again" (p. 262).

55. Mary Jo Bane and Robert W. Weiss, "Alone Together: The World of Single-Parent Families," *American Demographics*, May 1980, pp. 11–15, 48.

56. Robert W. Marans, Mary Ellen Colton, Robert M. Groves, and Barbara Thomas, *Measuring Restrictive Rental Practices Affecting Families with Children: A National Survey*, prepared for U.S. Department of Housing and Urban Development, Washington, D.C.: U.S. Government Printing Office, July 1980; Jane G. Greene and Glenda P. Blake, *How Restrictive Rental Practices Affect Families with Children*, prepared for U.S. Department of Housing and Urban Development, Washington, D.C.: U.S. Government Printing Office, July 1980.

57. If the shortage of low-cost rental housing leads to an increased incidence of moving in with parents, then it very likely also leads to earlier remarriages. A number of mothers in Bane & Weiss ("Alone Together") reported that moving in with parents, while saving money, also sacrificed privacy and fostered competition for control of the childrens' upbringing. Some of the women sought to retain parental autonomy by seeking a new husband.

58. *Annual Housing Survey: 1980*, Part A.

59. *Annual Housing Survey: 1980*, Part A.

60. U.S. Bureau of the Census, *Statistical Abstract of the United States: 1981*, Table 123, Washington, D.C.: U.S. Government Printing Office, 1982.

61. *Current Population Reports*, Series P-25, Nos. 310 and 311.

62. *Current Population Reports*, Series P-25, Nos. 311 and 521.

63. *Statistical Abstract of the United States: 1981*, Table 105.

64. The Act raised to 70 the legal age of mandatory retirement and other age-based job discrimination.

65. Wolfe, *Mauve Gloves & Madmen*, p. 123.

66. Michael E. Gleeson, "Housing Costs and the Elderly," *Journal of the American Real Estate and Urban Economics Association*, Vol. 8, No. 4, Winter 1980, pp. 387–94.

67. *Annual Housing Survey: 1980*, Part A.

68. John Shannon, "The Property Tax: Reform or Relief?" in George Peterson, ed., *Property Tax Reform*, Washington, D.C.: Urban Institute, 1973, pp. 25–52.

69. Gleeson, "Housing Costs and the Elderly."

70. Congressional Budget Office, *Homeownership: The Changing Relationship of Costs and Income, and Possible Federal Roles*, Washington, D.C.: U.S. Government Printing Office, 1977, p. 21.

71. See comments in Nelson N. Foote, et al. *Housing Choices and Housing Constraints*, New York: McGraw-Hill, 1960, p. 113.

72. U.S. Social Security Administration, *Social Security Bulletin*, monthly.

73. *Statistical Abstract of the United States: 1981*, Table No. 636.

74. U.S. House of Representatives, Select Committee on Aging, *Retirement: The Broken Promise*, Ninety-Seventh Congress, First Session, Washington, D.C.: U.S. Government Printing Office, May 1981.

75. See Robert B. Hudson, "Emerging Pressures on Public Policies for the Aging," *Society*, Vol. 15, No. 5, July/August 1978, pp. 3-35.

76. See Oscar Newman, *Design Guidelines for Creating Defensible Space*, pre-

pared for U.S. Department of Justice, Law Enforcement Assistance Administration, National Institute of Law Enforcement and Criminal Justice, Washington, D.C.: U.S. Government Printing Office, April 1976, pp. 69–100.

77. See Brian J. L. Berry and Quentin Gillard, *The Changing Shape of Metropolitan America: Commuting Patterns, Urban Fields, and Decentralization Processes, 1960–1970*, Cambridge, Mass.: Ballinger, 1977.

78. Schafer, *The Suburbanization of Multifamily Housing*, pp. 29–30.

79. Max Neutze, *The Suburban Apartment Boom*, Baltimore: Johns Hopkins University Press, 1968, pp. 53–54.

80. John H. Meyer, John F. Kain, and Martin Wohl, *The Urban Transportation Problem*, Cambridge, Mass.: Harvard University Press, 1965.

81. Schafer, pp. 28–29, 63.

82. Mahlon Straszheim, "Estimation of the Demand for Urban Housing Services from Household Interview Data," *Review of Economics and Statistics*, Vol. 55, February 1973.

83. Sanford R. Goodkin, Chairman, Sanford R. Goodkin Research Corporation, quoted in "Much More than Garden-Type Apartments," pp. 146–47.

84. Schafer, pp. 67–89.

85. In the case of the floor plan, this is after making an allowance for the number of bedrooms per dwelling unit.

86. U.S. Department of Housing and Urban Development, *Housing in the Seventies*, National Housing Policy Review, Washington, D.C.: U.S. Government Printing Office, 1974, p. 189.

87. While no figures are available for garden apartments, the National Association of Home Builders found that over 1949–77, building materials and on-site labor costs were reduced from 45.0 to 30.0 percent and to 24.0 to 16.7 percent, respectively, of a single-family dwelling. National Association of Home Builders, *NAHB Economic News Note*, Washington, D.C.: National Association of Home Builders, Economics Department, March 1977.

88. "NAHB Economic News Note."

89. For discussion of the principal abuse, known as "mortgaging out," see Charles Abrams, *The City Is the Frontier*, New York: Harper & Row, 1965; Martin Meyerson, Barbara Terrett, and William L. C. Wheaton, *Housing, People, and Cities*, New York: McGraw-Hill, 1962.

90. HUD estimated that on the average, Section 236 units cost 20 percent more to construct than comparable, privately-financed units. See U.S. Department of Housing and Urban Development, *Housing in the Seventies*, p. 112.

91. See Lee Rainwater, "Fear and the House-as-Haven in the Lower Class," *Journal of the American Institute of Planners*, Vol. 22, No. 1, January 1966, pp. 23–37; Alvin Schorr, *Slums and Social Insecurity*, Washington, D.C.: U.S. Government Printing Office, 1963.

92. 76 Stat. 778, 12. U.S.C.A., Sec. 1464 (Supp. 1962); 76 Stat. 779, 12. U.S.C.A., Sec. 1422 (Supp. 1962).

93. Richard F. Babcock and Fred P. Bosselman, "Suburban Zoning and the Apartment Boom," *University of Pennsylvania Law Review*, Vol. 111, 1963, pp. 1040–91.

94. Good discussions of the Act's provisions can be found in Babcock and Bosselman, pp. 1053–55; Chester Hartman, *Housing and Social Policy*, Englewood Cliffs, N.J.: Prentice-Hall, 1975, pp. 145–51.

95. Maury Seldin and Richard H. Swesnik, *Real Estate Investment Strategy*, New York: John Wiley & Sons, 1970, p. 154.

96. See Babcock & Bosselman, "Suburban Zoning and the Apartment Boom"; Anthony Downs, *Opening Up the Suburbs: An Urban Strategy for America*, New Haven: Yale University Press, 1973; Lee A. Syracuse, *Arguments for Apartment Zoning*, Washington, D.C.: National Association of Homebuilders, 1968; American Society of Planning Officials, *Apartments in the Suburbs*, Information Report No. 187, Chicago: American Society of Planning Officials, June 1964, pp. 2–3.

97. Babcock & Bosselman, p. 1046; John A. Parkins, Jr., "Judicial Attitudes Toward Multiple-Family Dwellings: A Reappraisal," *Washington & Lee Law Review*, Vol. XXVIII, 1971, pp. 224–25.

98. 72 N.J. 481, 371 A.2d 1192 (1977).

99. 67 N.J. 151 A.2d 713 (1975).

100. 402 U.S. 137 (1971).

101. 429 U.S. 252 (1977).

102. Ronald M. Shapiro, "The Zoning Variance Power: Constructive in Theory, Destructive in Practice," *Maryland Law Review*, Vol. XXIX, No. 1, Winter 1969, pp. 3–23.

103. New Jersey County and Municipal Government Study Commission, *Housing and Suburbs: Fiscal and Social Impact of Multi-Family Development*, Trenton, N.J.: State of New Jersey, County and Municipal Government Study Commission, June 1974, p. 15.

104. The list of favorable cost-revenue analyses of garden apartment projects is quite lengthy. Among those studies published during 1970 or after are: Robert W. Burchell, *Planned Unit Development: New Communities, American Style*, New Brunswick, N.J.: Center for Urban Policy Research, 1972; Frederick P. Clark & Associates, *Multifamily Housing Study: Phase I of the Town of New Castle*, New Castle, N.Y.: Town of New Castle, Planning Board, July 1971; Dartmouth Planning Board, *Fiscal Impact on the Town of Dartmouth, 1975*, Dartmouth, Mass.: Town of Dartmouth, August 1975; Paul Deibel, *Assessment of Residential Development Impact on School & Municipal Services*, Fort Collins, Colo.: City of Fort Collins, Planning Office, November 1975; Janesville Council-Manager's Office, *Cost Analysis: Revenues vs. Expenses per Type of Development*, Janesville, Wisc.: City of Janesville, City Manager's Office, July 1971; Malcolm G. Little, *Report of a Study of Housing Developments and Their Effects on County Fiscal Capacity*, Atlanta: Georgia Institute of Technology, School of Architecture, City Planning Program, September 1970; Louis K. Lowenstein, *Municipal Cost/Revenue Analysis for Planned Unit Developments*, Berkeley, Cal.: University of California, Institute of Urban and Regional Development, Center for Real Estate and Urban Economics, 1973; Maryland National Capital Park and Planning Commission, *Fiscal Analysis: Stage I, Germantown Master Plan*, Silver Spring, Md.: County of Montgomery, Planning Board, January 1974; Orange County Department of Planning, *Residential Uses, Students, and School Taxes in Orange County*, Goshen, N.Y.: County of Orange, Department of Planning, April 1975; George Sternlieb, et al. *Housing Development and Municipal Costs*, New Brunswick, N.J.: Center for Urban Policy Research, 1974; Westchester County Department of Planning, *School Taxes and Residential Development*, White Plains, N.Y.: County of Westchester, Department of Planning, November 1971.

105. U.S. Council on Environmental Quality, *The Costs of Sprawl*, Washington, D.C.: U.S. Government Printing Office, 1974.

106. For data on operating costs, see Institute of Real Estate Management, *Income-Expense Analysis: Apartments*, annually. For data on construction costs, see Michael Sumichrast, Gopal Ahliwalia, and Paul Rappoport, *Multifamily Component Cost Data*, Washington, D.C.: National Association of Home Builders, and Philadelphia: Applied Business Research Institute, 1981.

3

The Garden Apartment and its Residents: The View from the Census

Introduction

The previous chapter described the growth of the garden apartment market as an outcome of certain supply- and demand-side pressures. The current task is to identify and interpret nationwide shifts in its structural, financial, and residential characteristics, as documented by the 1970 Census of Housing and Annual Housing Survey Public Use Samples of 1978 and previous years. While the analysis centers on the garden apartment, it places the results in perspective with trends characterizing other types of housing, both renter- and owner-occupied, and examines changes in the distribution of household types according to stages in the family life-cycle.

The chapter contains six sections: 1) definition of a garden apartment according to several variables common to the Census and the Annual Housing Survey Public Use Samples; 2) examination of several major categories of structural defects indicated in the 1973 and 1978 Annual Housing Surveys and a comparison of their incidence for each type of dwelling; 3) examination of the financial characteristics of the rental housing stock, specifically rents and rent-income ratios; 4) analysis of renter demographic characteristics; 5) investigation of the reasons for moving into one's present unit and the average length of stay in one's dwelling; and 6) analysis of resident satisfaction according to numerical ratings and to what extent would certain neighborhood problems induce a resident to move.

What is a Garden Apartment?
A Census Perspective

Neither the Census of Housing nor the Annual Housing Survey identify "garden apartment" as a distinct housing category. The range of each data set, however, is broad enough to effectively isolate this form of housing from the rest of the stock through the controlled use of several variables.[1] Exhibit 3-1 lists nine Census constraints that, if applied simultaneously to a single observation, would delineate that dwelling as a garden apartment. That is, it would correspond to a garden apartment as observed in the real world. A dwelling unit must meet all nine criteria in order to be so defined. The following is a brief discussion of each constraint, with an asterisk placed after those that are especially crucial to the delineation of a garden apartment.

EXHIBIT 3-1

Definition of a Garden Apartment Through Use of
Annual Housing Survey and Decennial Census Variables

Code	*Description of Constraint*
H002	No units converted from a nonresidential use
H007	No units built prior to 1940
H008	No units with direct access through another unit
H009	No units in boarding house, hotel, or motel
H100	Rental units only (no owned, condominium, or cooperative units)
H101	No units in structure with less than five units
H103	No units in structure with commercial or other nonresidential use
H105	All units in 1-3 story structures
H106	No units in structure with passenger elevators

Source: U.S. Bureau of the Census, Data Uses Services Division, *Annual Housing Survey, 1978: National Core File*, Technical Documentation, 1980. All code numbers are derived from this source.

No unit converted from a nonresidential use—A number of dwellings potentially classifiable as garden apartments may have at some time in the past partially or fully accommodated commercial activity. Since actual garden units are zoned and built to be housed in entirely residential structures, these facsimiles, however few in number, must be excluded.

*No unit built prior to 1940**—There is a large reservoir of two- and three-story structures that cannot, even by loose definition, be considered as containing garden units. They consist primarily of apartment houses built at a time when garden apartments, if they had come into existence at all, were relative novelties. The year 1940 represents a reasonable cut-off point for their exclusion. First, the Annual Housing Survey provides only a single code for units constructed before that year. Moreover, the apartment house became a relic over the course of the 1940s. While garden units were not built in large numbers until the second half of the 1950s, most low-rise apartments constructed over the previous fifteen years were of the garden type. While there is no absolute assurance that the historical break is clean (a few of the early garden apartments may be eliminated and a few older-style apartment houses may be included), any potential overlap is negligible. It is necessary to emphasize that this criterion only applies to garden apartments and to no other type of housing.

No unit with direct access through another unit—A garden apartment does not have direct access to any other dwelling unit within the same building.

No unit is a boarding house, hotel, or motel—The elimination of pre-1940 housing would effectively eliminate the vast sum of SRO (Single Room Occupancy) group quarters from the garden apartment category. As a further precaution, however, all such units are removed from the sample anyway.

*Rental unit only**—As discussed in Chapter Two, many dwellings are identical to garden apartments in every respect, save for their cooperative, condominium, or fee simple tenure of ownership. They obviously must be eliminated from any sample that seeks to concentrate on rental units.

*No unit in structure with less that five units**—As multifamily housing, garden apartments are contained in structures having a sizeable number of units per structure. This eliminates all duplexes, triplexes, and quadplexes from consideration.

No unit in structure with commercial or other nonresidential use—Two- and three-story structures with a commercial establishment on the ground floor with apartments directly above are familiar mainstays of both small and large central business districts. Most of these structures are of pre-1940 vintage and are treated apart from garden units. As with the case of apartments in group quarters, the use of this factor further prevents any overlap.

*All units in 1-3 story structures**—The garden apartment unit is contained within a low-rise structure and, by Census definition, consists of three stories or less.[2]

No unit in structure with passenger elevators—Elevators are usually associated with mid- or high-rise buildings generally containing at least four stories. A few, however, are found in three-story structures as well. Since these structures are usually not of the garden type, it is necessary to eliminate them from the sample.

This section has thus developed a working definition of garden apartments for both Decennial Census and Annual Housing Survey Public Use Sample computation. While an identical match between actual and statistical garden apartments cannot be absolutely certified without gaining confidential knowledge of the actual units sampled, the list of stipulations is comprehensive to the point where it is nearly impossible for any non-garden units to have slipped into the sample. This possibility is further lessened by the exclusive use of suburban observations for all statistical comparisons. Although many garden apartments are located in cities and nonmetropolitan communities (see Exhibits 2-2 and 2-3), their residents may be significantly different in demographic composition. This is especially true in the case of cities, where subsidized units tend to be located. Since the Census of Housing does not distinguish either publicly-owned or privately-owned rent-subsidized units from all others (though the Annual Housing Survey does),[3] the 1970 sample would contain, to greater extent, the types of households that heavily benefit from subsidies: minorities, female-headed families with children, the elderly, and those near or below the poverty line. The somewhat different character of these types of households is muted by not including garden units located in central cities.

The following four sections summarize the key features of the Annual Housing Survey and the 5 percent 1970 Census of Housing Public Use Samples. In the case of the section pertaining to resident satisfaction and moving behavior, results were not available in the 1978 Annual Housing Survey tapes; thus, data for 1977 are used instead.

Indicators of Structural Quality

The continuous upgrading of the nation's housing stock since the first Census of Housing in 1940 has occasioned a secession by several analysts away from physical condition and toward cost as the appropriate yardstick for measuring housing deprivation.[4] By any constant historical standard, most rental housing in the United States is in good structural condition. Notwithstanding, there are noticeable differences in quality between the structural types indicated in Exhibit 3-2. Of nine common renter- and owner-occupied structural types, only high-rise rentals and detached owned units consistently exhibited fewer defects than garden apartments.[5] Most notably, in 1978 only 1.8 percent of all garden units had broken plaster of an area over one square foot, a figure even lower than that for high-rises. Although 7.7 percent of all garden apartments experienced cracks in ceilings and walls

EXHIBIT 3-2

Indicators of Structural Quality: 1973 and 1978

(in percentages, suburbs only)

	RENTER OCCUPIED						OWNER OCCUPIED		
PROBLEM	*Garden Apt.*	*2-3-4 Unit Structure*	*SFU Detached*	*SFU Attached*	*Mobile Home*	*High-Rise*	*SFU Detached*	*SFU Attached*	*Mobile Home*
Lacking Complete Plumbing Facilities									
1973	0.1	1.2	4.9	1.9	4.3	0.0	1.2	1.0	3.4
1978	0.6	0.1	2.6	1.1	0.0	0.0	0.5	0.8	1.3
% Change: 1973-78	+500.0	-86.7	-46.9	-42.1	--	--	-58.3	-20.0	-61.8
Cracks or Holes in Wall or Ceiling									
1973	5.0	7.8	10.8	8.7	2.9	5.2	2.4	3.5	1.3
1978	7.7	7.0	11.4	6.6	8.9	3.3	2.3	1.7	2.0
% Change: 1973-78	+54.0	-10.3	+ 5.5	-24.1	+206.9	-36.5	-4.2	-51.4	+53.8
Holes in Floor									
1973	0.5	1.6	5.1	3.1	1.5	0.0	0.6	1.0	0.0
1978	0.9	2.9	4.1	4.3	3.7	0.0	0.4	0.6	1.6
% Change: 1973-78	+80.0	+81.3	-19.6	+38.7	+146.7	--	-33.3	-40.0	--
Broken Plaster Over One Square Foot									
1973	8.1	16.1	18.5	14.5	3.1	11.4	6.6	8.2	1.3
1978	1.8	5.0	7.2	5.5	2.3	3.3	1.8	1.7	1.2
% Change: 1973-78	-77.7	-68.9	-61.1	-62.1	-25.8	-71.1	-71.1	-79.3	-7.7
Peeling Paint Over One Square Foot									
1973	NA	NA	NA	NA	NA	NA	NA	NA	NA
1978	3.8	4.3	8.0	7.3	2.3	3.3	2.2	1.7	1.6
% Change: 1973-78	--	--	--	--	--	--	--	--	--

Source: U.S. Bureau of the Census, Annual Housing Survey, Public Use Tapes.

during that year, most of the other rentals experienced that problem to a comparable degree.

The relative adequacy of the garden apartment's physical characteristics is very much a product of its recent emergence as a predominant housing choice. As indicated in the previous chapter, over 80 percent of all garden units existing in 1978 were constructed since March, 1960 and over half this number since March, 1970. The bulk of garden apartments, therefore, have not had significant time to deteriorate. Notice, however, that in three of four categories where data for 1973 are available, the incidence of problems in garden apartments rose over the following five years. This stands in contrast to the other housing types, where the dominant trend over 1973–78 had been almost exclusively one of improvement. It is possible that the explanation for this lies in the aging of the oldest portion of the garden apartment stock. However, most of the other structural types (excluding mobile homes) have much larger proportions of pre-1960 dwellings. This argument, then, implicitly rests on the assumption that the oldest garden apartments experienced a sizeable shortfall of maintenance relative to other structures during the 1970s.

Financial Characteristics

Rents

Several patterns are discernible in monthly rents, as indicated in Exhibit 3-3. First, garden apartments require higher rents than those of all other structural types, except for high-rise. In 1978, rents for studio, one-, two-, and three-bedroom units were $165, $215, $237, and $270, respectively. The one-bedroom figure for garden units is actually higher than the two-bedroom figure for all non-multifamily units.

Second, garden apartments displayed a marked consistency in rent increases by bedroom size. This stands in contrast to other dwellings, where an increase in one size outstripped an increase in another by over two-to-one.

Third, the increases over 1970–78, including those in garden apartments, were generally in excess—and sometimes well in excess—of the 49.0 percent Consumer Price Index increase for rents over this period. As published Annual Housing Survey data indicate, this situation is not unique to suburban rentals.[6] The inherent shortcoming of the Consumer Price Index is that it measures increases in a fixed bundle of housing services over time and therefore underestimates increases in newly-constructed units, which tend to provide more services than older ones. As one recent analysis of the problem concluded, "The module used in the CPI no longer is representative of the

EXHIBIT 3-3

Median Monthly Contract Rent by Bedroom Size: 1970 and 1978

(rounded off to the nearest dollar, suburbs only)

Housing Type and Number of Bedrooms	*1970*	*1980*	*% Change 1970-78*
Garden Apartment			
Studio	$100	$165	+ 65.0
One-Bedroom	135	215	+ 59.2
Two-Bedroom	151	237	+ 57.0
Three Bedroom	NA	270	--
2-3-4 Unit Structure			
Studio	48	103	+114.6
One-Bedroom	100	159	+ 59.0
Two-Bedroom	110	190	+ 72.7
Three-Bedroom	90	234	+160.0
SFU Detached			
Studio	NA	71	--
One-Bedroom	71	110	+ 54.9
Two-Bedroom	75	150	+100.0
Three-Bedroom	104	234	+125.0
SFU Attached			
Studio	78	NA	--
One-Bedroom	118	140	+ 18.6
Two-Bedroom	NA	198	--
Three-Bedroom	NA	240	--
Mobile Home			
Studio	NA	NA	--
One-Bedroom	NA	140	--
Two-Bedroom	107	148	+ 38.3
Three-Bedroom	NA	145	--
High-Rise			
Studio	120	210	+ 75.0
One-Bedroom	175	231	+ 32.0
Two-Bedroom	NA	392	--
Three-Bedroom	NA	NA	--

Source: U.S. Bureau of the Census, 1970 Census of Housing and 1978 Annual Housing Survey, Public Use Tapes.

real changes in the universe of rental facilities."[7] Lowry, for example, in controlling for changes in the rental housing bundle over 1970–80, found that the CPI rose 113 percent in contrast to the 74 percent as reported by the Bureau of Labor Statistics.[8]

Exhibit 3-4 illustrates the CPI underestimation of rent in newer units. Garden apartments constructed during 1970–78 exhibit an even greater set of increases over those constructed before 1960, with the exception of

EXHIBIT 3-4

Median Monthly Contract Rent by Bedroom Size and Year Unit Built, Garden Apartments: 1978

(rounded off to the nearest dollar, suburbs only)

	YEAR CONSTRUCTED				
Number of Bedrooms	*(1) 1940–3/60*	*(2) 4/60–3/70*	*(3) 4/70–1978*	*(2) ÷ (1)*	*(3) ÷ (1)*
Studio	$115	$174	$172	+51.3	+49.6
One-bedroom	190	220	222	+15.8	+16.8
Two-bedroom	210	235	249	+11.9	+18.6
Three-bedroom	256	256	315	0.0	+23.0

Source: U.S. Bureau of the Census, *1978 Annual Housing Survey*, Public Use Tapes.

studio units, where the rate of increase separating the two newer groupings is slight anyway.[9] This overall pattern provides support for the second component of the central research issue. Because there is a positive association between the newness of a unit and the rent it will yield, newer units will probably attract a tenantry with higher incomes and therefore attract a greater proportion of nuclear families.

Rent-Income Ratios

Several patterns emerge in the data on the rent-income ratios (Exhibit 3-5). First, the median ratio increased for all structure types where data were available. This is consonant with the overall nationwide rise from 20 to 25 percent over 1970–80. On the surface, the shift may indicate a severe problem, but two strongly mitigating factors must be taken into account: 1) per household consumption of rental services, in terms of both space and quality, increased over this period; and 2) incomes were stretched thinner as a result of the rapid rate of household formation and the subsequent decline in the per person household ratio (that is, household incomes lagged behind rents, but per capita incomes did not).[10]

EXHIBIT 3-5

Housing Type by Rent-Income Ratio: 1970 and 1978
(in percentages, suburbs only)

HOUSING TYPE	RENT-INCOME RATIO					
	Less Than 20%	20–24%	25–29%	30–34%	35% And Over	Median
Garden Apartment						
1970	40.6	13.0	------ 14.6 ------		31.7	22.1
1978	36.3	13.9	11.9	9.1	27.8	23.4
% Change: 1970-78	-10.6	+14.6	+43.8		-12.3	+ 5.9
2-3-4 Unit Structure						
1970	52.7	10.9	------ 15.5 ------		20.9	19.5
1978	31.4	14.0	12.5	9.0	33.0	25.2
% Change: 1970-78	-40.6	+28.4	+38.7		+57.9	+29.2
SFU Detached						
1970	51.0	16.8	------- 9.1 ------		18.1	19.6
1978	32.7	16.1	9.8	6.6	34.8	24.0
% Change: 1970-78	-35.9	- 4.2	+48.5		+92.3	+22.4
SFU Attached						
1970	52.9	29.4	------- 5.9 ------		11.8	18.9
1978	31.8	16.8	10.0	14.0	27.3	24.8
% Change: 1970-78	-29.9	-42.9	+137.3		+131.4	+31.2
Mobile Home						
1970	NA	NA	------- NA -------		NA	NA
1978	18.0	11.5	7.7	16.7	46.7	32.9
% Change: 1970-78	--	--	--		--	--
High-Rise						
1970	NA	NA	------- NA -------		NA	NA
1978	25.5	20.9	9.5	7.9	36.2	25.8
% Change: 1970-78	--	--	--		--	--

Source: U.S. Bureau of the Census, 1970 Census of Housing and 1978 Annual Housing Survey, Public Use Tapes.

Second, in 1978, garden apartments required the lowest median rent-income ratio of all rental dwellings, where they did not in 1970. This is a logical outcome of the large net outflow of nuclear families, especially those with children, from other types of units during that time.[11]

Finally, the percentage distributions are marked by polarity. Despite the overall median of 25 percent in 1978, approximately only one-fourth of the households in any rental structure spent between 20 and 30 percent of their incomes on rent. Even in the 20–34 percent range, no type of dwelling, including garden apartments, accounted for even close to one-half of all respondents. At the lower end, this suggests a growing number of renter households that desire to minimize rent expenditure in anticipation of eventual home purchase and/or those that cannot afford to spend a large portion of their income on rent. At the higher end (and somewhat less likely), this suggests a sizeable affluent tenantry willing to pay high rents for high quality.

Demographic Characteristics

Overview

The following section analyzes the demographic composition of garden apartment residents, frequently comparing it to the composition of other households. Of particular importance is the stage in the family life-cycle; this is the variable in which the statistical significance of change is examined. Data on age of household head, marital status, race, and education will illuminate the life-cycle shifts.

Household Structure

Exhibit 3-6 indicates how quickly the nuclear family has declined as a force of demand, from 50.1 percent of all households in 1970 to 36.4 percent in 1978. The youngest households, those under 35, accounted for most of the drop. Rather than being evenly distributed among other age brackets, however, the slack was primarily picked up by other household types under age 35. Female-headed households now account for over 15 percent of all households, with the under 25 and 25–34 groups experiencing large gains. The declining person per household ratio in the 1970s has thus affected garden apartments as it has the rest of the population.[12]

Age of Principal Wage Earner

Rental housing has traditionally been a respository of young households, and this is especially true of the garden apartment, as Exhibit 3-7 indicates. Almost two-thirds of all households in both 1970 and 1978 consisted of those headed by adults under 35. In fact, in each year, one-fourth of all

EXHIBIT 3-6

Garden Apartment Household Structure and Age of Principal Wage Earner: 1970 and 1978 (in percentages, suburbs only)

	1970	*1978*	*% Change: 1970-1978*
2-or-More Person Households			
Male Head, Wife Present			
Under 25 years	15.9	10.2	- 35.8
25-29 years	17.5	10.2	- 41.7
30-34 years	6.3	4.4	- 30.2
35-44 years	4.8	3.4	- 29.2
45-64 years	5.6	5.0	- 10.7
65 years and over	0.0	3.2	--
Total	50.1	36.4	- 27.3
Other Male Head			
Under 25 years	NA	3.2	--
25-29 years	NA	3.1	--
30-34 years	NA	0.6	--
35-44 years	NA	0.8	--
45-64 years	NA	0.0	--
65 years or over	NA	0.0	--
Total	2.4	7.7	+220.8
Female Head			
Under 25 years	0.0	4.1	--
25-34 years	3.2	5.4	+ 68.8
35-44 years	4.0	2.4	+ 40.0
45-64 years	2.4	2.2	- 8.3
65 years or over	0.8	1.1	+ 37.5
Total	9.6	15.2	+ 58.3
1-Person Households			
Under 25 years	10.3	6.0	- 41.7
25-34 years	10.3	16.1	+ 56.3
35-44 years	0.8	4.8	+500.0
45-64 years	7.1	6.1	- 14.1
65 years or over	8.7	7.7	- 11.5
Total	37.2	40.7	+ 9.4
All Households	100.0	100.0	

Note: "NA" refers to the fact that some categories contained too few responses to be conclusive.

Source: U.S. Bureau of the Census, 1970 Census of Housing and 1978 Annual Housing Survey, Public Use Tapes.

EXHIBIT 3-7

Age of Principal Wage Earner by Housing Type: 1970 and 1978

(in percentages, suburbs only)

Age	*RENTER OCCUPIED*						*OWNER OCCUPIED*		
	Garden Apartment	*2-3-4 Unit Structure*	*SFU Detached*	*SFU Attached*	*Mobile Home*	*High-Rise*	*SFU Detached*	*SFU Attached*	*Mobile Home*
Under 25									
1970	27.0	12.8	13.1	10.5	NA	NA	2.0	10.7	9.5
1978	23.5	19.3	13.9	18.8	34.4	7.7	1.4	3.0	8.6
% Change: 1970-78	-13.0	+50.8	+ 6.1	+79.1	--	--	-30.0	-72.0	-9.5
25-34									
1970	38.1	27.7	23.6	47.4	NA	NA	17.2	10.7	19.0
1978	39.2	30.9	36.2	32.3	31.4	13.4	20.3	26.2	19.2
% Change: 1970-78	+ 2.9	+11.6	+53.3	+31.9	--	--	+18.0	+144.9	+ 1.0
35-44									
1970	9.5	17.7	23.0	15.8	NA	NA	21.5	17.9	14.3
1978	11.1	14.4	18.0	23.3	15.3	3.2	22.8	20.4	11.8
% Change: 1970-78	+16.8	-18.6	-21.7	+47.5	--	--	+ 6.0	+14.0	+17.5
45-64									
1970	15.1	26.2	30.4	21.1	NA	NA	44.8	28.6	35.7
1978	14.2	19.3	22.3	15.2	14.2	21.5	39.8	34.2	33.0
% Change: 1970-78	- 6.0	-26.3	-26.6	-28.0	--	--	+11.2	+19.6	- 7.6
65 and Over									
1970	10.3	15.6	9.9	5.3	NA	NA	14.4	32.1	21.4
1978	12.0	16.1	9.6	10.4	4.3	54.2	15.8	16.2	27.4
% Change: 1970-78	+16.5	+ 3.2	-3.0	+96.2	--	--	+ 9.7	-49.5	+28.0

Note: "NA" refers to the fact that some categories contained too few responses to be conclusive.

Source: U.S. Bureau of the Census, 1970 Census of Housing and 1978 Annual Housing Survey, Public Use Tapes.

household heads were under 25, a figure exceeded only in the case of the mobile home. The brackets in which garden apartments were thinnest, 35–44 and 45–64, were those in which other rentals showed up considerably stronger.

Why do garden apartments tend to attract a younger clientele? First, they are compact units, only occasionally containing space that might be defined as excessive. Small households, very often childless couples and singles, are clearly candidates for this housing. Moreover, these apartments, more than other multifamily housing, contain open space and recreational amenities, so important in attracting persons in the most active years of their lives.

Marital Status

The decline of the family is further underscored in Exhibit 3-8, which shows that the percentage of married household heads in rental units decreased, while the percentage of single heads increased for all forms of housing, except for owner-occupied single-family attached. The proportion of divorced and separated households consistently exhibited large and sometimes threefold increases. This, of course, is part of a general social trend, yet its effects have been sharply felt in garden apartments. The increase among singles was relatively low only because its share of the total population in 1970 was already high. Moreover, the decrease in married households was the largest of all reported, except for 2–3–4 family structures. The percentage of divorced tenants in garden apartments, only a modestly high 8.7 percent in 1970, increased to 16.9 percent of the population by 1978, the highest share among all housing types.

The garden apartment is losing a sizeable portion of its traditional function as a houser of married couples and it is doing so at a high rate in comparison to other forms of housing. Given the current nationwide demographic trendlines, the central issue is not so much if, but rather, how much further this trend will continue before reaching bottom.

Stage in Family Life-Cycle

The litmus test of demographic compositional change is family life-cycle, which, as explained in Chapter One, is a more powerful research tool than either of its individual components—age of household head, marital status, and presence/age of children. Exhibit 3-9 indicates how the six-category model (single, married without children, married with children, female-headed family, empty nester, and elderly) is further partitioned into a ten-category model that will also serve the analysis in Chapter Four.

The age brackets indicated for the principal wage earners reflect the need for some standard of comparability between Census and non-Census resident samples. The 1972 study upon which the latter is based employed these

EXHIBIT 3-8

Marital Status of Principal Wage Earner by Housing Type: 1970 and 1978
(in percentages, suburbs only)

	RENTER OCCUPIED						OWNER OCCUPIED		
Marital Status	Garden Apt.	2-3-4 Unit Structure	SFU Detached	SFU Attached	Mobile Home	High-Rise	SFU Detached	SFU Attached	Mobile Home
Single									
1970	24.6	11.3	4.7	NA	NA	NA	2.4	16.1	4.8
1978	28.1	22.7	13.8	13.3	19.0	25.4	3.3	6.3	7.6
% Change: 1970-78	+14.3	+100.9	+193.6	--	--	--	+37.5	-60.9	+58.3
Married									
1970	51.6	63.1	71.2	NA	NA	NA	87.4	64.5	66.7
1978	38.1	42.1	57.2	49.9	55.7	33.7	80.5	69.2	61.5
% Change: 1970-78	-26.2	-33.3	-19.7	--	--	--	- 7.9	+ 7.3	- 7.8
Divorced									
1970	8.7	12.8	10.5	NA	NA	NA	1.9	3.2	9.5
1978	16.9	16.2	14.0	22.4	11.7	9.0	5.2	9.8	10.2
% Change: 1970-78	+94.3	+26.2	+33.3	--	--	--	+173.7	+206.3	+ 7.4
Separated									
1970	5.6	2.1	2.6	NA	NA	NA	0.6	0.0	2.4
1978	6.3	6.9	6.4	9.6	9.0	0.0	1.3	3.8	2.1
% Change: 1970-78	+12.5	+228.6	+146.2	--	--	--	+116.7	--	-12.5
Widowed									
1970	9.5	10.6	11.0	NA	NA	NA	7.6	16.1	16.7
1978	10.6	12.1	8.6	4.8	4.6	31.8	9.7	11.0	18.7
% Change: 1970-78	+11.6	+14.1	-21.8	--	--	--	+27.7	-31.7	+12.0

Source: U.S. Bureau of the Census, 1970 Census of Housing and 1978 Annual Housing Survey, Public Use Tapes.

EXHIBIT 3-9

Stages in the Family Life-Cycle

Stage	*Description*[2]
1	Single-person or unrelated household, principal wage earner (PWE) 35 or under
2	Married, PWE 35 or under; no children
3	Married, PWE 35 or under; youngest child, pre-school or kindergarten
4	Married, PWE 35 or under; youngest child, grammar school or older
5	Married, PWE 36-49; youngest child, grammar school or older
3a	[1]Female-headed household, PWE 35 or younger; youngest child, pre-school or kindergarten
4a	[1]Female-headed household, PWE 35 or younger; youngest child, grammar school or older
5a	[1]Female-headed household, PWE 36-49; youngest child, grammar school or older
6	Empty nester; married, single person, or unrelated household, PWE 36-64; no children
7	Elderly household; one or both adults 65 or older; no children

Note: In cases where a single mother cohabitates with an unrelated male, an increasingly frequent arrangement, the appropriate classification is "female-headed household," for reasons explained in Chapter One.

[2]There are inevitably certain households who will not fall under any of these categories.

Source: George Sternlieb, et al., Housing Development and Municipal Costs, New Brunswick, N.J.: Center for Urban Policy Research, 1974; John B. Lansing and Leslie Kish, "Family Life-Cycle as an Independent Variable," American Sociological Review, Vol. 22, No. 1, February 1957, pp. 512-19.

brackets as close-ended responses for adult ages. Hence, to have used other points of demarcation in 1980 (even with open-ended responses) would have been to reduce the degree of comparability to prior years.

The rationale for using the age of the youngest, rather than the oldest, child is that when a family has more than one child, the youngest is apt to be the last one to move out and establish his own household. When the oldest child or children move out, the parents do not become empty nesters; i.e., their stage in the life-cycle does not change. When the youngest moves out, it often indicates a change in their status. While the age of the oldest child as the primary consideration is not only permissible, but has in fact been effectively employed in research on moving behavior,[13] the use of the youngest is also justifiable.[14]

The central research issue thus examines the extent of decline in the proportions of Stages 2, 3, 4, and 5, especially the first two. Exhibit 3-10 provides the percentage breakdown of each life-cycle stage for all nine housing types. There are several conditions and trends that merit attention. First, as bolstered through re-examination of Exhibits 3-7 and 3-8, the nuclear family is diminishing as a source of garden apartment demand. In 1970, young childless couples (Stage 2) comprised 22.1 percent of all households; by 1978, this figure had dropped to 14.2 percent, a reduction of over one-third. For couples with children (Stages 3, 4, and 5), the figure decreased from 21.3 percent to 14.9 percent over this period. Even if marrieds age 36–49 with children (Stage 5) are eliminated, the cumulative decline would still come to almost 30 percent.

Where has the slack picked up? For one thing, there has been a large entry of singles aged 35 and under (Stage 1) in these units. Much of this has been due to the aging and subsequent economic independence of the young adults born of the baby boom. Some of it, however may also be due to the rising divorce rate, in which former marrieds have divorced and reverted back to Stage 1 status. Second, there was a 43.5 percent increase in the number of female-headed households with children (Stages 3a, 4a, and 5a), another indication of rising divorce and separation rates. Finally, the proportion of the elderly increased from 10.6 to 13.0 percent, offsetting the slight loss incurred by empty nesters.

The outflow of marrieds has also been telling in other types of dwellings, but the distribution of change is different. In garden units, the most severe loss occurred among childless couples, a traditional core of the rental market. Among other housing types for which 1970 data are available, the sharpest decline occurred in households with children. This held true for owner- as well as renter-occupied units. Deferred childrearing and an enormous influx of singles into these structures were both critical factors. While the rise of female-headed families has been fairly high in garden

EXHIBIT 3-10

Family Life-Cycle Stage by Housing Type: 1970 and 1978

(in percentages, suburbs only)

		RENTER OCCUPIED						OWNER OCCUPIED		
	Stage	Garden Apt.	2-3-4 Unit Structure	SFU Detached	SFU Attached	Mobile Home	High-Rise	SFU Detached	SFU Attached	Mobile Home
1	1970	23.0	7.0	4.7	NA	NA	NA	0.3	NA	0.0
	1978	34.3	20.6	18.3	13.7	22.1	14.3	2.4	7.0	5.9
	% Change: 1970-78	+49.1	+194.3	+289.4	--	--	--	+700.0	--	--
2	1970	22.1	13.0	6.3	NA	NA	NA	3.2	NA	10.0
	1978	14.2	10.4	10.0	7.8	17.3	4.5	5.8	5.8	6.7
	% Change: 1970-78	-35.7	-20.0	-58.7	--	--	--	+81.3	--	-33.0
3	1970	14.2	30.0	35.4	NA	NA	NA	22.5	NA	36.7
	1978	10.7	13.6	18.5	18.6	24.1	1.4	16.2	18.8	17.2
	% Change: 1970-78	-24.6	-54.7	-47.7	--	--	--	-28.0	--	-53.1
4	1970	0.9	1.0	3.1	NA	NA	NA	5.1	NA	3.3
	1978	2.1	1.9	3.9	6.3	1.7	0.0	3.9	3.0	3.3
	% Change: 1970-78	+133.3	+90.0	+25.8	--	--	--	-23.5	--	0.0
5	1970	6.2	8.0	22.0	NA	NA	NA	32.6	NA	6.7
	1978	2.1	5.1	13.5	8.5	1.7	0.0	34.1	20.7	4.5
	% Change: 1970-78	-66.1	-13.3	-38.6	--	--	--	+ 4.6	--	-32.8
3a	1970	0.9	3.0	9.8	NA	NA	NA	1.0	NA	0.0
	1978	3.8	3.8	4.7	8.2	7.1	1.8	0.9	1.4	--
	% Change: 1970-78	+322.2	+26.7	+487.5	--	--	--	-10.0	--	--
4a	1970	1.8	1.0	0.0	NA	NA	NA	0.7	NA	0.0
	1978	2.4	6.0	2.9	1.3	0.0	0.0	1.0	1.5	2.1
	% Change: 1970-78	+33.3	+500.0	--	--	--	--	+42.9	--	--

EXHIBIT 3-10 (Continued)

Family Life-Cycle Stage by Housing Type: 1970 and 1978

(in percentages, suburbs only)

Stage		RENTER OCCUPIED						OWNER OCCUPIED		
		Garden Apt.	2-3-4 Unit Structure	SFU Detached	SFU Attached	Mobile Home	High-Rise	SFU Detached	SFU Attached	Mobile Home
5a	1970	3.5	4.0	2.6	NA	NA	NA	0.1	NA	3.3
	1978	2.7	3.1	5.7	13.6	2.0	0.0	3.4	3.4	1.0
	% Change: 1970-78	-22.9	-22.5	+119.2	--	--	--	+3,300.0	--	-69.7
6	1970	16.8	11.0	9.4	NA	NA	NA	10.1	NA	20.0
	1978	14.9	5.3	11.2	10.6	19.1	21.3	10.5	17.5	21.3
	% Change: 1970-78	-11.3	-51.8	+19.1	--	--	--	+ 4.0	--	+ 6.5
7	1970	10.6	22.0	11.5	NA	NA	NA	23.5	NA	30.0
	1978	13.0	18.0	11.2	11.4	4.9	56.7	21.8	20.8	36.6
	% Change: 1970-78	+22.6	-18.2	- 2.6	--	--	--	- 7.2	--	+22.0

Note: "NA" refers to the fact that some categories contained too few responses to be conclusive.

Source: U.S. Bureau of the Census, 1970 Census of Housing and 1978 Annual Housing Survey, Public Use Tapes.

apartments, it has been even higher in most of the other dwellings, especially in 2-3-4 and detached single-family structures, where these households currently make up nearly 15 percent of the total.

The tests of statistical significance for shifts in life-cycle composition are presented in Exhibit 3-11. Changes in household life-cycle ratios in the garden apartment stock are analyzed as: 1) the aggregate of 1970 and 1978 responses; 2) the distribution of 1970 responses, by period of construction (1940–59 vs. 1960–March 1970); and 3) the distribution of 1978 responses, by period of construction (1940–March 1970 vs. April 1970–78).

The first set of data examines changes in household composition over the aforementioned eight-year period. Of interest here is the extent to which each type of household had shifted as a percentage of the total garden apartment tenantry, without respect to dwelling age. Since percentage for each stage is expected to travel in one direction, *decreasing* for young nuclear families (Stage 2, 3, 4, and 5) and *increasing* for all others, each test is one-tailed. Thus, a Z-score could be in the critical region of rejection (whether at the .01, .05, or .10 level) and still be statistically insignificant.

The second and third sets of data examine whether the results are affected by the age of the dwelling. The newer portion of the 1978 garden apartment stock should contain a tenantry that bears a closer resemblance to the 1970 distribution than does the older portion. It is essential to distinguish between the "1970, by Year Constructed" and "1978, by Year Constructed" data sets. The hypothesized outcome for the 1970 data is that no significant differences occur between units built during 1940–59 and during 1960–March 1970. This is because the year of observation (1970) preceded the period 1970–78. Thus, the percentage of all households accounted for by each life-cycle stage should exhibit little variation. The intent for the 1978 data, by contrast, is for significant differences to exist between units built prior to the 1970 Census and those built afterward. This is because 1978 represents the most recent year in which expected trends should have taken place. The trends in the rental market during the 1970s would dictate that a significantly *greater* portion of marrieds and a significantly *smaller* portion of other households surveyed in 1978 live in the post-March 1970 vintage units.

The instrument for measuring the significance of change is the difference-of-proportions test, which Blalock succinctly summarizes in *Social Statistics.*[15] Briefly, this is a variation of the difference-of-means test. Instead of examining means, however, the test examines the proportional breakdown of a given variable (life-cycle) the summation of which is 100 percent. Two independently drawn samples of sizes N_1 and N_2 are normally distributed around each proportion. By obtaining a pooled estimate of the standard error, it is possible to test whether or not the percentage difference

EXHIBIT 3-11

Stage in Family Life-Cycle of Garden Apartment Residents: 1970 and 1978
(in percentages, except for Z-scores)

	(All)			1970, By Year Constructed			1978, By Year Constructed		
Stage in Life-Cycle	*1970*	*1978*	*Z Score*	*1940-59*	*1960-70*	*Z Score*	*1940-3/70*	*4/1970-78*	*Z Score*
1	23.0	34.3	-2.51***	13.5	27.6	-1.68*	33.8	35.0	-1.09
2	22.1	14.2	2.32**	18.9	23.7	0.58	11.9	17.6	-5.84***
3	14.2	10.7	1.18	13.5	14.5	-0.10	11.1	10.0	1.22
4	0.9	2.1	-0.90	2.7	0.0	1.42	1.0	3.6	-8.67***
5	6.2	2.1	2.93***	2.7	7.9	-1.61*	1.8	2.5	-1.75*
3a	0.9	3.8	-4.83***	0.0	1.2	-0.67	3.5	4.2	-1.40
4a	1.8	2.4	-1.50*	2.7	1.2	0.56	2.1	2.8	-1.75
5a	3.5	2.7	0.53	5.4	2.4	0.83	2.3	3.2	-2.06
6	10.6	14.9	-1.31*	16.2	7.9	1.36*	17.0	11.6	5.43***
7	16.8	13.0	1.19	24.3	13.2	1.50*	15.4	9.3	6.49***
Total	100.0	100.0		100.0	100.0		100.0	100.0	
n =	113	2,203		37	76		1,214	819	

All tests are one-tailed.

*Significant at .10
**Significant at .05
***Significant at .01

Source: U.S. Bureau of the Census, 1970 Census of Housing and 1978 Annual Housing Survey, Public Use Tapes.

between two proportions of each life-cycle stage is large enough that the likelihood of it being due merely to sampling error is extremely low.

The first three columns in Exhibit 3-11 reveal that the aggregate 1970–78 change was statistically significant for life-cycle Stages 1, 2, 5, 3a, 4a, and 6. That is, for these categories of households, the shift in percentage was large enough to assume with a high degree of accuracy that no significant change had occurred. These households account for almost 75 percent of the 1978 sample. The results are significant at the .05 level in most cases and, with the exception of Stages 2, 4a, and 6, at the .01 level as well. In two additional stages (3 and 7), change occurred in an expected direction, though not to a significant degree. The two remaining stages (4 and 5a) proved the exceptions to the rule, with change occurring in the direction opposite from that expected. However, these accounted for less than five percent of all households in 1978. *On balance, therefore, the tenantry in garden apartments demonstrated a clear shift away from families over the course of the 1970s.*

The second and third trios of columns examine the extent of differences by structural age in the *1970 Census of Housing* and the *1978 Annual Housing Survey*, respectively. The 1970 data fulfilled expectations. In only four cases were differences significant and then, only at the .10 level, although much of the "success" here is due to the small size of the one-in-ten thousand sample. The proportion of singles, for instance, was twice as high in 1960–70 structures as it was in 1940–59 structures. Similarly, the proportions of empty nesters and the elderly in 1960–70 structures were approximately one-half what they were in older structures. Given that in each case, the percentage was initially quite substantial, had the sample size been boosted up to that of 1978, these differences would have almost unquestionably been significant at the .01 level as well. More conclusive are equivalent results found in the New Jersey resident sample (see Exhibit 4-4).

The 1978 sample, however, does contain a large number of cases. Differences are significant here at .10 for Stages 2, 4, 5, 6, and 7, and in most cases, at .01 as well. That is, marrieds (2, 4, and 5) comprised significantly larger portions of the aggregate tenantry in the newer units, especially childless ones (Stage 2), while empty nesters and the elderly comprised significantly smaller portions. Singles and female-headed households proved to be the anomalies, with greater proportions residing in newer complexes.

The results for both 1970 and 1978 indicate that age as well as life-cycle define demographic cleavages when differentiating by structural age. Newer units, despite their higher rents (see Exhibit 3–4), contain a greater portion of singles, despite these households' lower incomes in comparison to marrieds (see Exhibit 3–12). Newer complexes attract a younger clientele for several reasons. First, incomes are highest for childless couples and their childrearing demands are nonexistent. As such, they can afford to be more choosy about their residence. Though singles lack their potency, they have experienced a large increase in real income since 1970 and therefore could afford more expensive units. Second, singles tend to have a high preference for recreational amenities, and are willing to pay more to get them.[16] Finally, newer complexes tend to be located away from previously established communities, in outer ring suburbs and semi-rural areas.[17] This impacted most heavily upon the elderly (Stage 7), who aside from a lack of income with which to travel, tend to avoid residential choices where mass transit facilities are not nearby.[18]

Education

Garden apartment adults are by all reasonable accounts better educated than adults living in other forms of rental housing, and at least as well educated as homebuyers. They have, as Exhibit 3-12 indicates, the lowest portions of persons without a high school diploma and one of the highest portions of those with a college degree; over 25 percent held degrees in 1978.

Note, however, that the percentage of household heads with a postgraduate education actually fell by one-third, from 15.9 to 10.6 percent. Since a specialized education is prerequisite for a large cluster of high-salaried positions, it usually places the employee in a better position to afford a home. That is why the proportions of people with five or more years of college increased markedly for all homeowners and more than doubled in the case of townhouse owners.

Income

Exhibit 3-13 offers evidence of homeownership as a magnet for the affluent once-renter of the 1970s. Owners, who already had higher incomes than renters in 1970, widened their advantage. Each category of homeowner (by structural type) experienced an aggregate gain in median income, especially large in the case of SFU-detached owners. By contrast, with the exception of high-rises, there were no inflation-adjusted gains in renter medians.

In the context of their renter status, garden apartment households showed an overall 6.8 percent loss, which was considerably better than that of their counterparts in 2–3–4 unit single-family structures, yet worse than those in SFU-detached and high-rises.

Among individual households in garden units, the gain for singles was a whopping 30.9 percent. The garden apartment, like both the high-rise and single-family unit, tends to attract the upper end of the singles market. Marrieds without children gained in real income, while those with children lost. Those with children had the highest incomes for all household types except empty nesters in 1970, whereas this was no longer true eight years later.

EXHIBIT 3-12

Highest Level of Education Completed by Principal Wage Earner by Type of Housing: 1970 and 1978

(in percentages, suburbs only)

Level of Education	RENTER OCCUPIED Garden Apt.	2-3-4 Unit Structure	SFU Detached	SFU Attached	Mobile Home	High-Rise	OWNER OCCUPIED SFU Detached	SFU Attached	Mobile Home
Less than 12th grade									
1970	16.7	44.0	47.9	47.4	NA	NA	38.2	32.3	54.8
1978	16.2	30.6	32.2	32.4	44.3	26.1	23.1	20.8	43.9
% Change: 1970-78	- 3.0	-30.5	-32.8	-31.6		--	-39.5	-35.6	-19.9
High School Diploma (12th Grade)									
1970	31.7	28.4	29.8	26.3	NA	NA	30.4	35.5	28.6
1978	33.0	37.2	32.3	31.4	39.3	32.6	32.4	27.2	37.8
% Change: 1970-78	+ 4.1	+31.0	+ 8.4	+19.4		--	+ 6.6	-23.4	+32.2
1-3 Years College									
1970	21.4	13.5	10.5	5.3	NA	NA	13.4	3.2	9.5
1978	25.3	16.3	19.3	22.1	16.3	20.5	18.4	22.4	11.6
% Change: 1970-78	+18.2	+20.7	-83.8	+317.0		--	+37.3	+600.0	+22.1
4 Years College									
1970	14.3	5.0	6.3	10.5	NA	NA	9.2	22.6	7.1
1978	14.8	10.1	7.7	14.3	0.0	14.4	12.9	15.4	5.1
% Change: 1970-78	+ 3.5	+102.0	+22.2	+36.2		--	+40.2	-31.9	-28.1
5 Years or More of College									
1970	15.9	9.2	5.2	10.5	NA	NA	8.8	6.5	0.0
1978	10.0	5.9	8.5	0.0	0.0	6.4	13.2	14.3	1.5
% Change: 1970-78	-33.3	-35.9	+63.5	--	--	--	+50.0	+120.0	

Source: U.S. Bureau of the Census, 1970 Census of Housing and 1978 Annual Housing Survey, Public Use Tapes.

Contrast, for example, Stages 1 and 3. In 1970, Stage 3 households (principal wage earner 35 or under, youngest child pre-grammar school age) had a median figure exactly twice that of singles. In 1978, their edge had shrunk by barely over 20 percent. In 1970, Stage 5 households had a median income of almost 200 percent that of Stage 1 renters. By 1978, their edge had shrunk to only 60 percent. In the garden apartment market, even more so than in other segments of the rental market, there has been an outflow of households with children not only in relative proportions, but in relative financial potency as well. Many of those who remain renters are not likely candidates for homeownership in the near future, given that the expenses necessary to raise children reduce available funds for housing investment. This figure should be interpreted not so much as a problem, but as a measure of success among the bulk of affluent potential homebuyers in realizing their ambition.

The across-the-board decline in real incomes of empty nesters, even among owners of detached dwellings, is a curiosity. Presumably, the principal wage earners of many such households are in their peak earning years, yet in garden apartments, for example, their purchasing power fell by over one-third. This may be attributed to the impact of the trend toward early retirement, plus the rising proportion of divorced women among them.

Exhibit 3-14 indicates, at least for the most well-represented household types, that incomes tend to be higher in newer complexes. This is not surprising. These developments were constructed at a time when development, construction, and above all, financing costs had climbed to a higher level than that prior to the 1960s. The rents necessary to support these complexes were generally higher from the outset and had thus caused many low- and moderate- income households to look elsewhere for their rental accommodations.

Moving Behavior

Reasons for Moving

Exhibit 3-15 inquires into the principal reason why recent movers (within the past 12 months) had chosen to move. Leading all responses were those related to the workplace—either a change of job, or a desire to commute shorter distances to an existing one. Topping all forms of housing in this category was the garden apartment: fully 24.8 percent of all respondents in 1978 listed this as the primary motive. This figure outnumbered the combined totals for a desire for better housing or neighborhood. Garden units hold an attraction for singles, as evidenced by the 10.3 percent of those who wanted to establish their own household; this motive led all others related to a change in family situation. Finally, while garden apartment residents may

EXHIBIT 3-13

Stage in Family Life-Cycle by Total Household Median Income: 1970[3] and 1978 (rounded to nearest dollar, suburbs only)

Stage		RENTER OCCUPIED					
		Garden Apartment	2-3-4 Unit Structure	SFU Detached	SFU Attached	Mobile Home	High-Rise
1	1970	$ 8,000	$11,592	$ 6,384	$ --	$ NA[2]	$ --
	1978	11,000	9,699	9,701	9,999	7,869	15,049
	% Change: 1970-1978	+30.9	-16.3	+52.0	--	--	--
2	1970	15,960	16,968	12,180	--	--	--
	1978	18,055	15,107	18,001	10,203	9,883	25,390
	% Change: 1970-1978	+13.1	-11.0	+47.8	--	--	--
3	1970	16,800	12,768	12,768	12,096	NA[2]	NA[2]
	1978	13,286	12,000	12,615	12,461	6,051	NA[2]
	% Change: 1970-1978	-20.9	-6.0	-1.2	+3.0	--	NA[2]
4	1970	NA[2]	NA[2]	7,560	--	--	--
	1978	16,107	15,058	21,514	21,610	--	--
	% Change: 1970-1978	--	--	+184.6	--	--	--
5	1970	24,696	16,632	16,044	--	NA[2]	--
	1978	17,770	16,178	16,898	20,230	NA[2]	--
	% Change: 1970-1978	-28.0	-2.7	+5.3	--	--	--
3a	1970	NA	7,896	NA	--	--	--
	1978	5,593	5,696	4,797	9,892	--	NA[2]
	% Change: 1970-1978	--	-27.9	--	--	--	--
4a	1970	NA[2]	NA[2]	--	--	--	--
	1978	8,340	7,552	7,378	4,256	--	--
	% Change: 1970-1978	--	--	--	--	--	--
5a	1970	7,308	2,604	7,056	--	--	--
	1978	8,838	6,785	10,971	7,965	--	--
	% Change: 1970-1978	+20.9	+160.6	+55.4	--	--	--
6	1970	20,244	16,296	11,844	--	--	21,504
	1978	13,357	10,307	8,100	15,008	3,468	15,991
	% Change: 1970-1978	-34.0	-36.8	-31.6	--	--	-25.6
7	1970	7,728	4,116	5,880	NA[2]	NA[2]	NA[2]
	1978	5,011	5,199	4,032	3,445	NA[2]	6,206
	% Change: 1970-1978	-35.2	+26.3	-31.6	--	--	--
All Stages[1]	1970	12,936	12,306	12,235	16,464	6,137	9,744
	1978	12,050	10,000	11,951	11,000	6,006	10,000
	% Change: 1970-1978	-6.8	-18.7	-2.3	-33.2	-2.1	+ 2.6

EXHIBIT 3-13 (Continued)

Stage in Family Life-Cycle by Total Household Median Income: 1970[3] and 1978 (rounded to nearest dollar, suburbs only)

Stage		OWNER OCCUPIED		
		SFU Detached	*SFU Attached*	*Mobile Home*
1	1970	NA[2]	--	--
	1978	$16,460	$16,123	$11,095
	% Change: 1970-1978	--	--	--
2	1970	23,268	NA[2]	NA[2]
	1978	25,100	21,616	15,028
	% Change: 1970-1978	+7.9	--	--
3	1970	20,467	NA[2]	13,440
	1978	20,025	5,454	15,000
	% Change: 1970-1978	-2.2	--	+11.6
4	1970	20,076	NA[2]	NA[2]
	1978	21,501	23,654	20,771
	% Change: 1970-1978	+7.1	--	--
5	1970	23,659	30,072	NA[2]
	1978	25,300	26,042	19,463
	% Change: 1970-1978	+6.9	-13.4	--
3a	1970	6,720	--	--
	1978	8,451	NA[2]	5,275
	% Change: 1970-1978	+25.8	--	--
4a	1970	11,172	NA[2]	--
	1978	10,604	NA[2]	11,050
	% Change: 1970-1978	-5.1	--	--
5a	1970	7,476	--	NA[2]
	1978	13,028	11,040	--
	% Change: 1970-1978	+74.3	--	--
6	1970	23,772	NA[2]	9,576
	1978	14,000	18,864	--
	% Change: 1970-78	-41.1	--	--
7	1970	7,968	8,400	5,544
	1978	9,040	10,786	--
	% Change: 1970-78	+13.5	+28.4	--
All Stages [1]				
	1970	20,289	15,372	11,508
	1978	20,681	27,000	11,591
	% Change: 1970-78	+1.9	+36.6	+0.7

[1]Figures for "All Stages" do not include residual households not falling under any specific category.

[2]"NA" refers to the fact that some categories contained too few responses to be conclusive.

[3]All 1970 figures are weighted by 1.68, reflecting the change for all items in the Consumer Price Index over 1970-78.

Source: U.S. Bureau of the Census, 1970 Census of Housing and 1978 Annual Housing Survey, Public Use Tapes.

EXHIBIT 3-14

Total Household Median Income by Stage in Family Life-Cycle and Year Built, Garden Apartments: 1978

(suburbs only)

Stage	(1) Constructed 1940-3/60	(2) Constructed 4/1960-3/70	(3) Constructed 4/1970-78	(2) ÷ (1)	(3) ÷ (1)
1	$10,503	$10,775	$11,510	+ 2.6	+ 9.6
2	17,782	18,839	18,045	+ 5.9	+ 1.5
3	10,491	12,985	15,754	+23.8	+50.1
4	--	12,181	20,473	--	--
5	--	12,168	23,081	--	--
3a	5,677	7,792	3,453	+37.2	-39.2
4a	12,492	8,203	8,398	-34.3	-32.8
5a	8,195	9,414	8,840	+14.9	+ 7.9
6	11,961	13,649	13,612	+14.1	+13.8
7	3,858	6,314	4,380	+63.7	+13.5

Source: U.S. Bureau of the Census, 1978 Annual Housing Survey, Public Use Tapes.

be generally satisfied with their housing or neighborhood, a desire for an improvement in either was not as important a factor in bringing them to their present apartment as it was for residents of all other types of rental housing, excepting those in mobile homes, the low end of the totem pole.

Number of Years in Present Unit

It is difficult not to be struck by the extremely short periods of time that present garden apartment dwellers have lived in their unit, both in absolute and relative terms. According to Exhibit 3-16, the mean number of years for a garden apartment resident in 1978 was 2.01 years. This is far shorter than the result indicated in Chapter Five, and is suggestive of the enormous impact that leasing periods of less than one year (unlike New Jersey) have on a project's turnover rate.

Predictably, the latter two stages of the life-cycle, empty nesters (Stage 6) and the elderly (Stage 7) remained in their units for the longest mean periods.[19] Also predictably, singles (Stage 1) remained in their units for relatively short periods, reflecting the dominant pattern of singles in other housing types, renter and owner alike. Like marrieds, singles who rent a garden apartment frequently typify a "here today, gone tomorrow" pattern of turnover.

Since data for 1970 are not available as a result of a curious incongruity in the 5 and 15 percent Public Use Samples,[20] there is no way to measure the extent that the mean duration may have lengthened or shortened for a given

EXHIBIT 3-15

Main Reason for Moving Within the Last Twelve Months: 1977

(in percentages, suburbs only)

	RENTER OCCUPIED						*OWNER OCCUPIED*		
	Garden Apt.	*2-3-4 Unit Structure*	*SFU Detached*	*SFU Attached*	*Mobile Home*	*High-Rise*	*SFU Detached*	*SFU Attached*	*Mobile Home*
New Job/Closer Commute	24.8	15.9	19.0	21.0	17.3	5.1	16.9	14.4	12.7
Retirement	0.6	0.0	0.0	0.0	0.0	0.0	0.1	0.0	4.8
Attend School	4.2	2.3	0.5	0.0	0.0	5.1	0.2	0.0	2.4
Married	5.0	8.1	8.1	1.6	13.6	5.1	4.5	0.0	5.6
Separation/Divorce	6.8	5.8	2.0	2.9	8.2	0.0	1.3	0.0	0.0
Change in Size of Family	0.9	0.8	1.6	0.0	4.5	5.1	0.5	0.0	2.4
Wanted to Establish Own Household	10.3	12.0	9.3	4.8	19.1	10.2	3.7	3.1	7.1
Closer to Relatives	3.3	3.9	2.2	3.2	2.7	0.0	0.4	6.2	6.3
Wanted to Own Dwelling	NA	NA	NA	NA	NA	NA	24.4	43.3	14.3
Wanted Better Dwelling	5.3	4.1	7.2	8.1	0.0	0.0	8.2	3.1	2.4
Wanted Larger Dwelling	5.2	9.3	13.4	8.9	1.8	10.2	20.4	3.1	10.3
Wanted Better Neighborhood	3.6	3.9	5.2	4.8	2.7	5.1	6.4	0.0	4.0
Lower Rent or Housing Costs	5.4	7.6	5.2	5.6	8.2	0.0	1.7	10.3	4.0
Displacement	2.0	5.3	7.0	4.8	2.7	5.1	0.9	0.0	2.4
Other	22.6	21.0	19.3	34.3	19.2	51.0	10.4	16.5	21.3
Total	100.0	100.0	100.0	100.0	100.0	100.0	100.0	100.0	100.0

Source: U.S. Bureau of the Census, 1970 Census of Housing and 1978 Annual Housing Survey, Public Use Tapes.

EXHIBIT 3-16

Stage in Family Life-Cycle by Mean Number of Years Lived in Present Unit: 1978[1,3]

(suburbs only)

	RENTER OCCUPIED						OWNER OCCUPIED		
Stage	*Garden Apartment*	*2-3-4 Unit Structure*	*SFU Detached*	*SFU Attached*	*Mobile Home*	*High-Rise*	*SFU Detached*	*SFU Attached*	*Mobile Home*
1	1.20	0.65	1.06	1.83	0.80	0.85	2.31	0.55	0.55
2	1.06	0.96	1.35	0.77	0.82	1.17	1.54	0.48	2.55
3	1.25	1.73	1.90	1.88	0.80	2.50	2.96	2.29	2.81
4	1.83	2.92	1.13	2.08	1.00	--	3.80	1.79	1.83
5	1.15	4.74	3.07	4.81	2.00	--	8.92	12.49	3.30
3a	1.17	2.00	1.42	0.65	0.50	0.50	3.65	0.50	1.56
4a	1.62	2.73	2.07	4.50	--	--	5.25	1.71	4.13
5a	2.41	4.04	4.61	3.00	1.00	--	8.79	3.72	1.07
6	2.96	1.63	4.69	5.35	0.71	3.84	12.79	6.76	4.83
7	4.89	8.37	8.76	12.22	7.90	4.96	15.50	11.99	6.24
All Stages[2]	2.01	3.61	3.06	3.57	1.54	5.39	8.95	6.49	4.34

[1]Figures on duration in present dwelling were not available in the 5 percent sample of the 1970 Census of Housing.
[2]Figures for "All stages" do not include residual households not falling under any of the specified categories.
[3]Figures exclude units constructed from 1976 through 1978 to allow for sufficient time lag.

Source: U.S. Bureau of the Census, 1978 Annual Housing Survey, Public Use Tapes.

household type. However, it is worth noting that the short duration in garden apartments cannot be readily attributed to a large, sudden influx of residents in newly-constructed units. Cross tabulations revealed that among those residents of garden apartment units built during April 1970–1975 (allowing for a three-year time lag from a dwelling's construction to the 1978 Annual Housing Survey), 40 percent had moved into their present unit in the same year as the survey (1978), a figure comparable to that of residents in units constructed during 1940–60 (March) and during 1960–70 (March). The garden apartment clearly represents for many a short-term residential choice. Whether or not this represents a historical break remains unconfirmed.

Resident Satisfaction

Satisfaction with Dwelling and Neighborhood

Exhibit 3-17 indicates the overall perception held by residents of their dwelling and neighborhood condition. Approximately three-fourths of garden apartment residents rated their dwellings as either "good" or "excellent," with twice as many in the former category. While these figures are not as favorable as those of owner-occupants or high-rise renters, they do not vary from the overall pattern of satisfaction.

Just as it was not possible to compare length of residence in 1978 with that in 1970, neither was it possible to compare dwelling and neighborhood satisfaction between these two years. These variables were not included in the 1970 Census Questionnaire Form, nor for that matter in the first (1973) Annual Housing Survey. Moreover, at the time of this study, the 1978 sample had not been released, thus necessitating the use of the 1977 sample. The time elapse necessary to discern meaningful results is simply too short.

There is an association between the period during which a structure had been built and the degree to which its residents will view favorably both dwelling and neighborhood. Exhibits 3-18 and 3-19 indicate that with each increment of newness, the cumulative mean rating of each improved. This held true in all ten stages for dwelling rating and six out of ten for neighborhood rating. Yet the shifts were not particularly large in a number of instances and, therefore, would not have likely been statistically significant had a difference-of-means test been applied. For marrieds (Stages 2, 3, 4, and 5), the situation was different pertaining to dwelling rating: the improvement in the 4/70–77 period over the 4/60–3/70 period was quite substantial.

EXHIBIT 3-17

Housing Type by Overall Satisfaction with Dwelling and Neighborhood: 1977[1]
(in percentages, suburbs only)

	DWELLING RATING					*NEIGHBORHOOD RATING*				
	Excellent	*Good*	*Fair*	*Poor*	*Total*	*Excellent*	*Good*	*Fair*	*Poor*	*Total*
Renter-Occupied										
Garden Apartment	24.2	50.0	21.7	4.0	100.0	27.5	51.4	18.5	2.6	100.0
2-3-4 Unit Structure	21.1	53.9	20.5	4.4	100.0	27.0	51.2	17.9	3.9	100.0
SFU Detached	24.6	50.4	19.2	5.7	100.0	30.1	52.1	14.4	3.4	100.0
SFU Attached	26.2	40.6	28.1	5.1	100.0	24.4	49.1	21.1	5.4	100.0
Mobile Home	10.8	47.2	37.1	4.9	100.0	23.7	43.8	28.4	4.1	100.0
High-Rise	37.8	54.3	3.1	4.8	100.0	41.2	47.6	8.4	2.8	100.0
Owner-Occupied										
SFU Detached	51.1	42.7	6.0	0.2	100.0	46.8	43.7	8.6	0.9	100.0
SFU Attached	43.2	48.8	7.2	0.9	100.0	42.9	44.2	12.3	0.7	100.0
Mobile Home	34.9	48.3	11.9	4.9	100.0	37.9	46.3	13.8	2.8	100.0

[1]The 1978 Public Use Sample had not been released at the time of this research. Thus, 1977 data are used.

Source: U.S. Bureau of the Census, 1977 Annual Housing Survey, Public Use Tapes.

EXHIBIT 3-18

Stage in Family Life-Cycle by Mean Rating of Dwelling, Garden Apartments: 1977[1]

(in percentages, suburbs only)

	YEAR CONSTRUCTED				
Stage	*(1) 1940-3/60*	*(2) 4/1960-3/70*	*(3) 4/1970-77*	*(2) ÷ (1)*	*(3) ÷ (1)*
1	2.07	2.06	1.90	- 0.5	- 8.2
2	2.05	2.00	1.63	- 2.4	-20.5
3	2.01	1.85	1.67	- 8.0	-16.9
4	1.90	1.91	1.55	- 0.5	-18.4
5	1.82	1.49	1.44	-18.1	-20.9
3a	2.56	2.27	1.85	-11.3	-27.3
4a	2.24	2.10	2.03	- 6.8	- 9.4
5a	1.96	1.89	1.82	- 3.6	- 7.2
6	1.85	1.81	1.63	- 2.2	-11.9
7	1.67	1.58	1.45	- 5.4	-13.2
All stages[2]	1.87	1.76	1.64	- 5.9	-12.3

[1]Mean figures refer to scale from one to five, with "1" as "Excellent," "2" as "Good," "3" as "Fair," and "4" as "Poor."
[2]"All stages" does not include residual households that do not fall under any specific category.

Source: U.S. Bureau of the Census, 1977 Annual Housing Survey, Public Use Tapes.

Reasons for Moving as a Result of Neighborhood Problems

With the exception of single-family residents, who base their dwelling choice heavily upon the absence of potentially unfavorable neighborhood conditions, the overwhelming majority of residents in 1977 listed at least one problem existing in their neighborhood, as Exhibit 3-20 reveals. However, more importantly, approximately nine-tenths of those who did perceive a problem would not be willing to move as a direct result. Garden apartment residents closely adhere to this general pattern.

Those who indicated a desire to move usually gave more than one reason for doing so. The most common were street/highway noise, industries and businesses in the immediate vicinity, heavy traffic, and crime. Though commonly denoted as "urban" problems, they have come home to roost in the suburbs as well.

EXHIBIT 3-19

Stage in Family Life-Cycle by Mean Rating of Neighborhood, Garden Apartments: 1977[1]

(in percentages, suburbs only)

	YEAR CONSTRUCTED				
	(1)	(2)	(3)	(2) ÷ (1)	(3) ÷ (1)
Stage	*1940-3/60*	*4/1960-3/70*	*4/1970-77*		
1	1.91	1.99	1.73	+ 4.2	- 9.4
2	1.85	2.47	1.74	+33.5	- 5.9
3	1.94	1.85	1.81	- 4.6	- 6.7
4	1.80	1.78	1.69	- 1.1	- 6.1
5	1.77	1.57	1.56	-11.3	-11.9
3a	2.16	2.16	2.03	- 0.0	- 6.0
4a	2.32	2.29	1.81	- 1.3	-22.0
5a	1.92	1.91	2.18	- 0.6	+13.5
6	1.76	1.75	1.66	- 0.6	- 5.7
7	1.64	1.59	1.48	- 3.0	- 9.8
All stages[2]	1.80	1.75	1.64	- 2.8	- 8.9

[1]Mean figures refer to a scale from one to five, with "1" as "Excellent," "2" as "Good," "3" as "Fair," and "4" as "Poor."
[2]"All stages" does not include residual households that do not fall under any specific category.

Source: U.S. Bureau of the Census, 1977 Annual Housing Survey, Public Use Tapes.

Conclusion

This chapter has provided a Census-based overview of the key components of change in the garden apartment stock and its residents over the course of the 1970s. Garden apartments have indeed come to attract a significantly greater proportion of residents other than young nuclear families. When results are analyzed by the presence or absence of children in the units, the downturn occurred at a faster rate than nationwide for families without children, and at a slower rate than nationwide for families with children. The major exception among "nontraditional" households is the group of singles 35 and under, who have grown at a rapid rate in garden apartments and elsewhere. In newer units, this trend is less pronounced. Yet the ranks of singles in these newer apartments have swelled to over twice the figure of any other household stage. The young-old cleavage, like the married-nonmarried one, has come to figure prominently in the changing garden apartment market.

EXHIBIT 3-20

Perception of Neighborhood Problems and Wish to Move: 1977
(in percentages, suburbs only)

PROBLEM	RENTER OCCUPIED						OWNER OCCUPIED		
	Garden Apt.	2-3-4 Unit Structure	SFU Detached	SFU Attached	Mobile Home	High-Rise	SFU Detached	SFU Attached	Mobile Home
No undesirable neighborhood conditions	12.2	9.4	6.6	1.4	0.2	1.5	56.5	2.5	3.7
With undesirable neighborhood conditions	87.8	90.6	93.4	98.6	99.8	98.5	43.5	97.5	96.3
Household would not like to move	91.4	90.3	92.0	90.1	90.1	90.2	95.5	96.3	92.1
Household would like to move[1]	8.6	9.7	8.0	9.9	9.9	9.8	4.5	3.7	7.9
Street/highway noise	31.6	40.4	33.5	38.9	38.9	35.9	29.0	30.7	28.9
Heavy traffic	27.0	34.2	29.5	19.6	19.6	40.5	24.5	21.3	25.1
Streets in need of repair	9.3	12.9	18.5	36.3	36.3	8.2	15.9	6.5	25.3
Streets impassable	9.1	8.6	12.0	27.1	27.1	5.6	11.6	10.0	13.5
Inadequate street lighting	18.1	19.6	30.5	35.9	35.9	12.7	31.7	28.7	29.6
Crime	19.0	20.7	14.0	3.9	3.9	26.5	16.0	15.3	14.8
Trash, litter	10.9	12.4	14.7	12.7	12.7	8.5	12.5	13.2	13.1
Abandoned structures	4.1	5.2	7.1	4.9	4.9	11.1	3.4	6.0	5.0
Rundown housing	3.5	9.2	11.8	9.3	11.8	5.6	8.3	9.4	9.4
Industries/businesses	30.7	35.2	19.6	17.2	17.9	33.6	12.2	13.4	17.0
Odors, smoke, or gas	6.6	9.1	7.2	8.1	4.1	4.2	7.8	7.4	11.6
Airplane noise	19.9	21.3	6.4	29.4	27.1	17.9	20.1	16.4	24.4
Unsatisfactory public transportation	1.3	0.3	0.7	1.3	0.0	0.0	0.3	0.8	0.0
Unsatisfactory schools	0.4	1.3	1.0	1.9	0.0	1.4	0.5	0.3	0.0
Unsatisfactory shopping	0.3	0.4	0.6	0.8	0.0	1.4	0.2	0.7	0.4
Unsatisfactory police protection	1.1	0.7	0.9	0.0	0.0	2.9	0.2	0.7	0.4
Unsatisfactory recreational facilities	0.6	0.9	0.4	1.9	3.9	0.0	0.3	1.4	0.0
Unsatisfactory health clinics	0.6	0.5	1.0	2.9	2.0	0.0	0.2	0.7	1.7

[1]Respondents who would move as a result of neighborhood conditions frequently cited more than one reason for their doing so. This is why, for example, although 8.6 percent of all garden apartment households would move, individual categories sometimes yielded much higher figures.

Source: U.S. Bureau of the Census, 1977 Annual Housing Survey, Public Use Tapes.

What is the main implication of this? Garden apartments have come to serve less as "way stations" for marrieds than a decade before. While the duration of residence is also short for "nontraditionals," the fact that there are now far more of the latter households makes garden units increasingly dependent upon the more affluent young singles and childless divorcees for an adequate revenue base. Yet as condominiums, both new and converted, increase in popularity, they will siphon off many present and potential renters within this group. This will be especially true for the fast-growing segment of "singles" who are cohabitating couples of the opposite sex and who consequently have two incomes upon which to draw.

The vast portion of the garden apartment stock is still in sound condition, from the standpoint of both objective and subjective indicators. Whether it can remain so for many decades depends largely upon future patterns of household formation and upon how quickly substitute way-stations such as the condominium can further penetrate the housing market.

NOTES

1. The advantages of the Census and the Annual Housing Survey as data bases are described in William C. Apgar, Jr., "Census Data and Housing Analysis: Old Data Sources and New Applications," in Gregory K. Ingram, ed., *Residential Location and Urban Housing Markets*, Cambridge, Mass.: Ballinger, 1977, p. 140.

2. A few of the very early garden complexes do contain four stories. However, having been built during the 1920s and 30s, they would have been deleted from the sample anyway.

3. The questionnaire form in the Decennial Census does not make the distinction because it is self-enumerated, and the Census Bureau does not believe, based on prior field tests, that respondents would be able to accurately identify either the public ownership or rent-subsidized status of their unit. By contrast, the Annual Housing Survey form does make the distinction because enumerators are presumably trained to recognize cases falling into either of these categories. Telephone conversation with William Downs, Field Manager, Division of Housing, U.S. Department of Housing and Urban Development, April 23, 1980.

4. See Bernard J. Frieden and Arthur P. Solomon, *The Nation's Housing Needs: 1975–85*, Cambridge, Mass.: MIT-Harvard Joint Center for Urban Studies, 1977.

5. High-rise apartments, often "prestige" dwellings, command higher rents (see Exhibit 3-3) and have higher tenant incomes (see Exhibit 3-13) than garden apartments. It comes as little surprise, therefore, that they are in better structural condition.

6. U.S. Bureau of the Census, *Current Housing Reports*, Series H-150-78, Annual Housing Survey: 1978, Part A, "General Housing Characteristics for the United States and Regions: 1978," Washington, D.C.: U.S. Government Printing Office, 1980.

7. George Sternlieb and James W. Hughes, *America's Housing: Prospects and Problems*, New Brunswick, N.J.: Center for Urban Policy Research, 1980, p. 36.

8. Ira S. Lowry, *Rental Housing in the Seventies: Searching for the Crisis*, Santa Monica, Cal.: Rand Corporation, January 1982.

9. The year 1970 instead of 1972 is used as the point of demarcation of the newest portion of the stock in order to establish an eight-year time frame in order to observe market change, as was done in Chapter Four.

10. See Lowry, *Rental Housing in the 1970s*. The second point may be clarified by an example. Assume a nuclear family of four with an income of $30,000. Assume that two high school graduate offspring, given the ample availability of rental housing in their area, move out of their parents' home and into an apartment. Since their incomes (even if pooled together) are not likely to be even near the level of their parents, their effect upon the rent-income ratio would be to raise it. However, assume that the rental housing supply was far from ample. The likelihood of the offspring moving out early would not have been as great. As a result, they would not have contributed to the rising ratio.

11. See Exhibit 3-12. This statement applies only to 2–3–4 unit structures and single-family detached units, the only dwelling categories for which the 1970 data provided enough cases for conclusive results.

12. In 1970, the mean figures for persons per household in one-, two-, and three-bedroom units were 1.846, 2.500, and 4.111, respectively. By 1978, they had declined to 1.417, 2.295, and 3.528.

13. See Sheila J. Miller, "Family Life-Cycle, Extended Family Orientations, and Economic Aspirations as Factors in the Propensity to Migrate," *Sociological Quarterly*, Vol. 17, Summer 1976, pp. 323–35.

14. Moreover, it has been applied to housing research. See John B. Lansing and Leslie Kish, "Family Life-Cycle as an Independent Variable," *American Sociological Review*, Vol. 22, No. 1, February 1957, pp. 512–19; Robert Schafer, *The Suburbanization of Multifamily Housing*, Lexington, Mass.: Lexington Books, 1974.

15. Hubert M. Blalock, Jr., *Social Statistics*, 2nd ed., New York: McGraw-Hill, 1972, pp. 228–30.

16. Owens-Corning Fiberglas, "The Tenants' Point of View: A Survey of Garden Apartment Residents' Attitudes in Five Cities," *Urban Land*, February 1970, pp. 3–8.

17. Monmouth County Planning Board, *Multi-Family Housing in Monmouth County*, Freehold, N.J.: Monmouth County Planning Board, January 1973.

18. U.S. Department of Housing and Urban Development, Office of Metropolitan Development, *Tomorrow's Transportation*, Washington, D.C.: U.S. Government Printing Office, 1968. As the report summarizes (p. 17):

> If transit service continues to be reduced, many of these (elderly) nondrivers will be destined to be isolated more and more in their narrow neighborhood worlds, while all around them, the advantages of automobile mobility benefit the relatively affluent majority each year.

19. See the following for further evidence of this trait: C. G. Pickvance, "Life-Cycle, Housing Tenure and Intra-Urban Residential Mobility: A Causal Model," *Sociological Review*, Vol. 21, No. 2, May 1973, pp. 279–97; Stephen Golant, "The Housing Adjustments of the Young and the Elderly: Policy Implications," *Urban Affairs Quarterly*, Vol. 13, No. 1, September 1977, pp. 95–108.

20. See Appendix, in discussion under "Census Public Use Samples."

4

The Garden Apartment and its Residents: The View from a Statewide Survey

Introduction

This chapter draws upon a survey administered to garden apartment residents in towns and suburbs throughout the state of New Jersey, where an ample supply of garden units exists. Unlike Chapter Three, this analysis compares tenant characteristics not only as a function of two separate surveys (1972 vs. 1980), but also as one of the present survey demarcated by dwellings constructed before 1972 ("1980") vs. during and after 1972 ("1980a"). The intent of the first type of comparisons is to delineate historical change in garden apartment demand; the intent of the second is to identify how much of the change actually took place, when discounting new additions to the existing garden apartment stock. Prior to the discussion however, it will be necessary to develop a portrait of garden apartment dwellers based upon previous surveys.

Demographic Characteristics: Literature Summary

Overview

The growth of the garden apartment stock sharply accelerated during the late-50s and early-60s. Not surprisingly, studies of its residential composition began to appear in substantial numbers about this time. Much of the literature still consists solely of "head counts," and more specifically, of school children per dwelling unit ratios. This is because most garden apartment surveys have been conducted by suburban county and municipal planning agencies as an aid in determining the appropriateness of rental housing growth in their respective jurisdictions. Fiscal impact is a major issue that these agencies consider in evaluating individual development proposals,[1] and a leading component of the cost side of the ledger is the potential addition to existing public school enrollment. Sometimes these studies are limited exclusively to this issue. Others consider broader demographic concerns, such as occupation, income and race.[2] Since this study is far less concerned with dwelling unit multipliers than with family life-cycle and related variables, the former will not be discussed in this chapter.[3]

Family Life-Cycle

While several researchers have gathered data on one or more of the components of the household life-cycle—age of household head, marital status, and presence and age of children—only Schafer has combined them into a single variable. Dividing a Boston-area garden apartment sample into almost two dozen life-cycle categories, he found that singles and married couples without children predominated. The percentage of all married couples with children, in fact, did not equal that of married couples without children whose heads of household were younger than 30. Nor did it equal the figure for singles under 30. This research, conducted a decade ago, supports the argument that once a family commences its childrearing activity, it is increasingly predisposed toward purchasing a home, or, if it cannot afford to do so, rents a dwelling similar in appearance to the one it hopes to buy.

A statewide survey in Rhode Island conducted at about the same time revealed an over three-to-one ratio of married couples without children to those with children. Though the research does not contain a specific variable for life-cycle, it suggests a strong relationship between the presence of children in a nuclear family and a preference for homeownership.

Occupation

While suburbs have acquired a sizeable number of manufacturing and wholesaling firms over the past several decades, and while residential choice remains largely predicated upon proximity to the workplace, the empirical evidence indicates that adult garden apartment residents principally hold white-collar positions (professional, technical, managerial, sales, and clerical). In the Rhode Island study, for example, the ratio of white-collar employees to the total labor force was about 60 percent; in Boston and St.

Louis suburbs, this figure climbed to approximately 80 percent. In all cases, professional and technical employees accounted for the largest portion of the white-collar sector. As Schafer concluded from the Boston data, ". . .it is clear that the suburbs, including the outer suburbs involving one-half hour to one hour one-way commutes to work, are successfully competing with the central city to provide luxury apartments."[4]

Income

Generally, garden apartment residents are years away from their peak earning power, yet several studies conducted over the course of the mid-60s through the early 70s revealed that they form a relatively affluent portion of the renter population. In Woodbridge, New Jersey in 1965, the median income for garden apartment households was $8,314; for all households in that community, it was $8,207. In Greensboro, North Carolina in 1969, 67 percent of all garden apartment households had a total income of $8,000 or more; only 48 percent of the city's entire households fit into this upper category. While some of the other studies do not specifically compare garden apartment with total populations in the same sampling area and are therefore less useful, they too revealed sizeable incomes among the former.

In the context of the Census figures in Exhibit 3-13, it is difficult to avoid concluding that had these surveys been conducted very recently, the relative position of garden apartment residents would have been less favorable. Nationwide, real incomes of suburban garden apartment residents declined by almost ten percent; those of suburban homeowners gained, if only slightly.

Conclusion

Through the early-70s, garden apartment dwellers consisted of predominantly young, childless married couples who were well-educated and well-represented in white-collar positions. Compared to most renters, they had sizeable incomes. Whether or not this capsule reality has substantially shifted is a task for the next section to determine.

Demographic Characteristics: Baseline and Current Data

Household Structure

The nationwide decline of nuclear families as a proportion of all households during the past decade has been particularly acute in the existing garden apartment stock. Exhibit 4-1 reveals that in 1972, 38.0 and 30.8 percent of all garden apartment households consisted of husband-wife couples without and with children, respectively. By 1980, these figures had dwindled to

EXHIBIT 4-1

Household Structure: 1972, 1980, and 1980a
(in percentages)

	1972	*1980*	*% Change 1972-80*	*1980a*	*% Change 1972-80a*
Type of Household (All)					
Husband-wife couple, no children	38.0	24.4	- 35.8	42.3	+ 11.3
Husband-wife couple, with children	30.8	17.4	- 48.2	13.2	- 57.1
Male head with children, no wife present	0.3	0.6	+100.0	1.8	+500.0
Female head with children, no husband present	3.8	10.1	+165.8	7.0	+ 84.2
Primary individual(s), male principal wage earner	10.6	22.0	+107.5	20.7	+ 95.3
Primary individual(s), female principal wage earner	16.6	25.4	+ 53.0	15.0	- 9.6
Total	100.0	100.0		100.0	
n =	1,433	794		227	
Type of Household (Unrelated)					
One male or female, two or more relatives	NA	16.6	--	8.7	--
One male, one female	NA	51.1	--	56.5	--
Two males or two females	NA	24.4	--	26.0	--
One male, two or more females/one female, two or more males	NA	2.2	--	8.7	--
Three or more males/three or more females	NA	5.5	--	4.3	--
Total	--	100.0	--	100.0	--
Percent of all households with nonrelatives	--	11.3	--	10.1	--

Source: Center for Urban Policy Research, Garden Apartment Resident Survey, Summer-Fall 1980.

24.4 and 17.4 percent. Thus, barely over 40 percent of the garden units built prior to 1972 presently contain nuclear families. Each of the other four categories have taken up the slack. Both female- and male-headed primary individual households exhibited sizeable gains.[5] Even more remarkable was the rise in female-headed households with children from 3.8 to 10.1 percent of the total, clearly indicative of the increase in the divorce rate.

Note however, how these figures contrast with those for households in the newer (1980a) complexes. Here, the proportion of husband-wife couples without children actually rose to 42.3 percent. Yet that of couples with children fell even more precipitously, to 13.2 percent. Thus, the erosion of young married couples is a phenomenon limited primarily to the older portion of the stock, precisely that which was found in the national sample.

Both the 1980 and 1980a data indicate that slightly over ten percent of all households consist of two or more unrelated persons, with slightly over half this figure in both cases consisting of a male-female arrangement. The much lower figure in the newer complexes for "one male or female, two or more relatives" is accounted for by the fewer number of cases in which single women with children live with an unrelated male companion.

Age of Principal Wage Earner

Exhibit 4-2 indicates that the aggregate garden apartment tenantry grew older during 1972–80. While the share of principal wage earners aged 21–25 declined from 22.2 to 12.9 percent, the remaining brackets exhibited noticeable increases (although the under 21 bracket also exhibited a large percentage gain, its share was so minute in the first place, that the increase was

EXHIBIT 4-2

Age of Principal Wage Earner: 1972, 1980, and 1980a

(in percentages)

Age	*1972*	*1980*	*% Change 1972-80*	*1980a*	*% Change 1972-80a*
Under 21	0.8	1.4	+75.0	1.4	+75.0
21-25	22.2	12.9	-41.9	29.3	+31.9
26-35	36.4	38.7	+ 6.3	38.3	+ 5.2
36-49	13.3	15.6	+17.3	17.6	+32.2
50-64	11.9	13.3	+11.8	10.4	-12.6
65 and over	15.2	18.0	+18.4	3.2	-78.9
Total	100.0	100.0		100.0	
n =	1,424	790		222	

Source: Center for Urban Policy Research, Garden Apartment Resident Survey, Summer-Fall 1980.

almost meaningless). The general upward shift resulted partly from a portion of the tenants in 1972 remaining in their present units over the subsequent eight-year period and partly from the replacement in vacated units by older tenants.

However, for newer developments in the 1980 sample (1980a), the situation was quite different. Here, the 21–25 age bracket accounted for 29.3 percent of all households, a figure sizeably higher even than that of 1972, let alone 1980. In this case, the elderly were the principal losers; only 3.2 percent of all principal wage earners (PWEs) were 65 or over, less than one-fifth the total in the older complexes sampled in 1980. Again, the results point to a reduced presence of young marrieds in garden complexes as a whole, yet one which has not affected the newest portion of the stock.

Marital Status

Exhibit 4-3, like 4-1, indicates a decline in the overall married population during 1972–80, and a very large one for those in the existing complexes. In older developments, the proportion of singles doubled from 16.3 to 32.5 percent, while the separated, divorced, and widowed evidenced a sizeable gain as well.[6] In newer developments, singles increased, though by a lesser proportion, separated and divorced adults remained fairly stable, and the widowed dropped sharply, a reflection of the very small number of elderly households.

Family Life-Cycle Composition

Thus far, this section has analyzed shifts in various elements of the household life-cycle without examining shifts in the variable as a whole. Using the

EXHIBIT 4-3

Marital Status of Principal Wage Earner: 1972, 1980, 1980a

(in percentages)

Marital Status	*1972*	*1980*	*% Change 1972-80*	*1980a*	*% Change 1972-80a*
Single or unrelated household	16.3	32.5	+ 99.4	27.7	+ 69.9
Married	68.6	41.2	- 39.9	53.1	- 22.6
Separated	2.1	3.8	+ 81.0	4.5	+114.3
Divorced	3.6	11.0	+205.6	10.7	+197.2
Widowed	8.9	11.5	+ 29.2	4.0	- 55.1
Total	100.0	100.0		100.0	
n =	1,428	791		224	

Source: Center for Urban Policy Research, Garden Apartment Resident Survey, Summer-Fall 1980.

same classifications as indicated in Exhibit 3-9, Exhibit 4-4 pieces together the elements to focus on the central concern of this book: the potential erosion of the "traditional" young nuclear family garden apartment tenantry.

As with the equivalent Public Use Sample data in Exhibit 3-11, there are statistical tests, first, on the shift among each household type in the aggregate and, second, on the differences in composition produced by partitioning the data according to period of construction. Additionally, with respect to the first test, the more recent data are indicated in *weighted* and *unweighted* form. The purpose of weighting here is to ascertain if the change in each life-cycle stage *would have occurred had all 1980 observations (i.e. both 1980 and 1980a) contained a proportion of units built during or after 1972 similar to the proportion built in New Jersey as a whole.* Therefore, if expectations hold, the data should be statistically significant here as well as in the re-sample of existing units.

This weighting procedure was not performed on the national data because the 1978 Annual Housing Survey had already taken into account new construction over the 1970–78 period. For the sample here, new data pertained only to households residing in the same units surveyed in 1972. The weight was estimated by examining data on multifamily construction starts in New Jersey over 1972–80, estimating what portion of these were garden apartments, and further estimating what portion of these new additions comprised all garden units in the state in 1980. Approximately one-third of all units in the state existing in 1980 had been built during or after 1972, a figure of about 1.5 times the percentage of all households in these units sampled here. The weight, therefore, was 1.5.

The instrument measuring the significance of change, as before, is the difference-of-proportions test. As noted in Chapter Three, this test is applied to two or more *independently* drawn samples, and not to those consisting of matched pairs. Yet this precondition does not disqualify a comparison between 1972 and 1980 (existing) figures, even though the units in the later sample were selected to assure identical addresses. Note the following statement by Blalock:[7]

> . . .the whole aim of matching, or of using the same individuals twice, is to control as many variables as possible other than the experimental variable. The attempt is to make the two samples as much alike as possible, much more alike than if they had been selected independently.

Here, the experimental variable is not housing, but *households*. There is no assumption that the percentage distribution of life-cycle stages will necessarily be similar to those encountered in 1972. The 1980 sample does not

EXHIBIT 4-4

Stage in Family Life-Cycle of Garden Apartment Residents: 1972, 1980, 1980a
(in percentages, except for Z-scores)

Stage in Life Cycle	Re-Sample (Existing) 1972	1980	Z-Score	1972 vs. Weighted 1980 (All) 1972	1980	Z-Score	1972, by Year Constructed 1940-59	1960-71	Z-Score	1980, by Year Constructed 1940-71	1972-80	Z-Score
1	11.1	24.9	- 7.50***	11.1	25.1	-10.57***	11.7	10.7	0.56	24.9	25.7	- 0.24
2	24.8	13.4	6.20***	24.8	16.3	7.81***	19.7	27.5	-3.18***	13.4	37.3	-12.10***
3	23.2	10.5	15.12***	23.2	10.0	10.15***	14.0	28.1	-5.88***	10.5	6.8	1.57
4	1.7	2.3	- 0.97	1.7	2.2	- 1.02	1.1	0.9	0.36	2.3	1.5	0.71
5	2.8	1.9	1.27	2.8	1.8	1.95*	2.1	3.1	-1.11	1.9	1.5	0.38
3a	1.1	2.5	- 2.45**	1.1	2.5	- 3.01***	0.8	0.1	2.26**	2.5	1.9	0.50
4a	0.9	2.2	- 2.48**	0.9	2.1	- 2.73***	0.8	0.9	-0.14	2.2	1.0	1.18
5a	2.0	4.6	- 4.31***	2.0	4.6	- 4.06***	3.2	1.4	2.26**	4.6	3.4	0.75
6	16.3	18.3	- 1.18	16.3	18.1	- 1.38*	20.6	13.9	3.19***	18.3	17.0	0.43
7	16.3	19.2	- 1.65*	16.3	17.3	0.76	25.9	11.1	7.05***	19.2	3.4	5.51***
All stages	100.0	100.0		100.0	100.0		100.0	100.0		100.0	100.0	
n =	1,347	754		1,347	1,714		471	876		754	206	

All tests are one-tailed.

*Significant at .10
**Significant at .05
***Significant at .01

Note: Approximately four to seven percent of all households in each sample are unclassifiable and are not reflected in these or any subsequent figures by family life-cycle.
Source: Center for Urban Policy Research, Garden Apartment Resident Survey, Summer-Fall 1980.

consist of a variable that is being matched and, therefore, the difference-of-proportions test can indeed be applied.

The demographic shifts in existing units confirm the expected life-cycle shifts even more so than the national data, as the first trio of columns in Exhibit 4-4 indicates. Seven of the ten household life-cycle types evidenced significant shifts in an expected direction. They accounted for almost 80 percent of all respondents in existing 1980 units. Moreover, nuclear families, principal wage earner 36–49, youngest child at least in grammar school (Stage 5) and empty nesters (Stage 6) experienced change in a hypothesized direction, if not always significantly. The same results were yielded with weighted 1980 data, with the exception of the elderly, where the shift, while upward, was not significant.

Both data sets are indicative of a massive shift in the demand for rental housing, particularly at the younger end of the spectrum. Note that while the proportion of singles 35 and under (Stage 1) more than doubled, the proportion of marrieds 35 and under without children (Stage 2), and with the youngest child of kindergarten age or younger (Stage 3) each had fallen drastically. Where the latter two household types accounted for almost 50 percent of all households in 1972, they now account for less than 25 percent. This outflow of marrieds is too precipitous to have merely mirrored a statewide or nationwide decline; it had to have stemmed as well from a surge of homebuying among baby boom adults.

The latter two data sets in Exhibit 4-4 reveal that while significant differences may exist when dwellings are controlled for vintage, this tendency was actually more pronounced in 1972 than in 1980. In the earlier survey, percentage shifts were significant for six of ten household types, accounting for over 80 percent of all households in the then-new garden apartment stock. By contrast, shifts were only significant on two occasions in the 1980 observations. This finding is mitigated, however, when marrieds are broken down by the presence or absence of children. In 1972, the percentage of Stage 3 households (marrieds, 35 or under, youngest child, kindergarten or younger) in then-new 1960–71 units was twice the figure for the same households in 1940–59 vintage units. In 1980, however, it was lower in new units by almost one-third. For childless couples (Stage 2), the picture was markedly different. In 1972, their proportion in 1960–71 vintage dwellings was almost 50 percent greater than in 1940–59 units. In 1980, the proportion in new (1972–80) units nearly tripled to almost two-fifths of all households, despite the fact that the ratio of two-to-one bedroom units in the sample remained fairly constant.

Thus, *the already existing portion of the garden apartment stock is that in which the buildup of nontraditional households has been most pronounced.* Most notably, this portion contains the larger percentages of elderly and female-headed families, the two groups least able to absorb rising rents. The potential for a problem is clear, for in the oldest complexes, the necessity of rent increases, given high operating ratios, has been greatest (see Exhibit 5-1).

Education

Although levels of educational attainment among the American population continued to rise during the 70s, the garden apartment tenantry was left relatively untouched. In fact, the percentage of the various levels of college-educated principal wage earners actually declined during 1972–80 (see Exhibit 4-5). This would tend to support the notion that this type of housing serves a less upwardly mobile population—one consisting less of young married couples and more of singles (who are often enrolled in college), and of single mothers (who did not attain the level of education of their former spouses).

By contrast, residents of new complexes exhibited gains over the 1972 sample in all categories of college education, except for a negligible decline among those with a two-year Associate's Degree or two/three years of college. Among secondary wage earners, there was a substantially greater proportion of persons with at least a Bachelor's Degree.

Occupation

The results in Exhibit 4-5 suggest that fewer principal wage earners than before are engaged in occupations requiring an education beyond high school. The percentages of professional/technical and managerial/sales employees dropped by 27.5 and 11.9 percent, respectively (see Exhibit 4-6). On the other hand, clerical, service, and laborer positions exhibited sizeable gains. For 1980a the proportion of professional/technical employees decreased by 20.0 percent. However, managerial and sales employees increased by a prodigious 73.3 percent.

Among secondary wage earners, the percentages for all categories increased in the re-sampled developments, with managerial/sales, laborers, and students showing the most impressive gains. Among those living in newer complexes, the gains were even more striking. A full 30 percent were employed either in a professional/technical or managerial capacity. These gains are not merely the result of an erosion of married couples (and hence, of wives, who are usually the secondary wage earner of a married couple).[8] As Exhibit 4-7 indicates, in each household life-cycle category for married couples under 65, the percentage of working wives sharply increased, with the cumulative labor force participation rate rising from 41.4 to 61.9 percent. Among those in new complexes, the rate advanced to an even higher 73.5 percent. The greater rate of increase can be readily explained by the

EXHIBIT 4-5

Highest Level of Education Completed by Principal and Secondary Wage Earner: 1972, 1980, and 1980a

(in percentages)

EDUCATION	*1972*	*1980*	*% Change 1972-80*	*1980a*	*% Change 1972-80a*
Principal Wage Earner					
Less than high school diploma	8.0	6.9	-13.8	3.6	-55.0
High school diploma/1 year college	32.9	42.7	+29.8	33.6	+ 2.1
Associate's, business, or trade school degree/2-3 years college	14.8	12.4	-16.2	14.5	- 2.0
B.A. or equivalent/Working on M.A. or equivalent	29.1	23.5	-19.2	30.5	+ 4.8
M.A. or equivalent/Working on Ph.D. or equivalent	10.6	10.3	- 2.8	12.7	+19.8
Ph.D. or equivalent	4.8	4.2	-12.5	5.0	+ 4.1
Total	100.0	100.0		100.0	
n =	1,409	758		220	
Secondary Wage Earner					
Less than high school diploma	NA	5.4	--	3.6	--
High school diploma/1 year college	NA	57.1	--	52.9	--
Associate's, business or trade school degree/2-3 years college	NA	14.2	--	16.7	--
B.A. or equivalent/Working on M.A. or equivalent	NA	15.9	--	19.6	--
M.A. or equivalent/Working on Ph.D. or equivalent	NA	5.9	--	5.8	--
Ph.D. or equivalent	NA	1.5	--	1.4	--
Total	--	100.0	--	100.0	
n =	--	408	--	138	

Source: Center for Urban Policy Research, Garden Apartment Resident Survey, Summer-Fall 1980.

EXHIBIT 4-6

Occupational Status of Principal and Secondary Wage Earners: 1972, 1980, and 1980a

(in percentages)

Occupation	1972	1980	% Change 1972-80	1980a	% Change 1972-80a
Principal Wage Earner					
Professional and technical	33.5	24.3	- 27.5	26.8	- 20.0
Managerial and sales	21.0	18.5	- 11.9	36.4	+ 73.3
Clerical	9.0	12.2	+ 35.6	10.5	+ 16.7
Craftsman	8.2	7.8	- 4.9	5.9	- 28.0
Operative	5.7	5.8	+ 1.8	7.3	+ 28.0
Service worker	3.1	5.0	+ 61.3	5.0	+ 61.3
Laborer	1.8	5.0	+177.8	1.8	0.0
Retired	14.3	18.1	+ 26.6	4.5	- 68.5
Student	1.8	1.0	- 45.4	0.0	--
Unemployed/Disabled	1.4	2.2	+ 57.1	1.8	+ 28.6
Military	0.3	0.0	--	0.0	--
Total	100.0	100.0	100.0	100.0	
n =	1,422	778		220	
Secondary Wage Earner					
Professional and technical	12.7	13.9	+ 9.4	17.8	+ 40.1
Managerial and sales	2.2	6.9	+213.6	12.3	+459.0
Clerical	16.6	21.1	+ 27.1	30.1	+ 81.3
Craftsman	0.4	0.9	+125.0	1.4	+250.0
Operative	0.7	0.9	+ 28.6	0.7	0.0
Service worker	3.5	4.4	+ 25.7	7.5	+114.2
Laborer	0.4	4.2	+950.0	1.4	+250.0
Retired	9.6	15.3	+ 59.4	5.5	- 47.4
Student	2.1	5.6	+166.7	1.4	- 33.3
Unemployed/Disabled	2.4	4.2	+ 75.0	1.4	- 41.6
Housewife	49.3	22.3	- 54.8	22.6	- 54.2
Military	0.0	0.2	--	0.0	--
Total	100.0	100.0		100.0	
n =	1,081	431		146	

Source: Center for Urban Policy Research, Garden Apartment Resident Survey, Summer-Fall 1980.

EXHIBIT 4-7

Stage in Family Life-Cycle by Percent of Married Couples Under Age 65 with Two Wage Earners: 1972, 1980, and 1980a

(in percentages)

Stage in Family Life Cycle	*1972*	*1980*	*% Change: 1972-80*	*1980a*	*% Change: 1972-80a*
2	64.0	88.8	+ 38.8	78.5	+22.7
3	16.6	38.4	+131.3	27.3	+64.6
4	42.9	60.0	+ 39.9	80.0	+86.6
5	38.9	61.5	+ 58.1	66.7	+71.5
6	43.6	48.8	+ 11.9	75.0	+72.0
All couples under 65[1]	41.4	61.9	+ 49.5	73.5	+77.5

[1]"All couples under 65" includes residual households that do not fall under any specific category. Figures exclude cases where one or both adults were either students or retirees.

Source: Center for Urban Policy Research, Garden Apartment Resident Survey, Summer-Fall 1980.

larger portion of Stage 4, 5, and 6 employees and by the much higher absolute number of Stage 2 employees despite a lower participation rate.

Income

Household incomes in re-surveyed units experienced absolute gains, but when adjusted for areawide Consumer Price Index increases, they actually fell, as Exhibit 4-8 reveals. Many former garden apartment occupants are being replaced not only by households with lower incomes (Stages 3a, 4a, 5a, and 7), but also by households with lower (inflation-adjusted) incomes within each life-cycle stage. Only Stages 1, 2, and 5 had higher incomes in 1980. While the cumulative 1980 median of $19,581 is high in comparison to the nationwide median, it suggests a weakening of the revenue base necessary to support operating costs. The figure is actually substantially less than its equivalent for 1972, when allowing for an 84.0 percent increase in the overall Consumer Price Index for the New York-Northeastern New Jersey area. On the other hand, it is instructive to note that the fast-growing singles market (Stage 1) had 1980 incomes well above $20,000, an indication that garden units attract the more affluent of these households. The decreases in Stages 3 and 4 were far more marked than the increases in Stages 2 and 5. The singles' growth in real income is surely a strong buffer against the overall downward trend. Garden apartments, more than other rental accommodations, provide an added attraction to the upper crust of suburban market households.

EXHIBIT 4-8

Stage in Family Life-Cycle by Median Total Household Income: 1972, 1980, and 1980a

Stage	*1972*[2]	*1980*	*% Change: 1972-80*	*1980a*	*% Change: 1972-80a*
1	$21,608	$22,899	+ 6.0	$24,765	+14.6
2	24,795	25,111	+ 1.3	25,859	+ 4.3
3	22,618	18,250	-19.4	20,000	-11.6
4	26,285	18,750	-28.7	25,000	- 4.9
5	22,164	25,000	+12.8	32,500	+46.6
3a	12,511	8,156	-34.8	15,000	+19.9
4a	15,946	13,571	-14.8	10,000	-37.3
5a	14,604	13,014	-10.9	13,750	- 5.9
6	22,842	18,375	-19.6	22,857	+ 0.1
7	14,006	7,873	-43.8	9,166	-34.6
All stages[1]	22,994	19,581	-14.8	24,980	+ 8.6

[1]"All stages" includes residual households that do not fall under any specific category.
[2]All figures for 1972 are inflated by 84.0 percent, the June 1972-August 1980 Consumer Price Index increase for all items in the New York City-Northeastern New Jersey area.

Source: Center for Urban Policy Research, Garden Apartment Resident Survey, Summer-Fall 1980.

With the exception of Stage 4a (of which there were extremely few cases), households in new complexes had uniformly higher incomes than those in re-surveyed ones. The overall difference was 27.6 percent, with married couples without children (Stage 2)—the largest component in this sample—having only a slightly higher figure. This is why the aggregate median was sizeably higher than most of its individual components.

Exhibit 4-9 indicates the distribution of mean responses, by income bracket, regarding which homebuying households planned to move within three years, and anticipated major difficulties in affording a home. In the literal sense, homebuying may involve "difficulties," however minor, for households with incomes as high as $100,000. The present concern is with problems of such a magnitude as to restrict potential homebuyers to renter status for much longer periods of time than they wish to accept.

Within all income brackets, except $7,500–9,999 (who are not likely to be able to afford a home, whatever they may believe to the contrary), residents of the older complexes were more optimistic about their homebuying opportunities. This is probably because so many residents of the newer developments cited homeownership as the predominant objective of a planned move, but not a realizable one within the near future (see Exhibit 4-14).

EXHIBIT 4-9

Anticipation of Major Difficulty in Being Able to Afford a Home by Total Household Income: 1980 and 1980a

(means only)[1]

Income	*1980*	*1980a*	*% Difference: 1980a÷80*
Under $5,000	1.00	--	--
$5,000-$7,499	1.00	--	--
$7,500-$9,999	2.60	3.00	+15.4
$10,000-$14,999	2.17	1.43	-34.1
$15,000-$19,999	2.81	2.44	-13.2
$20,000-$24,999	2.61	2.09	-19.9
$25,000-$34,999	3.00	2.55	-15.0
$35,000 and over	4.69	3.12	-33.5

[1]Mean figures refer to a scale of anticipated major difficulty of being able to afford a home, with "1" as "Yes, definitely" and "5" as "Definitely not." They include only those respondents who plan to move within three years and who plan to buy a home.

Source: Center for Urban Policy Research, Garden Apartment Resident Survey, Summer-Fall 1980.

EXHIBIT 4-10

Contract Rent: 1972, 1980, and 1980a

(in percentages)

Contract Rent	*1972*	*1980*	*% Change: 1972-80*	*1980a*	*% Change: 1972-80a*
Under $150	18.6	0.7	- 96.2	0.0	--
$150-$199	56.0	4.5	- 92.0	0.0	--
$200-$249	24.0	14.7	- 38.7	0.0	--
$250-$299	1.4	31.7	+2,164.7	5.7	+307.1
$300-$349	0.0	35.8	--	33.6	--
$350-$399	0.0	9.8	--	34.6	--
$400 and over	0.0	2.7	--	26.1	--
Totals	100.0	100.0		100.0	
Median (Nearest Dollar)	$175	$296	+ 69.1	$360	+105.7

Source: Center for Urban Policy Research, Garden Apartment Resident Survey, Summer-Fall 1980.

Housing Costs

That newer complexes have higher rents is evident in Exhibit 4-10. While the median rent increased in re-surveyed complexes from $175 to $296, or 69.1 percent,[9] it increased to $360, or 105.7 percent in complexes constructed during or after 1972. Virtually all units rented for at least $300 in the latter group and over sixty percent rented for at least $350.

The year-round monthly average utility bill (gas and electricity) cost 25 percent more in the newer complexes (see Exhibit 4-11). Much of this difference, however, may simply be due to the fact that since their residents have higher incomes, they are less apt to exercise austerity in controlling thermostat temperatures during winter months. Of households using at least one of four available amenities separate from contract rent (garage/carport, swimming club, carpeting, and balcony/patio), renters in the newer complexes spent 140 percent more for them. This was due to: 1) the greater availability of these amenities in these developments; 2) the higher cost of their operation; and 3) the greater willingness of residents to pay the extra fees.[10]

Garden Apartment Residents and Their Living Environment: Literature Summary

Overview

Empirical research on the attitudinal and behavioral characteristics of garden apartment residents has been limited to approximately a half-dozen studies,[11] few of which are comprehensive in scope. There are a number of problems with their data bases. First, there is frequently a scant variety of questions in the sample questionnaire. Second, there is sometimes an insufficient variety of responses available to a respondent. Third, there is little cross tabulation between two or more variables. Finally, there is only sporadic calculation of a mean or a median for data on interval variables. However, despite these shortcomings, the studies do provide a fair approximation of the major indicators of satisfaction and moving behavior.

Length of Stay in Present Unit

The evidence from the late-60s and early-70s suggests relatively rapid rates of turnover within garden apartment complexes. In studies in Kansas City, Monmouth County, Greensboro, and Nashua, the percentages of tenants living in their present unit for less than one year were 33.5, 34.1, 66.5, and 58.7 percent, respectively. In fact, over one-third of the respondents in the latter two cases had lived in their units for less than six months. The recurring pattern in these studies was that of young marrieds and singles whose stay in that dwelling had been brief.

EXHIBIT 4-11

Utility and Additional Amenity Costs: 1980 and 1980a

(in percentages)

	1980	*1980a*	*% Difference 1980a ÷ 80*
Utilities			
Under $10	0.4	0.0	--
$10-$19	27.6	12.3	- 55.4
$20-$29	41.0	36.9	- 10.0
$30-$39	18.3	18.7	+ 2.2
$40-$49	7.1	8.4	+ 18.3
$50-$69	4.6	10.3	+ 123.9
$70 and over	1.0	13.3	+1,230.0
Totals	100.0	100.0	
Median (nearest dollar)	$24	$30	+ 25.0
Amenities[1]			
Under $5	15.4	8.7	- 43.5
$5-$9	19.9	19.6	- 1.5
$10-$19	63.5	14.1	- 77.8
$20-$29	0.0	31.5	--
$30 and over	1.2	26.1	+2,075.0
Totals	100.0	100.0	
Median	$10	$24	+ 140.0

[1]Figures for amenities reflect only those households who pay a fee for the use of at least one amenity. There are a minority in both the new and old development samples. All residents paid separate utility bills from rent, save for water.

Source: Center for Urban Policy Research, Garden Apartment Resident Survey, Summer-Fall 1980.

Anticipated Moving Behavior

A brief tenure of accumulated residency in one's apartment does not necessarily translate into a brief anticipated remaining tenure in that apartment. In all cases, the majority of tenants planned to remain in their present dwelling for at least two years, and in Johnson County and Greensboro, almost one-fourth planned to remain for at least another four years. Data on motives, unfortunately, are scant. In Johnson County, the primary reasons were closer commuting distances and job transfers, while in Monmouth County, it was home purchase. The most frequently anticipated form of housing for movers in St. Louis and Monmouth Counties was a private detached home, while in Johnson County, with its high proportion of empty nesters, another apartment (type unspecified) was the most likely destination.

Satisfaction with Neighborhood

The availability of data here is very limited. Only a survey conducted in the late-60s by Owens-Corning Fiberglas among garden apartment residents in Detroit, San Francisco, Minneapolis-St. Paul, Atlanta, and Washington, D.C. suburbs requested respondents to rate various features of their apartment complex. One a one-to-five scale ("1" as "excellent," "2" as "very good," "3" as "good," "4" as "fair," and "5" as "poor"), the mean ratings of recreational amenities, general appearance, and parking facilities were 2.89, 3.93, and 2.81, respectively. Garden apartments, therefore, rated slightly better than "good" in two categories and slightly better than "fair" in the other.

Reason for Choosing Present Development

Low cost, attractive physical appearance, a desire to rent, low maintenance effort, and proximity to work were the most frequent reasons cited for selecting a development among studies where these data were available. However, the results exhibit a large degree of variation even within these categories. For example, in suburban St. Louis, over fifty percent of the respondents cited proximity to work as the overriding reason for selecting their present complex. In Greensboro, by contrast, less than ten percent mentioned this as a factor, even though the interviewee had more than one choice.

Willingness to Pay Higher Rent

The Owens-Corning and Schafer studies constitute impressive efforts to gauge a tenant's willingness to pay for added project amenities. Owens-Corning asked tenants to express their willingness to pay a cited sum of rent for each of sixteen amenities that consisted of various household appliances, larger storage area, garage space, and various recreational facilities. The two principal findings were that: 1) singles were far more disposed to be "extremely" or "very" interested in paying additional rent than married couples with or without children; and 2) with the exception of a swimming pool, residents were far more reluctant to pay for added recreational amenities than appliances, even given a modest cost difference between the two overall categories. Schafer developed a hedonic index of thirty-two amenities (including location). Adult recreational facilities, personal security, and outdoor recreational facilities, as composite measures, accounted for over half the mean monthly rent.

Conclusion

The garden apartment residents in these studies share several traits. They are young marrieds or singles whose duration in their current residence is fairly brief. Their moves to their present dwelling originate at least as much from a desire for proximity to the workplace and for minimization of rental expenditures as they do from the appeal of the dwelling, complex, or immediate neighborhood. Though they are moderately satisfied with structural conditions, with the exception of singles, they are reluctant to pay higher rent for added services or amenities.

Garden Apartment Residents and Their Living Environment: Baseline and Current Data

Length of Stay in Present Unit

One of the supporting research issues of this book is the twin possibility that: 1) traditional occupants of garden apartments, whose propensity to move had been already high, are remaining in their present units for even shorter periods; and 2) nontraditional occupants are remaining in their present units for longer periods. As a consequence, the overall tenure of garden apartment residents may have actually lengthened because the proportion of marrieds is thinning. The format in Exhibit 4-12 is similar though not identical to that in 4-4. As before, unweighted and weighted data are compared with 1972 data. Also as before, figures for 1972 are divided into 1940–59 and 1960–71 periods of dwelling construction.

The difference lies in the two statistical controls applied here. First, responses from any project opened for occupancy more recently than three years prior to the fieldwork could not be included. This stipulation allowed for an adequate time elapse for mobility patterns to emerge. In that the newest apartments built during 1960–71 were actually completed in 1968, responses from complexes completed after 1977 during the 1972–80 period are necessarily deleted here. Second, responses from complexes surveyed in 1972 that were built prior to 1964 were also deleted. This was done to ensure that the longest possible length of stay for any household in either sample would be eight years.

Exhibit 4-12 indicates the significance of the shifts in mobility with respect to household life-cycle. Because the figures here are grouped means rather than grouped proportions (as was the case in Exhibit 4-4), the *difference-of-means* (t-values) rather than the difference-of-proportions (Z-values) test serves as the appropriate measuring instrument.

The overall mean period spent in a garden apartment lengthened from 3.22 to 5.08 years during 1972–80, an increase of 57.8 percent. With the

EXHIBIT 4-12

Stage in Family Life-Cycle by Number of Years Lived at Present Address: 1972, 1980, and 1980a

(in means, except for t-scores)

Stage in Life Cycle	Re-Sample (Existing)			1972 vs. Weighted 1980 (All)[1]			1972, by Year Constructed[1]			(1972)	(1980)[1]	
	1972	1980	t-Score	1972	1980	t-Score	1940-59	1960-71	t-Score	1964-68	1972-77	t-Score
1	1.76	2.75	-3.62***	1.77	2.58	-4.06***	1.70	1.79		1.70	1.48	1.16
2	1.82	2.33	-2.45	1.82	2.10	-1.77	2.04	1.76		2.04	1.61	1.89*
3	2.28	2.58	-1.28	2.28	2.51	-1.16	2.79	2.13		2.73	1.94	1.74*
4	3.30	4.53	-1.38	3.30	4.32	-1.34	5.25	2.76		5.25	2.00	1.09
5	4.09	6.70	-2.12	4.09	6.22	-1.88	5.73	3.20		5.25	1.83	1.72*
3a	1.72	2.30	-0.83	1.72	2.28	-1.24	1.88	1.66		1.88	2.06	0.30
4a	3.04	2.58	0.62	3.04	2.49	0.86	3.88	2.63		3.88	0.88	1.76
5a	3.98	5.57	-1.42*	3.98	5.33	-1.64*	3.78	4.23		3.79	3.25	0.74
6	4.80	7.30	-4.19***	4.80	6.81	-4.54***	6.11	3.96		6.01	3.02	3.08
7	6.36	9.81	-1.42*	6.36	9.65	-5.95***	8.32	3.91		8.43	3.17	5.02
All stages	3.22	5.08		3.35	4.69		4.90	2.60	931***	4.87	2.01	
n =	1,346	751		1,445	1,809		472	973		772	203	

All tests are one-tailed.

*Significant at .10
**Significant at .05
***Significant at .01

[1]The final three columns reflect the necessity of eliminating bias. Units surveyed in 1980, built during 1972-80, but completed after 1977 had to be deleted due to the insufficient lag time between the unit's opening for occupancy and the time of the sample (the most recent units in the 1940-71 grouping were actually opened in 1968). Likewise, units surveyed in 1972 and completed prior to 1964 had to be deleted due to the possibility that tenants would have lived in such units for more than eight years.

Source: Center for Urban Policy Research, Garden Apartment Resident Survey, Summer-Fall 1980.

minor exception of Stage 4a (female-headed families, mother 35 and under, youngest child grammar school or older), *every type of household increased its length of residence*. Thus, while nonmarrieds increased their length of stay, marrieds did so as well, contrary to expectations. While the latter's increase was generally not as pronounced as that of the former's, and while the period during which marrieds remain renters (in any dwelling) may very well be as short as ever, their duration of residence has unquestionably lengthened. These figures show a considerably longer length of stay than those of the 1978 Annual Housing Survey Public Use Sample. The disparities can be explained by market conditions between the nationwide and New Jersey garden apartment markets. In New Jersey, vacancy rates are comparatively low, rents are high, and the financial risks of premature moving are likewise high.[12] Additionally, the near-universality of one-year leases in the state, as opposed to those of shorter periods often found elsewhere (especially in the South and West), serves to discourage tenancies of less than one year.

When the entire 1980 data set was weighted to account for new additions to the stock, the figures remained significant for each stage that had yielded significant results in the previous data set. Indeed, the degree of association was stronger here, especially among the elderly.

Does the age of the structure make a difference with these data? According to Exhibit 4-12, it would make an extremely large one, at least in the case of households surveyed in 1972. Since moving behavior was expected to differ according to structural age only insofar as the entire sample was concerned, t-tests could not have been conducted for individual household types. However, as a result of the greater preponderance of younger households in newer buildings, the overall length of stay was much smaller, and also significant to the .01 level. Comparing the 1964–68 period (1972 survey) with the 1972–77 period (1980 survey), the results are significant for only a few households, and then, only at the .10 level. Even when exercising strict controls over maximum and minimum lengths of stay for both samples, thus insuring comparability, the duration in newer complexes was much lower for each type of household. With the passage of time, therefore, the newest portion of the garden apartment stock has become less able to retain its tenants over sizeable durations.

Anticipated Moving Behavior

The findings in Exhibit 4-13 indicate divergences between moves planned within one and three years. Among older households, if respondents anticipated remaining in their present unit for at least one year, they replied likewise for three years. Among younger households, however, a three-year

EXHIBIT 4-13

Stage in Family Life-Cycle by Moving Plans
Within One and Three Years: 1980 and 1980a

(means only)[2]

	Within One Year			*Within Three Years*		
Stage	*1980*	*1980a*	*% Difference: 1980a÷80*	*1980*	*1980a*	*% Difference: 1980a÷80*
1	3.39	2.93	-13.6	2.10	1.73	-17.6
2	3.23	2.78	-13.9	1.76	1.45	-17.6
3	2.99	2.36	-21.1	1.85	1.14	-38.4
4	3.16	2.25	-28.8	2.00	1.25	-37.5
5	2.59	3.00	+15.8	1.94	3.00	+54.6
3a	3.64	3.67	+ 0.8	2.86	1.67	-41.6
4a	3.61	2.71	-24.9	2.89	2.00	-30.8
5a	3.91	3.74	- 4.3	3.72	2.63	-29.3
6	4.24	2.50	-41.0	2.18	1.50	-31.2
7	4.66	4.42	- 5.2	4.37	4.43	+ 1.4
All stages[1]	3.69	3.05	-17.3	2.37	1.89	-30.8

[1]"All stages" includes residual households that do not fall under any specific category.
[2]Mean figures refer to a scale from one to five, with "1" as "Yes, definitely moving" and "5" as "Definitely not moving." Thus, a negative sign denotes an increased willingness to move.

Source: Center for Urban Policy Research, Garden Apartment Resident Survey, Summer-Fall 1980.

tenure was not a likely eventuality; in fact, virtually every married couple under 50 viewed a move within that time as probable or definite.

Residents of new complexes, with few exceptions, anticipate a forthcoming move more frequently than those in older complexes. In fact, among marrieds with children, almost every single respondent believed that a move was definite within three years; for other households, excepting the elderly and couples with children of grammar school age or older, mean scores were only slightly lower (i.e. closer to "Definitely not"). This supports the panel data of Butler, et al., in which there was a strong correlation between high occupational status (a characteristic of residents in 1980a complexes) and moving plans.[13]

Do these figures help predict mobility? A planned move is obviously not the same as an actual move. There are inevitably households who intend to move, but do not follow through with their plans; there are others who do not intend to move, but for whatever reason, move anyway. Rossi, for example, found that among those who planned to remain in their units within eight months, 96 percent actually did so.[14] As the author concluded, "A family's reported intentions about moving can be taken as a good indicator of how that family will behave." More recently, Van Arsdol, Sabagh, and Butler found that between 40 and 70 percent of those planning to move within a year followed through with their intent.[15] These studies, however, do not account for those who desire to move, but owing to financial or other circumstances, realize that they cannot and, therefore, do not indicate any "plans" to move. As Varady maintains, ". . .studies of factors affecting moving plans may provide broader understanding of sources of dissatisfaction with residential environment than can be obtained from studies of actual behavior."[16] Exhibit 4-14 reveals a number of such factors. Heading the list was the desire to own a home. One-third of all respondents in old complexes and nearly one half of those in new developments cited this as the overriding consideration. Such a difference is not surprising, in that far more residents of the latter consisted of young married couples—prime candidates for first-time homebuying. Nor is it surprising that this reason would rank highest in either case. The desire for homeownership was found to be a significant determinant of moving plans by Speare,[17] Michelson, et al.,[18] Zimmer,[19] Nathanson,[20] and Morris.[21] Journey-to-work considerations—expressed as either a change in place of employment or a desire for a shorter commute—ranked second in both samples, while a desire for a better neighborhood ranked third—again, in both samples.

EXHIBIT 4-14

Main Reason for Planning to Move from Present Unit: 1980 and 1980a

(in percentages)

Reason	*1980*	*1980a*	*% Difference: 1980a÷80*
Wants to own home	33.5	48.9	+46.0
New job/commuting	14.3	16.7	+16.8
Better neighborhood	12.3	8.9	-27.6
Better dwelling	9.0	4.2	-53.3
Larger dwelling (unrelated to increase in family size)	7.8	3.6	-53.8
Lower rent/housing costs	6.3	7.1	+12.7
Marriage	4.3	0.6	-86.0
Change of region or climate	2.5	2.4	- 4.0
Attend/leave school	2.0	1.2	-40.0
Retirement	1.5	0.0	--
Other	4.0	6.5	+62.5
Total	100.0	100.0	
n =	400	168	

Source: Center for Urban Policy Research, Garden Apartment Resident Survey, Summer-Fall 1980.

Satisfaction with Present Dwelling

Exhibit 4-15 provides the results of a difference-of-means test for each stage in the life-cycle with respect to overall dwelling rating.[22] The expectation is that due to wear and tear in the existing stock, ratings will have become more negative for all household types.

In six of ten cases, the perception had worsened over the 1972–80 period. However, in only three of the ten (one-tailed) tests were shifts significant, and they represented stages whose combined total of 1980 households was approximately ten percent. The aggregate rating for all ten types actually grew more favorable, from 2.22 to 2.10 on a 1-to-5 scale, with "1" as "very good" and "5" as "very poor." Similar results occurred when the 1972 data were compared with weighted 1980 data.

Is satisfaction with the dwelling unit significantly less in older complexes, where rents are lower and operating costs higher? Quite the contrary, in not one instance were differences statistically significant. Among five household types, especially young marrieds, newer developments provided less favorable responses, despite the preponderance of dual income households.

Reason for Choosing Present Development

Respondents were asked in Exhibit 4-16 to cite the single most important reason for choosing their present complex. Ranking highest for each sample were proximity to work, rent level, desirability of the surrounding neighborhood or community, necessity of acquiring an apartment immediately, and size, design, or attractiveness of the apartment's interior. A location near work was by far the strongest factor; many garden apartment residents preferred to take the time and expense necessary to find an apartment close to work rather than remain in their previous housing and commute longer distances. A fairly significant number of respondents cited the need to find an apartment—any apartment—within a short time. The conspicuousness of garden complexes due to their visibility from highways and boulevards, their familiarity as community landmarks, and their extensive advertisements in newspapers, draws many "quick fix" households to their confines, especially single mothers and young households of all types.

Large differences between responses in new and old complexes occurred in "Rent level" and "Management allowed pets." Understandably, far fewer residents of newer, more expensive complexes cited rent level as a factor. Also noteworthy is the greater willingness of managers in newer complexes to allow pets, particularly dogs. Many households with dogs flock to the few complexes where they are allowed, however unpleasant they view some of the complex's features.

EXHIBIT 4-15

Stage in Family Life-Cycle by Satisfaction with Present Dwelling: 1972, 1980, and 1980a

(means only, except for t-scores)[1]

Stage in Life Cycle	Re-Sample (Existing) 1972	Re-Sample (Existing) 1980	Re-Sample (Existing) t-Score	1972 vs. Weighted 1980 (all) 1972	1972 vs. Weighted 1980 (all) 1980	1972 vs. Weighted 1980 (all) t-Score	1972, by Year Constructed 1940-59	1972, by Year Constructed 1960-71	1972, by Year Constructed t-Score	1980, by Year Constructed 1940-71	1980, by Year Constructed 1972-80	1980, by Year Constructed t-Score
1	2.29	2.13	1.56	2.29	2.13	1.78	2.17	2.35	1.13	2.13	2.15	-0.23
2	2.29	2.12	1.57	2.29	2.17	1.63	2.15	2.35	1.65**	2.12	2.29	-0.23
3	2.52	2.37	1.14	2.52	2.40	1.25	2.32	2.58	1.76**	2.37	2.71	-0.70
4	2.35	3.00	-2.12**	2.35	2.92	-2.15**	2.60	2.28	-0.70	3.00	2.50	0.63
5	2.11	2.21	-0.37	2.11	2.19	-0.37	1.80	2.22	1.89**	2.21	2.00	0.22
3a	2.00	2.67	-1.57*	2.00	2.76	-2.01	1.75	2.10	0.52	2.67	3.50	1.34
4a	2.42	2.25	0.46	2.42	2.24	0.61	2.25	2.50	0.36	2.25	2.50	-0.53
5a	2.04	2.58	-2.00**	2.04	2.59	-2.23**	1.93	2.17	0.70	2.58	2.00	0.68
6	2.06	2.15	-0.83	2.06	2.13	-0.75	1.98	2.13	1.12	2.15	1.94	0.69
7	1.88	1.90	-0.22	1.88	1.90	-0.19	1.68	2.14	3.49***	1.90	1.71	0.45
All stages	2.22	2.10		2.22	2.18		2.02	2.37		2.10	2.20	
n =	1,333	720		1,333	1,648		465	868		721	206	

All tests are one-tailed.

*Significant at .10
**Significant at .05
***Significant at .01

[1]Mean figures refer to a scale from one to five, with "1" as "Very good" and "5" as "Very poor."

Source: Center for Urban Policy Research, Garden Apartment Resident Survey, Summer-Fall 1980.

EXHIBIT 4-16

Most Important Reason for Choosing Present Development by Stage in Family Life-Cycle: 1980 and 1980a

(in percentages)

	1	2	3	4	5	3a	4a	5a	6	7	All Stages[1]
Reason (1980)											
Location near work	29.3	23.5	26.0	17.6	50.0	21.4	6.3	36.7	28.7	10.8	24.6
Rent level	26.1	26.5	16.9	23.5	0.0	14.3	37.5	13.3	9.3	9.2	17.4
Neighborhood/Community	14.1	12.2	14.3	17.6	28.6	7.1	18.8	10.0	27.1	37.7	20.4
Needed apartment immediately	17.2	21.4	21.4	11.8	11.8	35.7	18.8	10.0	9.1	5.4	15.2
Size/design of units	6.5	10.2	10.4	11.8	14.3	14.3	6.3	16.7	7.0	11.5	9.3
Liked/knew people here	1.6	3.1	10.4	11.8	0.0	7.1	0.0	10.0	0.0	13.1	5.6
Management allowed pets	1.6	0.0	0.0	0.0	0.0	0.0	6.3	0.0	0.0	7.1	1.3
Other	3.7	3.0	3.0	5.9	0.0	0.0	0.0	3.3	9.3	10.8	7.8
Total	100.0	100.0	100.0	100.0	100.0	100.0	100.0	100.0	100.0	100.0	100.0
n =	184	98	77	14	14	14	16	30	129	130	745
Reason (1980a)											
Location near work	20.0	32.5	35.7	66.7	0.0	0.0	0.0	14.3	22.9	0.0	28.2
Rent level	6.7	9.1	7.1	0.0	0.0	0.0	0.0	0.0	5.7	0.0	8.2
Neighborhood/Community	33.3	18.2	0.0	0.0	0.0	25.0	0.0	0.0	14.3	71.4	15.5
Needed apartment immediately	17.0	11.7	13.3	0.0	0.0	25.0	0.0	71.4	14.3	0.0	15.9
Size/design of units	20.0	14.3	21.4	33.3	100.0	50.0	50.0	14.3	14.3	0.0	15.0
Liked/knew people here	3.8	0.0	13.3	0.0	0.0	0.0	0.0	0.0	0.0	0.0	1.4
Management allowed pets	11.3	11.7	0.0	0.0	0.0	0.0	0.0	0.0	17.1	0.0	10.9
Other	6.7	2.6	0.0	0.0	0.0	0.0	50.0	0.0	11.5	28.6	5.0
Total	100.0	100.0	100.0	100.0	100.0	100.0	100.0	100.0	100.0	100.0	100.0
n =	53	77	14	3	3	2	2	7	35	7	203

[1]"All stages" includes residual households that do not fall under any specific category.

Source: Center for Urban Policy Research, Garden Apartment Resident Survey, Summer-Fall 1980.

Neighborhood Problems

Respondents were asked to cite whether they viewed each of nineteen neighborhood conditions as a problem. As Exhibit 4-17 shows, ten categories in the re-surveyed developments and twelve in the newer ones were cited as problems by at least ten percent of all households. At the top of the list were lack of public transportation, street/highway noise, crime, and heavy traffic; ranking at the bottom were boarded up/abandoned structures, unsatisfactory schools, presence of nonresidential land uses, and lack of access to adequate health care facilities.

There was a fairly even distribution of differences in the levels of problem identification between 1980 and 1980a developments. In ten of the categories, problems were noted more frequently by the former; in the remaining nine, they were cited more frequently by the latter. It is striking that responses from newer developments should have ranked unfavorably even

EXHIBIT 4-17

Existence of Neighborhood Problems: 1980 and 1980a

(in percentages)[1]

Problem	*1980*	*1980a*	*% Difference 1980a÷80*
Street (highway) noise	20.4	18.5	- 9.3
Heavy traffic	18.6	12.5	- 33.9
Streets or roads in need of repair/open ditches	16.8	31.0	+ 84.5
Roads impassable due to snow or water	17.3	18.1	+ 4.6
Poor street lighting	11.4	11.1	- 2.6
Crime	19.3	11.6	- 39.9
Trash, litter, or junk	14.4	18.5	+ 28.5
Boarded up/abandoned structures	0.7	0.5	- 28.4
Occupied housing in rundown condition	5.8	0.9	- 84.5
Nonresidential activity	3.2	5.1	+ 51.4
Odors, smoke, or gas	6.6	12.0	+ 81.8
Airplane or train noise	7.6	23.6	+210.5
Unsatisfactory public transportation	21.7	25.0	+ 15.2
Unsatisfactory schools	2.4	2.3	- 4.2
Unsatisfactory shopping	4.7	7.9	+ 68.1
Unsatisfactory police protection	5.6	3.2	- 42.9
Unsatisfactory recreation facilities	14.5	20.8	+ 43.4
Unsatisfactory health clinics/hospitals	3.2	6.0	- 12.5
Unsatisfactory parking space	16.8	14.0	- 16.7
n =	696	216	

[1]Percentage figures refer to a choice within each particular category.

Source: Center for Urban Policy Research, Garden Apartment Resident Survey, Summer-Fall 1980.

to this extent. It would seem that the more recent the construction, the less likely would be the presence of problems associated with areas of high-density development.

A problem may be perceived in severity ranging from nearly nonexistent to calamitous, an issue Exhibit 4-18 addresses. There are four potential responses—"Does not bother," "Bothers a little," "Bothers very much," and "Bothers so much would like to move"—and the table provides the percentage breakdown for the most important of them, the latter two.[23]

While bearing in mind that the figures shown here are percentages of the percentages in Exhibit 4-17 (and, in some cases, very small ones), a large proportion of residents view problems in their neighborhoods as something more than minor irritants. For re-surveyed developments, the combined total of "Very much" and "Would like to move" in fourteen of nineteen problem categories exceeded 40 percent, and, in three others, it came very close to that figure; in new complexes, this was true of twelve categories. For six categories in older complexes, over 10 percent of the respondents felt so strongly about a problem that they were willing to move. In newer complexes, this was true of eleven categories, each usually containing an even greater proportion of potential movers. For highway noise, streets in need of repair, lack of parking space, and several other conditions, the totals were astronomically higher. That a garden apartment complex is old appears to have little negative effect on neighborhood or community pride among its residents.

The Garden Apartment as a Long-Term Substitute for Homeownership

Although many residents of garden apartments view their housing arrangements as satisfactory, and even gratifying, they rate them a poor second to homeownership as a long-term housing choice. Exhibit 4-19 examines the potential extent of this view. Not surprisingly, the elderly were the only households who consistently viewed the garden apartment as a good substitute, as many had already been homeowners. Among other categories, the most prevalent response was that it was "definitely not" a good substitute. On the other hand, even among young households, the most likely candidates for future homeownership, there were about 30–40 percent who felt the garden unit to be an adequate proxy.

Interviewees often provided explanations as to why their apartments were good or poor substitutes (they were allowed more than one choice). Topping the list of favorable responses in both new and old complexes were that these apartments provide many advantages of private dwellings, such as open space, tranquility, and privacy, and do not require a heavy maintenance burden. Ranking highest by far among the "poor" group was the in-

EXHIBIT 4-18

Percent of Residents Reporting Neighborhood Problems That Bothered Them Very Much or So Much That They Would Like to Move: 1980 and 1980a

(in percentages)[1]

Problem	Bothers Very Much (1980)	Bothers Very Much (1980a)	% Difference 1980a ÷ 80	Bothers So Much Would Like to Move (1980)	Bothers So Much Would Like to Move (1980a)	% Difference 1980a ÷ 80
Street (highway) noise	18.3	32.5	+ 77.5	6.3	15.0	+ 138.1
Heavy traffic	23.6	35.7	+ 51.2	7.1	10.7	+ 50.7
Streets or roads in need of repair/open ditches	20.5	37.3	+ 18.1	0.9	13.4	+1,389.9
Roads impassable due to snow or water	23.7	41.0	+ 21.7	0.8	10.3	+1,187.5
Poor street lighting	35.5	29.2	- 17.7	3.9	0.0	--
Crime	36.1	30.8	- 14.7	12.8	26.9	+ 110.2
Trash, litter, junk	28.9	27.5	- 4.8	10.3	10.0	- 2.9
Boarded up/abandoned structures	0.0	0.0	--	0.0	0.0	--
Occupied housing in rundown condition	35.0	50.0	+ 42.9	15.0	0.0	--
Nonresidential activity	14.3	18.2	+ 27.3	14.3	9.1	- 36.4
Odors, smoke, or gas	22.2	23.1	+ 4.0	6.7	11.5	+ 71.6
Airplane or train noise	5.7	17.6	+208.8	0.0	9.8	--
Unsatisfactory public transportation	36.7	28.3	- 22.9	2.0	7.5	+ 275.0
Unsatisfactory schools	29.4	20.0	- 32.0	17.6	40.0	+ 127.3
Unsatisfactory shopping	28.1	17.6	- 37.4	0.0	11.8	--
Unsatisfactory police protection	36.8	28.6	- 22.3	15.8	28.6	+ 81.0
Unsatisfactory recreational facilities	33.7	42.2	+ 25.2	6.9	8.9	+ 29.0
Unsatisfactory health clinics/hospitals	36.4	38.5	+ 5.8	0.0	7.7	--
Unsatisfactory parking space	32.8	36.7	+ 11.9	1.7	16.7	+ 882.4

[1]Percentage figures refer to a choice within each particular category.

Source: Center for Urban Policy Research, Garden Apartment Resident Survey, Summer-Fall 1980.

EXHIBIT 4-19

Perception of Garden Apartment Renting as a Substitute for Homeownership by Stage in Family Life-Cycle: 1980 and 1980a

(in percentages)

	STAGE IN LIFE-CYCLE										
	1	*2*	*3*	*4*	*5*	*3a*	*4a*	*5a*	*6*	*7*	*All Stages*[1]
Renting As a Substitute (1980)											
Yes, definitely	20.9	25.8	19.4	23.1	38.5	21.4	25.0	26.9	32.8	60.3	31.4
Yes, probably	17.0	17.5	16.7	23.1	7.7	21.4	12.5	11.5	25.0	16.5	17.5
Not sure	6.0	4.1	5.6	7.7	15.4	0.0	18.8	15.4	10.2	10.7	8.1
Probably not	11.5	7.2	18.1	0.0	15.4	14.3	0.0	7.7	6.3	2.5	8.9
Definitely not	44.5	45.4	40.3	46.2	23.1	42.9	43.8	38.5	25.8	9.9	34.1
Total	100.0	100.0	100.0	100.0	100.0	100.0	100.0	100.0	100.0	100.0	100.0
Mean[2]	3.42	3.29	3.43	3.23	2.77	3.36	3.25	3.19	2.67	1.85	2.96
n =	187	97	72	13	13	14	16	26	128	121	716
Renting As a Substitute (1980a)											
Yes, definitely	20.4	27.3	42.9	66.7	100.0	25.0	0.0	28.6	42.9	71.4	33.8
Yes, probably	9.3	7.8	14.3	33.3	0.0	0.0	50.0	14.3	5.7	14.3	8.7
Not sure	5.6	2.6	0.0	0.0	0.0	0.0	0.0	0.0	8.6	0.0	4.6
Probably not	9.3	10.4	14.3	0.0	0.0	0.0	0.0	0.0	14.3	0.0	9.6
Definitely not	55.6	51.9	28.6	0.0	0.0	75.0	50.0	57.1	28.6	14.3	43.4
Total	100.0	100.0	100.0	100.0	100.0	100.0	100.0	100.0	100.0	100.0	100.0
Mean[2]	3.70	3.52	2.71	1.33	1.00	4.00	3.50	3.14	2.80	1.71	3.20
n =	54	77	14	3	3	4	2	7	35	7	219

[1]"All stages" includes residual households that do not fall under any specific category.
[2]Mean figures refer to a scale from one to five, with "1" as "Very good," and "5" as "Very poor."

Source: Center for Urban Policy Research, Garden Apartment Resident Survey, Summer-Fall 1980.

ability of renting to provide the financial advantages of homeownership. Almost one-half of the re-surveyed sample and almost two-thirds of the new sample cited this as a factor. Lack of privacy and space in a multi-family environment also accounted for a sizeable share of responses.

Willingness to Pay Higher Rent

Any rational tenant would prefer not to pay higher rent in lieu of any improvement in his or her housing situation. However, some might be willing to pay more if the increase led to the addition and/or improvement of certain services and amenities. Exhibit 4-20 reveals that even given this inducement, rent increases, however small, have a very limited appeal. With household life-cycle as an independent variable, the cumulative mean scores for 1980 and 1980a complexes were 3.82 and 3.89, respectively, on a one-to-five scale, with five representing the lowest degree of willingness to pay. There was relatively little intra-group variation.

What types of improvements and additions are sought by those who are willing to pay higher rent? As shown in Exhibit 4-21, the first preference is for better maintenance. Almost half the willing residents in the 1980 sample preferred to have the management target the added revenues for this purpose. A sizeable portion of respondents also would have increases set aside for groundskeeping, insulation, replacement of household appliances, and improved laundry machine operation.

Conclusion

The results of the statewide survey confirm the expectations of the central research question even more than did the nationwide sample. Garden apartment complexes serve the younger married population far less now than during the early-70s. This is especially true among those with young children. Their places have been taken by singles, single mothers, the elderly, and empty nesters, in descending order of importance. In newer complexes, there has been no decline—but actually, a large increase—in childless couples. These and the national findings suggest a cleavage among the tenantry divided along lines of age as well as family life-cycle. Residents of newer developments tend to consist far more of a young, upwardly mobile population than their counterparts in older complexes. They are better-educated, more frequently employed in high-salaried white-collar positions, and are more willing and likely to purchase a home within a few years. Thus, the early-70s only partly represent a historical point in time from which socioeconomic differences among garden apartment renters have grown increasingly distinct. With the aging of the existing stock have come many of the changes observed in then-recently built developments. This filtering process

EXHIBIT 4-20

Willingness to Pay Higher Rent in Return for More or Better Services and Amenities by Stage in Family Life-Cycle: 1980 and 1980a

(in percentages)

	STAGE IN LIFE CYCLE										
	1	2	3	4	5	3a	4a	5a	6	7	All Stages[1]
Willingness to Pay Higher Rent (1980)											
Yes, definitely	18.1	17.7	17.4	30.8	0.0	38.5	25.0	14.8	12.4	5.5	14.8
Yes, probably	15.3	8.3	2.9	30.8	23.1	7.7	0.0	7.4	7.0	8.6	9.8
Not sure	5.6	7.3	8.7	0.0	23.1	0.0	6.3	14.8	9.3	4.7	7.1
Probably not	13.6	17.7	14.5	0.0	0.0	7.7	12.5	7.4	13.2	22.7	15.1
Definitely not	47.5	49.0	56.5	38.5	53.8	46.2	56.3	55.6	58.2	58.6	53.2
Total	100.0	100.0	100.0	100.0	100.0	100.0	100.0	100.0	100.0	100.0	100.0
Mean[2]	3.57	3.72	3.90	2.85	3.85	3.15	3.75	3.81	4.28	4.28	3.82
n =	177	96	69	13	13	13	16	27	129	128	716
Willingness to Pay Higher Rent (1980a)											
Yes, definitely	18.5	15.6	7.1	0.0	33.3	0.0	50.0	0.0	8.6	0.0	15.2
Yes, probably	11.1	14.3	0.0	0.0	0.0	0.0	0.0	0.0	0.0	16.7	9.2
Not sure	1.9	2.6	0.0	0.0	0.0	0.0	0.0	0.0	8.6	0.0	3.2
Probably not	13.0	13.0	7.1	50.0	66.7	0.0	0.0	42.9	11.4	50.0	15.7
Definitely not	55.6	54.5	85.7	50.0	0.0	100.0	50.0	57.1	68.6	33.3	56.2
Total	100.0	100.0	100.0	100.0	100.0	100.0	100.0	100.0	100.0	100.0	100.0
Mean[2]	3.76	3.77	4.64	4.50	3.00	5.00	3.00	4.57	4.35	4.00	3.89
n =	54	77	14	2	3	4	2	7	34	6	216

[1]"All stages" includes residual households that do not fall under any specific category.
[2]Mean figures refer to a scale from one to five, with "1" as "Yes, definitely," and "5" as "Definitely not."

Source: Center for Urban Policy Research, Garden Apartment Resident Survey, Summer-Fall 1980.

EXHIBIT 4-21

Items Which Added or Improved Would Induce a Tenant to Pay Higher Rent: 1980 and 1980a

(in percentages)

Addition or Improvement[1]	*1980*	*1980a*	*% Difference 1980a ÷ 80*
Improve maintenance	46.6	33.9	- 27.3
Improve or replace laundry machines/increase laundry room hours	7.4	15.1	+104.1
Improve groundskeeping	10.2	11.3	+ 10.8
Make major structural improvements or additions/build garages	14.8	11.3	- 23.6
Build swimming pool or other recreational amenity/include existing swimming pool or other recreational amenity in rent	35.2	33.9	- 3.7
Install carpeting or drapes/include existing carpeting or drapes in rent	6.3	5.7	- 9.6
Install or replace dishwasher, air conditioner, sink garbage disposal, or other household appliance	13.7	7.5	- 45.3
Tighten screening process of prospective tenants	4.5	7.5	+ 66.7
Improve insulation/install story windows	15.3	5.7	- 62.7
Include heat, electricity, or air conditioning in rent	4.0	5.7	+ 42.5
Improve security/replace locks or doors	5.7	9.4	+ 64.9
n =	176	53	

1Respondents were allowed more than one choice. They include only those interviewees who expressed a definite or probable willingness to pay higher rent.

Source: Center for Urban Policy Research, Garden Apartment Resident Survey, Summer-Fall 1980.

suggests that some of the uniqueness of tenant composition in newer complexes may become less pronounced over time.

Moreover, while there are substantially fewer marrieds, the shift has not necessarily resulted from a lessening appeal of the garden apartment. Rather, it has come about because of the sharp nationwide decline of marrieds as a proportion of all households and of their purchase of homes. Thus, as a "processor" of young households during their renting years, garden apartments have performed quite efficiently—so efficiently, in fact, that their pool has begun to atrophy.

The propensity to remain in the same dwelling for longer periods of time is endemic to almost all stages of the life-cycle. Yet this has been due not so much to increases in satisfaction (which were by any reasonable standard rather minimal), but to a net influx of types of households whose incomes are insufficient to buy a home and to a declining availability of moderate-cost housing within commuting ranges. In complexes built since the early-70s, the propensity to move, as measured by intentions, is greater than that of residents in older complexes, while the indicators of environmental satisfaction generally rank lower. Despite Brian J. L. Berry's contention that a "love of newness" has pervaded the logic of American suburbanization,[24] the resident of a new garden apartment complex has a limited affinity for his or her abode. To a certain degree, this is a by-product of high expectations. These are people who, for the most part, have known the comforts of a private home (their parents') for most of their lives, for whom the purchase of one looms near on the horizon, and for whom there is little else that can adequately substitute, even as a stop-gap measure. For young affluent households, especially marrieds, the garden apartment is not an acceptable proxy, as a set of amenities, as a lever of investment, nor as a source of self-esteem. And the more recent the construction, the more likely it is to contain precisely these households.

NOTES

1. The discussion here excludes George Sternlieb, et al., *Housing Development and Municipal Costs*, New Brunswick, N.J.: Center for Urban Policy Research, 1974, whose findings will be compared with those of the current resident survey later in this chapter.

2. See Carl Norcross & John Hysom, *Apartment Communities: The Next Big Market*, Washington, D.C.: Urban Land Institute, Technical Bulletin No. 61, 1968; Woodbridge Department of Planning and Development, *Garden Apartment Evaluation*, Woodbridge, N.J.: Township of Woodbridge, Department of Planning and Development, August 1968; Sherry Manus, *Apartment Resident Survey*, Greensboro, N.C.: City of Greensboro, Planning Department, May 1970; St. Louis County Planning Department, *Apartments in St. Louis County*, Clayton, Mo.: County of St. Louis, Planning Department, March 1972; Monmouth County Planning Board,

Multifamily Housing in Monmouth County, Freehold, N.J.: County of Monmouth, Planning Board, January 1973; Robert Schafer, *The Suburbanization of Multifamily Housing*, Lexington, Mass.: Lexington Books, 1974. All of the discussion in this section is drawn from the above material. The Schafer volume is by far and away the most authoritative source.

3. For a broad listing of studies whose sole focus is the multiplier issue, see Robert W. Burchell and David Listokin, *The Fiscal Impact Handbook: Estimating Local Costs and Revenues of Land Development*, New Brunswick, N.J.: Center for Urban Policy Research, 1978, pp. 378–429.

4. Schafer, *The Suburbanization of Multifamily Housing*, p. 107.

5. The extremely high proportion of "primary individual(s), female principal wage earner" is potentially misleading. A lot of these households consisted of single and widowed elderly women. The 40.9 percent difference between 1980 and 1980a for this category is due almost entirely to the fact that in the latter sample, there were far fewer elderly households.

6. Among Stage 1 households, especially those in pre-1972 vintage complexes, the single population only occasionally consisted of the young adult fresh out of high school or college. This is evident from examining Exhibits 4-2 and 4-3. While 32.5 percent of the 1980 sample had never married, the total 25 and under population was less than 15.0 percent—and a portion of this latter figure consisted of married couples. Thus, the large majority of singles were older than 25. The trend toward delayed marriages has been highly felt in garden apartment complexes.

7. Hubert M. Blalock, Jr., *Social Statistics*, 2nd ed., New York: McGraw-Hill, 1972, p. 233.

8. See Lynda Lytle Holmstrom, *The Two-Career Family*, Cambridge, Mass.: Schenkman, 1974.

9. The increase in median rents for the New York-Northeastern New Jersey area, where most of the interviews took place, was 62.7 percent over June 1972–August 1980 (the median months, chronologically, during which sampling took place in the respective surveys).

10. In fact, in four of the older complexes, the management closed its swimming pool during the entire summer of 1980 due to a lack of willing applicants. If representative of cases nationwide, a strategy of charging for the use of community recreational facilities separate from rent may frequently backfire.

11. See Norcross & Hysom; Hysom; St. Louis County Planning Department; Monmouth County Planning Department. See also Owens-Corning Fiberglas, "The Tenants' Point of View: A Survey of Garden Apartment Residents' Attitudes in Five Cities," *Urban Land*, February 1970, pp. 3–8; Nashua Planning Board, *Apartment Survey Results*, Nashua, N.H.: City of Nashua, Planning Board, June 1973.

12. See U.S. Bureau of the Census, *1978 Annual Housing Survey*, Public Use Sample.

13. E. W. Butler, M. D. Van Arsdol, Jr., and G. Sabagh, "Spatial Mobility Differentials by Socioeconomic Status, Intergenerational and Career Social Mobility," paper presented to American Sociological Association Meeting, Washington, D.C.; August–September 1970.

14. Peter Rossi, *Why Families Move: A Study in the Social Psychology of Urban Residential Mobility*, Glencoe, Ill.: Free Press, 1965.

15. M. D. Van Arsdol, Jr., G. Sabagh, and E. W. Butler, "Retrospective and Subsequent Metropolitan Residential Mobility," *Demography*, Vol. 5, 1968, pp. 249–67.

16. David Varady, "White Moving Plans in a Racially Changing Middle-Class

Community," *Journal of the American Institute of Planners* (now *Journal of the American Planning Association*), Vol. 40, No. 5, September 1974, p. 368.

17. Alden A. Speare, Jr., "Home Ownership, Life-Cycle Stage, and Residential Mobility," *Demography*, Vol. 7, No. 4, November 1970, pp. 449–58.

18. William Michelson, D. Belgue, and J. Stewart, "Intentions and Expectations in Differential Residential Selection," *Journal of Marriage and the Family*, Vol. 35, No. 1, February 1976, pp. 189–96.

19. B. G. Zimmer, "Residential Mobility and Housing," *Land Economics*, Vol. 49, 1973, pp. 334–50.

20. Constance A. Nathanson, "Moving Preferences and Plans Among Urban Black Families," *Journal of the American Institute of Planners*, Vol. 40, No. 5, September 1974, pp. 353–59.

21. Earl W. Morris, "A Normative Deficit Approach to Consumer Satisfaction," paper presented to the Marketing Science Institute Workshop on Consumer Satisfaction/Dissatisfaction, Chicago, April 11-13, 1976.

22. No results are provided here for neighborhood rating because this variable was not examined in the 1972 baseline study (Sternlieb, et al., *Housing Development and Municipal Costs*). Hence, there is no basis for historical comparability.

23. This scale is developed from the Annual Housing Survey.

24. Brian J. L. Berry, "The Decline of the Aging Metropolis: Cultural Bases and Social Process," in *Post-Industrial America: Metropolitan Decline & Inter-Regional Job Shifts*, George Sternlieb and James W. Hughes, ed., New Brunswick, N.J.: Center for Urban Policy Research, 1975, p. 175.

5

Summary and Recommendations

Summary and Interpretation of Major Findings

The directions of the demographic trends uncovered in the previous two chapters are hardly startling. There has been a relative decline in the United States of married couples and a relative gain in singles, single mothers, and the elderly during the last twenty years, and these trends have accelerated over the last ten. These shifts, far from being endemic to garden apartment dwellers, have affected the tenant composition of virtually all forms of housing, owner- and renter-occupied alike. Nor is it startling that non-nuclear family households constitute at least a moderate force in the garden apartment market. A garden apartment is a compact multifamily rental dwelling usually containing from three to five rooms. It is not intended for large households who typically consist of families with many children. What *is* startling are the dimensions of the shifts over a mere eight-year period. In the early-70s, a "small household" in a garden apartment more often than not meant a reasonably young married couple whose children, if any, were few in number and only occasionally of school age. Their length of stay in each apartment was brief, and they sought to own a good home in a good neighborhood in the not too distant future. While still present among the overall garden apartment tenantry, and very much so among the tenantry of the newer units, they are nonetheless a fading force. In relative terms, about one-third to two-fifths of the "marrieds" in the garden apartment market during the early-70s are no longer there.[1] There are two overwhelming reasons for this sharp drop—a drop that is well in excess of that for the nation as a whole.

First, the then-fairly recently married young couples have bought homes over the interim period. While some have remained renters, these households remain the exceptions. In 1980, the homeownership rate for married couples in the 30–44 age bracket was approximately 82 percent.[2] For these people, buying into the American Dream was an act not to be denied. With interest rates apparently on the way down as of early 1983, many current renter couples under 30 will follow suit. Whatever the cost, homeownership remains almost as realizable as it is tempting. As Tucillo explains:

> While the increase in the relative price of housing has made it somewhat more difficult in terms of current cash flow to acquire housing, it has also increased the wealth of those currently owning houses and has enabled them to afford new ones. The experience of current owners stimulates the demand for housing by those who currently do not own. Housing has been perceived as a sound investment available to the majority of households, and the relative rise in house prices reflects this rise in demand as much as it reflects the increases in the supply price of housing.[3]

As interpreted in the previous chapter, the loss of marrieds from the garden apartment market is not a "problem" from a broad social standpoint. Quite the contrary, in light of the homeownership ratio cited above, it is an indication that the working American family has remained financially mobile. No doubt some of the buyers acted too fast and too soon by encumbering themselves with a monthly mortgage debt beyond their capability.[4] Notwithstanding, gains in home values have exceeded the overall Consumer Price Index for almost every year since 1970,[5] and have worked in the long run to benefit even many of these buyers.

Second, the American household has gone through an "unbundling" process that has reduced the nuclear family's share of all households to about 60 percent.[6] In other words, even had the propensity for marrieds to choose garden apartments as a form of residence remained constant, their portion of the tenantry would have fallen anyway. The reasons behind this trend are not difficult to fathom. Singles tend to leave their parents' home at earlier ages, particularly as college enrollment rates continue to rise. They also remain single for longer periods of time. There are, of course, exceptions. It is still quite common, for example, especially in small towns and rural areas, for young adults to get married almost as soon as they have graduated from high school. Yet the trend is undoubtedly toward more frequent and earlier establishment of single households, lasting for longer periods of time. Rising divorce and separation rates have created large numbers of adults who live apart from the structures of the nuclear family. This means that with each termination of a marriage, the number of "traditional" households falls by one and the number of "nontraditional" households increases by two. In addition, pension plans and cost-of-living adjustments for Social Security have freed many elderly persons from dependence upon offspring.

All of this has flooded the market with households who generally do not have the purchasing power of married couples.[7] Nuclear families have increased in absolute numbers, but their gain has been far outstripped by those of "nontraditionals." Consequently, their choices of dwelling are often limited to apartments. On the surface, this would indicate a huge untapped reservoir of garden apartment demand.

Closer examination, however, reveals that the garden apartment market is not likely to expand at a rapid pace. This is not to imply that the garden apartment is a spent force. The vast majority of rental starts will continue to be of this configuration, especially as the cost of producing elevator structures climbs nearly out of proportion.[8] Yet the likelihood of a massive rental boom, either in the short- or medium-range future, is remote. Increasingly, the 1969–73 period is shaping up to have been a brief phenomenon, not to be repeated. Aside from the changing composition and housing consumption patterns of nuclear families, why should this be so?

First, there are several housing forms—most notably, condominiums and accessory apartments—that are cutting into the garden apartment's way-station function. During 1979–80, the average sale price of a condominium was approximately 20 percent less than that for all homes tabulated in the National Association of Realtors' monthly, *Existing Home Sales*.[9] As a result, condominiums, especially low-rises, have attracted many households, including singles, who would normally have rented for a prolonged period of time prior to purchasing a single-family dwelling. So potent is this source of demand that over 100,000 conversions took place during the first nine months of 1979 alone.[10] As for accessory apartments—rentals created by partitioning the basement, attic, or story of an existing private dwelling—there has been a recent and substantial increase. In Minneapolis, an estimated five percent of the total housing stock consists of these apartments.[11] Two researchers calculated that within the existing nationwide housing stock, anywhere from 3.38 million to 8.46 million of these units, legal and illegal, could be produced.[12] Primarily, the tenants are single- and two-person households (and often related to the building's owner), the prime source of demand for garden apartments.[13] Over and above these alternatives, the private home as a rental choice has demonstrated recent growth:

early in 1982, the Census Bureau reported an increase of over 300,000 single-family rentals since 1979.[14]

Equally noteworthy have been tangible signs of the federal government's reversal of support for rental construction. In 1980, roughly half of all rental starts received rent subsidy commitments and an added one-third received mortgage insurance.[15] This may be the last hurrah for intervention of this magnitude. The 1983 Federal Budget, all but approved by Congress as of this writing, authorizes almost no units to be built under the Section 8 New Construction or Public Housing programs. HUD's total obligational authority for Fiscal 1983 would be only \$13.4 billion, a drop from \$38.7 billion for Fiscal 1981.[16] The Reagan Administration's Task Force on Housing argues that while government has played an important role in expanding and upgrading the nation's housing stock, it has done so only by incurring an enormous burden upon the taxpayer, and with little cost-efficiency. The homebuilding industry, "cosseted" for so long, must now stand on its own accord.[17]

The implications for the garden apartment market are evident. The only way that garden apartment production can experience a sharp resurgence is to attract long-term, hard-core renters. And who are these renters? For the most part, they are people who cannot buy homes because their jobs (assuming they are employed) do not provide them with incomes sufficient to do so. Without subsidies, reaching them via new construction will be difficult. Both the Census and statewide research in this book have firmly indicated that newer complexes rent for a good deal more than those built prior to the 1970s. With interest rates on construction loans fluctuating between 15 and 21 percent for most of the past three years, new garden units may require even higher rents than units built during the last decade. The likely direction of support from Washington is the replacement of the production of new rentals with a consumer-oriented housing allowance program. This will expand the residential mobility of the housing-poor, but will do little to add garden apartments to the existing inventory.

In summary, the garden apartment has become an institution, but one whose limits have become apparent. Given the diminishing federal support for rental housing, the emergence of substitutes in the "compact" housing market, and the changing patterns of household formation, garden apartments remain way-stations, but in a sense significantly different from that of a decade ago. Increasingly, for garden apartment tenants, the formation (or re-formation, as the case may be) of a nuclear family is an anticipated rather than a previous decision.[18] Given income differences between family and non-family households, existing garden apartments will have a difficult enough time attracting middle-income tenants even without new construction at close to early-70s levels.

Public Policy and the Garden Apartment

Introduction

How can public officials apply the findings of this study to their decision-making? This section outlines the feasibility of pursuing certain strategies in four general areas: 1) management and improvement of the existing apartment stock; 2) stimulation of new production; 3) relaxation of certain forms of state and local regulation affecting new and existing rental housing, particularly garden apartments; and 4) reduction of development costs through reduction of the size and quality of the product. Each discussion will relate, where appropriate, the "what ought to be" with the basic findings of Chapters Three and Four. Often, especially in the discussion of new production, it will be necessary to subsume the discussion of garden apartments under the more encompassing rubric of rental housing.

Conservation of the Existing Stock

It is difficult to consider the preservation of garden apartments as an issue of the same order as the rehabilitation of deteriorating structures in predominantly low-income neighborhoods. Rising operating costs have affected all types of rental properties over the past decade, but the brunt has been borne by apartment houses built prior to the 1930s. Garden apartments are still relatively late bloomers in the housing industry. They do not yet require the more costly kinds of property rehabilitation, such as heating, electrical, and plumbing system replacement, kitchen cabinet replacement, wall re-plastering, and floor retiling. Over four-fifths of all garden apartments existing in 1978 were built no earlier than 1960, and over two-fifths no earlier than 1970. Yet while their ability to withstand wear and tear is yet to be really tested, it is not an entirely unknown quantity.

Recent data developed by the Institute for Real Estate Management lend an air of both optimism and pessimism to extrapolations of how gracefully garden apartments will age. *Income-Expense Analysis* indicates that the operating ratios (total operating expenses divided by total collections) of garden apartments, like those of other apartments, increase with the age of the structure (see Exhibit 5-1). In 1979, garden apartment buildings constructed in 1968 or later incurred an operating ratio of 44.5 percent. For buildings constructed during 1961–67, 1946–60, and 1931–45, these figures were 48.8, 56.0, and 58.5 percent, respectively.[19] The same general pattern occurred among the other three structural types. Counterbalancing this has been: 1) a less pronounced increase in the ratio with age for garden apartments than for other rental structures; and 2) an overall *decline* in the ratio over the latter half of the 70s for all structures of all age ranges, with the ex-

EXHIBIT 5-1

Operating Ratios for Apartment Buildings by Period of Construction: 1975–79
(Total Expenses Divided by Total Collections)

		Year Structure Built			
Building Type	*Year*	*1931-45*	*1946-60*	*1961-67*	*1968 and After*
Elevator	1979	63.3%	59.8%	50.8%	47.9%
	1978	65.5	59.7	52.5	50.0
	1977	68.6	59.6	53.6	50.8
	1976	65.7	59.8	55.1	51.1
	1975	63.5	60.2	56.3	50.2
Low Rise (12-24 units)	1979	57.5	51.7	44.0	43.5
	1978	63.9	54.0	44.1	44.8
	1977	62.1	54.6	46.3	44.5
	1976	60.1	54.8	48.1	45.3
	1975	62.6	54.7	48.8	45.3
Low Rise (25 units and over)	1979	66.1	55.2	48.3	44.0
	1978	64.8	54.7	49.1	46.6
	1977	62.3	57.1	49.4	46.9
	1976	62.8	54.7	50.9	49.0
	1975	60.9	55.3	50.4	53.6
Garden	1979	58.5	56.0	48.8	44.5
	1978	63.2	58.2	50.4	46.0
	1977	59.6	58.7	51.0	48.0
	1976	61.9	61.6	52.3	51.1
	1975	61.3	57.8	52.3	50.9

Source: Institute of Real Estate Management, Income-Expense Analysis: Apartments. Chicago: National Association of Realtors, Institute of Real Estate Management, 1980, p. 32.

ception of 1931–45 low-rises with more than twenty-four units. If many garden apartment developments seem to be in serious financial trouble, such a reality is not supported by these figures.

Examined in greater depth, however, this situation becomes somewhat more somber. First, no matter how favorable operating ratios and net operating incomes may have become, they must be placed in the context of general price inflation. According to Ira Lowry's recent estimates, the net operating return (income available for debt service, depreciation, and equity) for all rental units during the 1970s increased by 34 percent.[20] Given the change in the rental component of the Consumer Price Index, this represented a real decrease in net purchasing power of 37.0 percent, and a real increase in the overall operating ratio of 29.0 percent. Lowry also capitalized this return at 1980 interest rates and found that in constant dollars, rental property values fell by nearly 50 percent. According to *Income-Expense Analysis*, the overall net return for garden apartments grew by approximately 60 percent during 1970–79. In constant dollars, however, this represented a downward shift of approximately 6 percent.[21]

Second, the escalation of heating fuel and electric costs has especially burdened the older garden apartment stock. In 1979, these two operating components took slightly over 17 cents per collected rental dollar in complexes built during 1970 or afterward. In the same year, these components took over 28 cents of each rental dollar in complexes built during 1920–45.[22] The latter is a particularly staggering sum, and very likely some owner-operators of these developments have deferred needed maintenance outlays in lieu of instituting sizeable rent increases. The sheer magnitude of this problem is recounted in the experiences of a contractor who recently converted a master-metered garden apartment complex in Forest Hills, Queens into private homes:

> It costs an average of $200 per tenant per (winter) month just to heat these (garden apartment) buildings as rentals and that is not even providing decent heat. The costs of heating is the crux of the problem. It is much less efficient than in vertical buildings because we are heating crawl spaces and empty areas between apartments—areas where we don't collect a dime in rent.[23]

Third, there is a large stock of garden complexes that requires refinancing of balloon mortgages. Since the term of standard non-amortizing apartment mortgages is approximately ten to fifteen years, this would include many developments constructed during the boom years of the early-70s. Typically, building owners do not pay the remaining principal at the end of the period; instead, they negotiate with the lender to establish a new term at prevailing interest rates.[24] Those presently coming due face interest rates of over 12 percent, a level that could potentially constrict cash flow.

Fourth, there is growing case-by-case evidence that the potential for structural and site deterioration has begun to materialize. The following recent capsule summaries may be weathervanes for what could happen to a much larger portion of garden complexes only a few decades from now.

- In Queens, New York, there is a large stock of pre-1960 garden apartment complexes comprising approximately 24,000 units. In 1979, New York City's Department of Housing Preservation and Development conducted a field survey of these projects, many of which had been financed under the Section 608 Program with long-term mortgages up to thirty years. The Department observed that about twenty percent of the units were in "poor" condition and an additional forty percent were in the "beginning stages" of deterioration.[25] The worst of these projects, American Gardens, constructed in 1950, is now "totally vacant and sealed up." Its declining market value has adversely affected values of adjacent properties.

● At the Edgemere-at-Somerset complex in Franklin Township, New Jersey, a similar downturn has occurred. Constructed during the early-60s as a semi-luxury development and insured by FHA, Edgemere had deteriorated to such an extent that by 1980, local housing inspectors had uncovered at least 3,000 code violations in the 400-unit complex—despite its exemption from the local rent levelling ordinance, since HUD holds the mortgage.[26]

● In Southeast Washington, D.C., Stanton Hill had been built in the mid-60s as a moderate-income garden apartment development. By the end of the 70s, however, one observer described its condition as such:

> Stanton Hill. . .is in decline—not yet a slum, but with enough evidence of decay to indicate that the end is in sight unless there is a substantial transfusion of hard cash for repairs and maintenance. . . Trash litters the grass-and-dirt entrance to the buildings. Sidewalk lamps are broken off. Sidewalks and the parking lot pavement are sagging and cracked; one building is boarded up because of fire damages.[27]

Having lost $101,500 on the 412-unit project in 1979, one of the co-owners remarked, "We don't have the funds to pay the operating losses. We're not going to continue to pour money into it."

● Among the sample developments of this study, there were several cases of marked deterioration. Like Edgemere and Stanton Hill, these complexes had been built during the mid-60s, and like those two, they contained numerous housing code violations. In some instances, violations took the form of extensive peeling of exterior paint, and potholes in driveways and parking lots. In others, they were more serious—heating and plumbing systems were in disrepair.

The majority of garden developments have yet to reach the more ominous of these crossroads, nor will any necessarily do so over the next several decades. At present, they are in superior structural condition to most types of rental housing, even to those located exclusively in suburbs (see Exhibit 3-2). Yet these capsule summaries do not offer an encouraging prognosis for several reasons. First, they were built after World War II, and in some cases, after 1960. Second, they were built for an unsubsidized (and, thus, reasonably affluent) tenantry. Third, they are located in suburbs or in sections of cities that are far removed from the confines of slum neighborhoods. The evidence suggests that the ability of landlords to absorb rising operating costs, with or without rent control, may be seriously impaired long before a structural shell may be considered ready for demolition. Finally, referring back to the findings in this study, there is the demographic factor. The older complexes, where operating costs are rising more rapidly, are the focal points of the highest increases in elderly and female-headed households. Marrieds, by contrast, particularly financially mobile ones, if they choose to rent a garden apartment, are more likely to move to newer complexes.

To reiterate, it would be premature to infer from this discussion a problem of crisis proportions. Having emerged at a recent point in history, garden apartments, even of moderate cost, have yet to be truly affected by the disinvestment-decay-disinvestment cycle that plagues the very bottom end of the rental stock. It would be myopic, however, to deny that this process may cast a pall over a much larger number of complexes by the end of this century.

There are a number of federal programs with a proven track record in providing cost-effective rehabilitation. Unfortunately, their applicability to garden apartments is limited. First, a number of programs, such as Section 312, are targeted primarily or exclusively for one-to-four family structures. Second, even in multifamily programs, garden apartments are at a competitive disadvantage with older apartments for funding; their overall condition does not warrant the targeting of large sums of money toward structural improvements. Third, the feasibility of any program, even the most successful, must be considered in the current political context. It takes no particular insight to see that housing subsidies hardly qualify as a major budgetary priority of either Congress or the Reagan Administration. Given the constraints, there should at least be an expansion of the Section 8 Moderate Rehabilitation Program. If the objective here is to upgrade as many apartments as possible, using as little money as possible, a good many garden units might prove eligible under this program.

New Construction: How Much Is Enough?

A decade ago, multifamily rental housing was a bellweather of the construction industry. Approximately 750,000 multifamily units intended for rental occupancy were built annually during 1971–73, the overwhelming majority of them garden apartments. This figure plummeted to less than 300,000 during both 1975 and 1976, rose to over 400,000 annually during 1977–79, dropped to less than 300,000 once more in 1981, and to less than 250,000 for 1982.[28] These diminished levels of new starts, accompanied by an increased incidence in rental conversions to condominiums and continued high demolition rates, have strongly contributed to the below-five percent nationwide rental vacancy rates over the last few years. The situation has moved several analysts to imply or recommend that only a return to production levels close to the halycon period of a decade ago can avert disastrous consequences.[29]

Yet would a high-production strategy of this magnitude really be feasible, given current and future patterns of rental demand? Even according to the strongly pro-growth National Association of Home Builders, an average annual level of new starts of between 400,000–450,000 units, allowing for inventory losses, would accommodate rental demand through the 1980s.[30] Two researchers from MIT estimate that the consumption of rental multifamily units (five or more units in a structure) would increase by a total of only 1,965,000 units (less than 200,000 annually) during 1980–90, assuming a medium fertility rate.[31] As with NAHB's estimate, this figure allows for inventory losses.

A sharp boost in rental production would flood the market with units that would be fairly expensive to build, and would attract many existing tenants whose moderate incomes would support necessary debt service and operating expenses only with substantial difficulty.[32] As Exhibit 4-8 indicates, incomes in newly-constructed garden complexes are fairly high, but they represent a limited layer of demand. Once this layer thins, new complexes would invariably have to draw upon the less affluent. Over time, the replacement of homebuying tenants with those of equivalent purchasing power will become an increasingly difficult task, given the overall outflow of nuclear families. Net operating returns may lag behind those of other real property investments, and subsequently builders, lacking a front-end government commitment, will avoid projects not commanding peak rentals. This is precisely what has already begun to happen. Reversing the process would require a ratio of subsidized-to-total rental starts well in excess of the fifty percent level of 1980–81, and perhaps an even further reduction of the current depreciation write-off period of fifteen years for all classes of real property.[33]

Some of the rigidity in the present rental market will ease, as the pent up demand for homeownership continues to be released. The market for apartments is currently tight because young adults born during the 1946–59 baby boom have yet to completely enter the first-time homebuying age bracket of 25–34. In a few years, however, they will have done so, and the ranks that replace them will become progressively thinner. The Census Bureau projects that beginning in 1985, the number of households headed by persons under 25 may dwindle by as much as 122,000 annually until 1985.[34]

Further, the ability of first-time homeseekers to acquire their portion of the good life has not appreciably diminished. No matter how frequent the claim that this segment of the population "can no longer" afford a home, the reality, as pointed out in Chapter Two, is that approximately 22 percent more married households in the 25–34 age bracket were homeowners in

1980 than in 1974.[35] These households usually experience difficulty in buying a first home, yet they are willing to make the sacrifice, as Breckenfeld notes:

> . . .more and more young people in their late twenties, single or married, have been buying homes in recent years. . .They have been digging deeper and deeper into their own (and their parents') pockets to make down payments and, as rising prices and interest rates have continued to lift monthly mortgage payments to Himalayan heights, committing 35 or even 40 percent of their income to housing, a quantum jump from 25 percent minimum that lenders would usually permit only a few years ago.[36]

Nor is this a recent phenomenon. In the late-1950s, for example, a major builder characteristically remarked: "They (young homebuyers) will do without a car, TV, country club, anything to have a home for their kids in a good neighborhood. They strap themselves, sacrificing almost everything else to get a home."[37] The rise of the two-earner married household in garden units (see Exhibit 4-9) and elsewhere provides the first-time homeseeker with an added financial potency.

Thus, renter marrieds traditionally have substituted housing for nonhousing consumption in anticipation of acquiring a set of economic and noneconomic rewards associated with homeownership, however extreme the initial hardships. The stretching of housing expenditure-to-income ratios well beyond the traditional 25 percent standard (and the flexibility with which lenders apply this standard) is indicative not only of the importance that these households place on "getting on the train" early, but of their overall *success* in accomplishing this goal as well.

The tempting financial carrot of homeownership explains their eagerness. Diamond computed that after taking appreciation and income tax deductions for interest and property tax payments into consideration, the costs of owning actually declined by 30 percent over 1969–79.[38] Brueggeman and Peiser concluded that homeownership yielded a far greater internal rate of return than what renters could derive from equivalent investments in corporate bonds.[39] Boehm and McKenzie calculated that a 1.0 percent increase in the perceived rate of home price appreciation led to a 1.56 percent increase in the quantity of housing bought.[40]

The severity of price increases has also been exaggerated. For one thing, 1970 usually serves as the baseline year for measuring price changes. Yet, because of the high level of Section 235-subsidized units built that year, it overestimates the magnitude of the rise that would have taken place under more conventional circumstances.[41] Second, price increases would be lower if the quality of the housing bundle remained constant. The Census Bureau's "Price Index of New One-Family Homes Sold" indicates that when adjusting for dwelling size and amenities, much of the rise in the cost of homes built since 1967 would not have taken place.[42] Finally, the overall reduction of the down payment ratio since 1970 has particularly benefitted first-time buyers. According to National Association of Home Builders' figures, the median downpayment for this group fell below ten percent of the sales price by 1976.[43] The image of the young homebuyer-as-Prometheus being somewhat misleading, the argument for rapid apartment growth is probably likewise so.

However, it must be emphasized that garden apartments should continue to serve as the bulwark of the growth that will occur. Despite extensively documented evidence of a back-to-the-city movement, suburbanization remains the predominant pattern of residential development. Within the same SMSA, central city-to-suburb moves exceeded suburb-to-central city moves by 172.9 percent during March 1975–March 1979. Even within the 18–34 age bracket, where a disproportionately large number of the latter moves occur, the former was still 122.1 percent higher.[44] In the suburbs, where buildable vacant land is most abundant and employment growth most pronounced, apartments will be most needed. And for reasons previously outlined, no type of apartment has been so conducive to suburban growth as the garden unit.

State and Local Laws

Rent Control

One of the ironies of the housing market during the 1970–82 (May) period was the Consumer Price Index rise of 146.9 percent for all items and only 101.4 percent for rents,[45] yet simultaneously, the growing nationwide clamor for rent control. Tenants have been increasingly unwilling to bear the costs of maintaining rental property at a time when some of the major components of overall increase are beyond their ability to control. As Anthony Downs elucidates:

> Tenants cannot retaliate when distant farmers or Arab Oil sheiks raise their prices, but their landlords' immobile properties are captive hostages of the local government. Hence, in communities containing high fractions of tenants, strong political protests led to rent controls.
>
> In theory, all rent control systems allow owners to 'pass through' major increases in expenses to their tenants so they can maintain a competitive return on equity. But political pressure from tenants—who vastly

> outnumber landlords—always persuades rent control administrators to prevent rents from rising as fast as expenses, thus penalizing owners.[46]

Until the late-1960s, the only city that did not remove its wartime rent control had been New York. Over the past fifteen years, however, many other municipalities have enacted ordinances of their own. Among them are suburban communities that contain hundreds of garden apartments.

The previous discussion established a case for a moderate-production strategy of garden apartment growth. It does not necessarily follow that rent control (or levelling) will significantly hamper that growth. Opponents of rent control note that developers are hesitant about building in communities where rent revenues are inherently limited, even under "moderate" ordinances, where the possibility always looms that local officials may reduce the allowable ceilings.[47] Yet as long as new construction is exempt from coverage (which is the case in over 100 New Jersey communities with ordinances), this argument is inapplicable. Moreover, there is evidence that rent-controlled apartments do not necessarily experience more decay than non-controlled apartments.[48] While a moderate rent control ordinance will neither expand nor improve the apartment stock, it can make it more affordable to renter households not receiving a subsidy, and can accomplish this without unduly inhibiting the operator's cash flow.

Condominium Conversion Control

HUD's exhaustive study in 1980 on condominium conversions revealed that during 1970–79, 328,000 apartments were converted to condominiums, about 226,000 of them during the last three years of that period and 108,000 alone during the first three quarters of 1979. Another 1.1 million additional units will have been converted over 1980–85.[49] Many rental conversions have resulted from declining real operating margins. As Lowry explains:

> Landlords whose rent receipts are lagging behind their costs often find it quite profitable to convert, either directly or through an intermediary purchaser. . .The remarkable feature of these conversions is that the change in tenure sometimes doubles or triples the market value of the property. Under those circumstances, conversion generates enough cash to retire the former owner's mortgage, reimburse displaced tenants, and brighten the lives of any number of middlemen.[50]

The fact, however, that not all displacees, even with adequate compensation, can find suitable replacement shelter, has led to controls on conversion activity, particularly in California, Connecticut, and Washington, D.C. While conversions can reduce the available rental stock, there are several reasons why governmental bodies should view the imposition of stringent limitations with caution. First, the extent to which conversion has occurred on a localized basis has been exaggerated, even by the real estate community. In Chicago, for example, an extensive tax map search indicated that the total number of condominium conversions was less than one-half of what had actually been claimed by local tenant organizations.[51] Second, and more importantly, extreme measures would eliminate a vital conduit toward homeownership for a number of young households: the condominium. This is especially important for the affluent portion of the singles' market, which does not need the space of a detached dwelling and in many cases, cannot afford its cost.[52] As one recent condominium buyer in his late-20s analogized, "It's really like buying a first car. Your first car is always a clunker. You work on it and learn how to fix it. Now, we'll know what we want in a house."[53]

At the same time, convertors should provide relocation assistance, particularly for elderly and disabled tenants. If they will not voluntarily do this, local governments should compel them to do so. A display of sensitivity toward the displacee would benefit the landlord as well as the tenant, first, because existing tenants offer a substantial market for home purchase and, second, because rental payments by those who do not purchase still represent a continued source of income, especially important during the initial stages of conversion.[54]

Exclusionary Zoning

Suburban communities continue to receive criticism for their exclusion of certain categories of land use (especially multifamily dwellings) from their zoning ordinances that facilitate housing opportunities for low- and moderate-income households. The judiciary in *Oakwood at Madison*,[55] *Mount Laurel*,[56] and similar decisions[57] played a vigilant role in weakening these barriers during the 70s. The underlying assumption was that decent, safe, and sanitary housing, as a basic necessity of life, is entitled to constitutional protection.[58] A municipality with sizeable vacant tracts of land zoned for residential purposes has within its power the capacity to determine the access of less affluent citizens to this necessity. Consequently it should be required to provide its fair share of the regional housing need of low- and moderate-income households.

More often than not, garden apartments have been the unspoken subject of the debate. Suburban communities are relatively unwilling to make a concession to other forms of rental housing. High-rises smack of high density, and mobile homes of the rural and semi-rural poor. The garden apartment is the best possible solution to local officials. Though garden apartment demand, as noted before, is likely to slacken off during the latter half of this decade, outer ring communities still bear a strong responsibility toward promoting their growth, since they contain tracts of land readily available for assemblage. Nor would the garden apartment's promotion necessarily engender suburban sprawl. As Mallach explains:

> By fostering sprawl, exclusionary zoning bears the brunt of the responsibility for the massive conversion of farmland that characterizes American suburban development. The only additional factor that can be considered of comparable significance in terms of its impact on the wasteful pattern of suburban development, is the absence of any meaningful regional planning in all but a handful of the metropolitan areas of the United States, and the resulting patterns of land use control at the local level, grounded in the most parochial of interests and prejudices. Extensive evidence exists to show that the exercise of local land use controls in suburbia tends to be oriented toward a combination of maximizing fiscal advantage (hence the mad scramble for commercial and industrial ratables) and maintaining what are perceived to be desireable socioeconomic characteristics on the part of residents of the community.[59]

Several qualifications must be made here, however. The effort to break down exclusionary zoning ordinances should be cognizant of the following considerations.

First, public officials must be careful to distinguish between—rather than lump together (as they so often do)—the housing needs of low- and moderate-income households. The crucial difference between the two is that a low-income household cannot afford new housing without a deep subsidy; a moderate-income household can, given certain adjustments by itself and the developer. New garden apartments are more expensive than old ones—and it is "new" (or, more accurately, as-of-yet) structures toward which efforts must be engaged.

Second, the fact that suburban communities may appear to be employing exclusionary practices does not necessarily mean that they are actually doing so. Schafer, in analyzing the zoning ordinances of several dozen Boston-area communities, found that many of those which formally excluded garden apartments in their zoning ordinances still permitted their construction.[60] The relationship between unmet housing demand and the stringency of the ordinance was statistically insignificant.

Finally, and most importantly, while the zoning ordinance can be used as an effective tool for expanding rental housing opportunities in the suburbs, it cannot build the housing if the demand is not there.[61] The fact that communities with large tracts of vacant, residentially-zoned land may not have experienced much recent apartment construction (even with "inclusionary" ordinances) may be more a result of the diminishing appeal of renting than of their resistance to recent court decisions.

Energy Conservation Codes

On the matter of energy conservation, the necessity of government activism leaves little room for question. Over the next several years, the costs of heating and electricity may prove to be even more burdensome for rental property operation. There are opportunities for state, county, and local government to develop performance-based standards for energy conservation in new and existing garden apartment complexes. These need not take a punitive tack. In relative degree of coercion, they can take the form of removal of barriers to energy conservation, encouragement of energy conservation, and mandates for certain energy-saving measures. The first category removes regulations that lead to energy waste (e.g., excessive yard and setback specifications, prohibitions on solar collectors, excessive street widths required by subdivision ordinances), the second involves the creation of various incentives for builders and landlords to conserve energy (e.g., density bonuses, tax rebates), and the third involves the imposition of numerous requirements upon developers and owners to adopt energy conservation measures.

The front-end costs may be difficult for a landlord to absorb, but they could be offset within a reasonably short period. As one example, the management of an all-electric California garden apartment complex performed a complete retrofit, including a switch from master to separate metering. The payback period was only 3.45 years, with management passing on a monthly savings of $10 to tenants in studio apartments, and $14 to those in one-bedroom units.[62] Tenant acceptance of this measure was reasonably positive. While some households inevitably moved out due to a reluctance to pay their own heating bills, the vacancies were quickly filled.[63]

Environmental Controls

Beginning in the 1960s and accelerating in the 1970s, public concern over ecologically-injurious consequences of development, such as soil erosion, air pollution, groundwater pollution, and wetland dredging, has resulted in the enactment of numerous laws at all levels of government to mitigate these consequences. These laws either prohibit or restrict development in certain designated areas or mandate builders to comply with certain procedures related to environmental protection (e.g. special plat review, environmental impact statements) prior to receiving approval for a proposal.

Such measures impose procedural and substantive costs upon builders. The germane issue is whether the benefits conferred upon their jurisdictions are worth the restrictions placed upon the productive power of the homebuilding industry. A number of observers have argued "no," often vehemently. Some have focused specifically upon housing-related issues,[64] while others have broadened their opprobrium to include the entire environmentalist movement.[65] All have concluded that suburban officials who restrict new development are responding to short-sighted and often hypocritical pressures placed upon them by their respective local electorates. "Elitist" residents of upper middle-income suburbs feign interest in a public issue, environmental protection, in order to promote a private concern—maintaining high property values.

Garden apartments figure heavily in this controversy. Adopting the argument of the critics for the time being, the imposition of environmental laws may have impaired the mobility of housing firms and consumers in several ways. Garden apartments have become increasingly less affordable to the low- and moderate-income households who need them most. This is because the younger households are far more likely to rent than own anyway, and as practically all new apartment construction in the suburbs is currently of the garden type, further promulgation of these laws will inhibit their ability to find decent housing near the workplace. Likewise, the creation of environmental review procedures, with their attendant fees and delays, tends to dissuade the small developer from absorbing these front-end costs. Indeed, these procedures may have induced large developers to scale down their garden projects, where the potential for hostile political response is muted. Moreover, once a given supply of land is protected from development, owners of unprotected land, realizing the increased scarcity of their asset, will be more likely to speculate.[66] The irony of this, as Frieden notes, is not only a more expensive product, but also one unable to realize the very anti-sprawl intent of these procedures.

Several empirical studies, however, suggest that the cost of compliance is only modest in relation to the total project cost. Richardson concluded that a developer's compliance with the New Jersey Coastal Area Facility Review Act added only $125 to the total cost of a garden apartment in one shore community.[67] This figure represented 5.7 percent more than the entire subdivision process for garden apartment proposals in communities where the Act did not apply, and only about one percent more than the average development and construction cost of an 800-square foot two-bedroom garden apartment built in New Jersey in 1975.[68] Muller and James, in examining several housing development proposals in southeastern Florida and metropolitan San Diego, found that compliance with state Environmental Impact Statements added only $386 and $165 (1.4 and 0.6 percent, respectively) to the total development and construction cost of a new private dwelling.[69] Environmental Analysis Systems, Inc., in examining the impact of the California Environmental Quality Act, found that for all housing, compliance added $150 per total unit cost.[70] More dramatically, Nicholas, et al. concluded that during 1978–79, Florida's implementation of the American Land Institute's Model Land Development Code added $4,698 to the cost of a new private dwelling within the same market area, but that virtually the entire increase was due to delay rather than compliance. Thus, the problem was due to a lack of streamlining in the approval process rather than to the harshness of the standards themselves.[71]

Moreover, empirical studies have tended to avoid examining the benefits of environmental regulation. This is because while costs can be measured in terms of a single tangible entity (i.e. a dwelling), benefits are extremely diffuse and therefore difficult to measure. Given both the benefit analysis that has yet to be performed and the cost analysis that has been performed, there is little reason to believe that the removal of environmental safeguards would greatly reduce the cost, increase the supply, or improve the quality of future garden apartment development.

Cost Reduction and Structural Quality

Reduction of Interior Square Footage

Reducing gross leasable square footage has a limited capacity to hold down rents. Given the shrinking ratios of children per unit,[72] some complexes consequently need a lower proportion of two- and three-bedroom units. In some cases, a den may replace the second or third bedroom without incurring a shortage of garden units for households with children. There are, however, serious difficulties involved in reducing the average size per room. For one thing, this strategy would discourage households with one or more young children from seeking such units, since the children may share the same bedroom or have to sleep in the living room. Further, it may induce higher turnover among single and two-adult households at the younger end of this market from seeking such units (since they may share the same bedroom). Young adults generally have a high income elasticity for household durable goods.[73] In practical terms, given rising incomes, they will need sufficient space to house their newly-purchased furniture, bookcases, record albums, and television sets.[74] The more fortunate among them will seek larger rental quarters, whether or not of garden design.

Reduction of Material and Labor Costs

A cut-rate approach to material and labor costs (and hopefully rents) would be even more questionable. Though such a strategy would provide an initial cost reduction, it would very likely fail its more important test—the long-run savings in utility and maintenance outlays. For example, where energy conservation standards are not instituted, developments tend to have excessively thin window panes, drywalls, and ceilings. These features rebound to the owner in the form of higher heating bills and an expensive (if performed) retrofit. As another example, the hiring of unskilled labor may save on wage costs, but is more likely to result in loose guard railings, squeaking floors, and improperly installed doors, caulking, window frames, and studs. That repairing these defects requires paying for added wages as well as materials should be fairly obvious.

There are no doubt imperatives in keeping construction costs down to realistic levels. The garden apartment represents a moderate-cost approach to the problem of housing a nation. Yet there are clear limits as to how much the product can be stripped down in order to reach progressively lower layers of demand without the use of rent subsidies. Cheaply-built developments in lieu of subsidies represent an attempt to hit two targets with one arrow. They are too expensive to attract most of the poor and they are too unappealing to attract any among the non-poor but those who need to find housing quickly; i.e., the most mobile among singles, marrieds and single parents. To the latter group, these complexes represent housing of necessity rather than of choice, a fact mirrored all too often in their excessively high turnover rates. Ironically, they provide the very fuel for the traditional bases of opposition to suburban apartment growth; that apartments are detrimental to community character, that they attract "transients" (instead of real citizens), and that they are "slums of the future." The larger these developments are, the greater the likelihood will be that they will raise suspicions of nearby area residents faced with similar proposals, and the lesser the likelihood that these proposals will obtain even preliminary approval.

Conclusion

This book has assembled a substantial reservoir of information and data on the state of garden apartment dwellings and households in the 1970s and 80s. The demand for garden apartments among young nuclear families has markedly diminished, with the decline occurring, particularly in complexes constructed over a decade ago. Some of this fallout has been due to their willingness to live in newer, more expensive garden units, given their higher incomes. Their departure has left a vacuum filled by a less affluent tenantry consisting heavily of singles and to a lesser extent, female-headed families and the elderly. Like the marrieds whom they have replaced, their propensity to move has somewhat diminished. And like them, they are relatively content with their dwelling and neighborhood.

The shrinkage of marrieds within the rental market has been the dominant reality of the changing demand for garden apartments. The shift has occurred due to both their declining proportionate share of all American households and to the enhanced appeal of homeownership in the inflationary period of the last several years. The maturing of baby boom adults should, at least until the late-80s, push this trend along further. While their replacements, particularly singles, are affluent to a certain degree, they are not as affluent as marrieds. As such, the meeting of operating expenses may prove to be an especially vexing problem.

There is relatively little that government can do to reverse or otherwise alter these demographic trends over the next several years and probably on through to the close of the century. However, there is much that government can do to accommodate them in its decisionmaking, first, by preventing the growing garden apartment stock from falling into disrepair and, second, by making it readily available and affordable to households for whom renting has become a long-term adjustment to their own economic fortunes. This will probably require an expansion of the role recommended for it by the Reagan Administration. Yet an activist approach would be worth the effort. Garden apartments are, in the main, habitable and attractive places to live. That they will remain so may be questionable if the degree of success in meeting the nation's rental housing needs is interpreted solely in terms of the number of new starts.

NOTES

1. This statement refers to the type of household, not to the actual households themselves.

2. U.S. Bureau of the Census, *Current Housing Reports*, H-150-80, "Annual Housing Survey: 1980," Part A: General Housing Characteristics, Washington, D.C.: U.S. Government Printing Office, 1982.

3. John Tucillo, *Housing and Investment in an Inflationary World: Theory and Evidence*, Washington, D.C.: Urban Institute, 1980, p. 19.

4. The devotion of an unusually high ratio of household income to mortgage payment is currently endemic to certain local markets. For example, *U.S. Housing Markets* recently reported that San Diego has "the country's most psychologically depressed housing market" and the nation's highest ratio of mortgage payment to income. See Advance Mortgage Corporation, *U.S. Housing Markets*, Subscribers' Special Report, February 5, 1982.

5. See Tucillo, *Housing and Investment in an Inflationary World*, p. 1.

6. U.S. Bureau of the Census, *Current Population Reports*, Series P-20, No. 371, "Percent Distribution of Families by Number of Own Children Under 18 Years Old: 1950 to 1981," Washington, D.C.: U.S. Government Printing Office, May 1982.

7. For a general discussion of recent income disparities by household type, see George Sternlieb and James W. Hughes, "Faster to Stay in Place: Family Income and the Baby Boom," *American Demographics*, June 1982, pp. 17–20.

8. For evidence as this applies to Section 8 New Construction projects, see U.S. General Accounting Office, *Section 8 Subsidized Housing—Some Observations on Its High Rents, Costs, and Inequities*, Washington, D.C.: U.S. General Accounting Office, CED-80-59, June 6, 1980, pp. 14–39.

9. U.S. Bureau of the Census, "Annual Housing Survey: 1979" and "Annual Housing Survey: 1980," Part A, General Housing Characteristics; National Associa-

tion of Realtors, *Existing Home Sales*, Chicago: National Association of Realtors, monthly.

10. U.S. Department of Housing and Urban Development, *The Conversion of Rental Housing to Condominiums and Cooperatives: Causes, Incidence, and Effects*, Washington, D.C.: U.S. Government Printing Office, August 1980; summarized in John A. Casazza, "The Condominium Conversion Phenomenon," *Urban Land*, November 1980, pp. 3–5.

11. Philip L. Clay, "Improving the Utilization of the Existing Housing Stock: The Case of Accessory Apartments," paper presented to a conference sponsored by the Joint Center for Urban Studies of MIT-Harvard and Lincoln Institute for Land Policy, July 1, 1982.

12. Anne Vernez-Moudon and Chester Sprague, "Housing Conservation: Infill and Consolidation," draft paper, June 1982, quoted in Clay, "Improving the Utilization of Existing Housing Stock," p. 9.

13. Clay, pp. 14–17.

14. Cited in Advance Mortgage Corporation, advertisement brochure for *U.S. Housing Markets*, Detroit: Advance Mortgage Corporation, 1982.

15. See Ira S. Lowry, *Rental Housing in the 1970s: Searching for the Crisis*, Santa Monica, Cal.: Rand Corporation, January 1982, p. 11; George Sternlieb, "Comment," *Urban Affairs Quarterly*, Vol. 17, No. 2, December 1981, pp. 144–45.

16. "The Incredible Shrinking HUD," *Housing*, Vol. 61, No. 3, March 1982, p. 19.

17. Office of the White House, *Report of the President's Commission on Housing*, Advance Edition, Washington, D.C.: Office of the White House, April 1982; see also Robert Lubar, "Housing's Unsheltered Future," *Fortune*, March 8, 1982, pp. 86–90.

18. One may take note of several examples of this trend in certain local markets (see Advance Mortgage Corporation, advertisement brochure for *U.S. Housing Markets*, 1982, comments by one Philadelphia apartment operator on the outflow of young singles from his project and their replacement by households with children). Notwithstanding, the trend does not appear to be interrupted on a massive scale.

19. Since this index is a ratio, at least some of the differences can be attributed to higher rent collections (the denominator) in newer complexes.

20. Ira S. Lowry, *Rental Housing in the 1970s: Searching for the Crisis*, pp. 31–32.

21. Institute of Real Estate Management, *Income-Expense Analysis: Apartments*, Chicago: National Association of Realtors, Institute of Real Estate Management, annually.

22. *Income-Expense Analysis*, 1980 edition, pp. 25–26. These figures include common areas (stairwells, laundry rooms, corridors, etc.) as well as individual apartments.

23. Alan Oser, "Garden Apartments in Queens Becoming Private Homes," *New York Times*, November 23, 1980.

24. This arrangement is mutually beneficial. Lenders avoid the likelihood of having to acquire and manage the property in case of default. Owners can deduct most of their mortgage payments from their Federal income tax.

25. William G. Blair, "The Garden Apartment as a Rental on Decline in City," *New York Times*, November 23, 1980.

26. George Wirt, "Franklin Township Girds for Housing Showdown," *Newark Star-Ledger*, October 16, 1980. The project's condition has become noticeably worse since this article first appeared. In fact, the windows to many units are boarded up.

27. Kenneth Bredemeier, "Stanton Hill's Decline Sharpens Rent Issue," *Washington Post*, April 9, 1980.

28. U.S. Bureau of the Census, *Construction Reports*, Series C-20-18-3, "Housing Starts," Washington, D.C.: U.S. Government Printing Office, March 1982.

29. See, for example, U.S. General Accounting Office, *Rental Housing: A National Problem that Needs Immediate Attention*, Washington, D.C.: U.S. General Accounting Office, CED-80-11, November 8, 1979; Testimony of various witnesses in U.S. House of Representatives, Ninety-Sixth Congress, Second Session, *Hearing Before the Subcommittee on Housing and Community Development of the Committee on Banking, Finance, and Urban Affairs*, Washington, D.C.: U.S. Government Printing Office, 1980.

30. John Pitkin and George Masnick, *Projections of Housing Consumption in the U.S., 1980 to 2000, by a Cohort Method*, Annual Housing Survey Study No. 9, Washington, D.C.: U.S. Department of Housing and Urban Development, Office of Policy Development and Research, November 1980, p. 76.

31. Uriel Manheim, *Rental Housing in the 1980s*, Washington, D.C.: National Association of Home Builders, 1980, pp. 4–5.

32. A similar argument is made in Lowry, *Rental Housing in the 1970s*; Anthony Downs, "Public Policy and the Rising Cost of Housing," *Real Estate Review*, Vol. 8, No. 1, Spring 1978, pp. 27–38.

33. Economic Recovery Tax Act of 1981, P.L. 97–34, Title II.

34. U.S. Bureau of the Census, *Current Population Reports*, Series P-25, Nos. 310 and 311, "Estimate and Projected Population, by Age and Sex, 1950 to 2010," Washington, D.C.: U.S. Government Printing Office, 1980.

35. U.S. Bureau of the Census, "Annual Housing Survey: 1974," and "Annual Housing Survey: 1980," Part A, General Housing Characteristics. Even more telling, approximately half of this increase took place during 1979–80 alone (see "Annual Housing Survey: 1979").

36. Gurney Breckenfeld, "A Decade of Catch-Up for Housing," *Fortune*, April 7, 1980, p. 98.

37. Quoted in Charles E. Silberman and Todd May, "The Coming Changes in Housing," *Fortune*, April 1959, p. 91.

38. Douglas B. Diamond, "The Next Housing Crisis," *Real Estate Review*, Vol. 10, No. 3, Fall 1980, pp. 65–71.

39. William B. Brueggeman and Richard B. Peiser, "Housing Choice and Relative Tenure Prices," *Journal of Finance and Quantitative Analysis*, Vol. 14, No. 4, November 1979, pp. 735–51.

40. Thomas P. Boehm and Joseph A. McKenzie, "Inflation, Taxes, and the Demand for Housing," *Journal of the American Real Estate and Urban Economics Association*, Vol. 10, No. 1, Spring 1982, pp. 25–38.

41. Anthony Downs, "Public Policy and the Rising Cost of Housing," *Real Estate Review*, Vol. 8, No. 1, Spring 1978, p. 28.

42. U.S. Bureau of the Census, *Current Housing Reports*, Series C-27, "Price Index of New One-Family Homes Sold," Washington, D.C.: U.S. Government Printing Office, annually.

43. National Association of Home Builders, *Characteristics of New Homes Sold*, Washington, D.C.: National Association of Home Builders, annually.

44. U.S. Bureau of the Census, *Current Population Reports*, Series P-20, No. 353, Table 10, "Geographic Mobility: March 1975 to March 1979." Washington, D.C.: U.S. Government Printing Office, August 1980, p. 25.

45. U.S. Department of Labor, Bureau of Labor Statistics, *CPI Detailed Report*, Washington, D.C.: U.S. Government Printing Office, monthly.

46. Anthony Downs, *The Future of Rental Housing*, Washington, D.C.: Brookings Institution, 1979.

47. This point was made by a New Jersey garden apartment developer who has built in communities with rent levelling ordinances enacted after construction. Interview with Samuel Herzog, Village Associates, East Brunswick, New Jersey, November 28, 1980.

48. Herbert Selesnick, *Rent Control: The Case For*, Lexington, Mass.: Lexington Books, 1976; John Ingram Gilderbloom, "Moderate Rent Control: Its Impact on the Quality and Quantity of the Housing Stock," *Urban Affairs Quarterly*, Vol. 17, No. 2, December 1981, pp. 123–42.

49. U.S. Department of Housing and Urban Development, *The Conversion of Rental Housing to Condominiums and Cooperatives.*

50. Lowry, *Rental Housing in the 1970s.*

51. Richard Roddewig, "Condomania or Condophobia?" *Real Estate Issues*, Vol. 5, No. 1, Summer 1980, pp. 16–31.

52. U.S. Department of Housing and Urban Development, *The Conversion of Rental Housing to Condominiums and Cooperatives.*

53. Quoted in Robert Lindsay, "High Housing Costs Create a Grudging Condominium Generation," *New York Times*, May 25, 1980.

54. See Casazza, "The Condominium Conversion Phenomenon," p. 4.

55. 72 N.J. 481, 371, A.2d 1193 (1977).

56. 67 N.J. 151, 336, A.2d 173 (1975).

57. See *Urban League of Greater New Brunswick v. Carteret*, 142 N.J. Super. 11, 359 A.2d 526 (1976); *Kennedy Park Homes Association v. Lackawanna*, 317 F. Supp. 669 (WDNY. 1970), affd., 436 F.2d 108 (CA 2nd, 1970), cert. deb., 401 U.S. 1010 (1971); *Appeal of Girsh*, 437 Pa. 237, 263 A.2d 395 (1970); *Warth v. Seldin*, 4-22 U.S. 490 (1975); *Berenson v. Town of New Castle*, 38 N.Y. 2d. 102, 341, N.E. 2d 236, 378 N.Y. S.2d 672 (1975); *Surrick v. Upper Providence Township*, 476 Pa. 182, 382, A.2d 105 (1977); *Township of Willistown v. Chesterdale Farms, Inc.*, 462 Pa. 445, 341 A.2d 466 (1975); *Associated Home Builders of Greater Eastbay, Inc. v. City of Livermore*, 17 Cal. 3d 582, 557 P.2d 473, 135 Cal. Rptr. 41 (1976).

58. See Frederick W. Hall, "An Orientation to Mount Laurel," in Jerome G. Rose and Robert E. Rothman, eds., *After Mount Laurel: The New Suburban Zoning*, New Brunswick, N.J.: Center for Urban Policy Research, 1977, pp. 3-31.

59. Alan Mallach, "Exclusionary Zoning Litigation: Setting the Record Straight," *Real Estate Law Journal*, Vol. 9, No. 4, Spring 1981, pp. 275-310.

60. Robert Schafer, *The Suburbanization of Multifamily Housing*, Lexington, Mass.: Lexington Books, 1974, pp. 91-100.

61. See, especially, Jerome G. Rose, "Myths and Misconceptions of Exclusionary Zoning Litigation," *Real Estate Law Journal*, Vol. 8, No. 2, Fall 1979, pp. 99-124.

62. Judith C. Ricker, "The Retrofit of a Master Metered Apartment Complex: A Case Study," *Journal of Property Management*, Vol. 45, No. 3, May/June 1980, pp. 52–56. This, of course, did not take into account the added costs to the tenants who now had to pay their own electric bills.

63. See Ricker; also Institute of Behavioral Sciences, University of Colorado, *Encouraging Energy Conservation in Multifamily Housing: RUBS and Other Methods of Allocating Energy Costs to Residents*, Washington, D.C.: U.S. Department of Energy, June 1980.

64. Bernard Frieden, *The Environmental Protection Hustle*, Cambridge, Mass.: MIT Press, 1979; "Environmental Politics," *Urban Land*, March 1977; "The New Regulation Comes to Suburbia," *The Public Interest*, No. 55, Spring 1979, pp. 15-27; Anthony Downs, "Comments on Session I," in Robert W. Burchell, ed., *Frontiers of Planned Unit Development: A Synthesis of Expert Opinion*, New Brunswick, N.J.: Center for Urban Policy Research, 1973, pp. 73-83.

65. William Tucker, "Environmentalism and the Leisure Class," *Harper's*, December 1977, pp. 49-80; A. Lawrence Chickering, "Why Are There No Blacks in the Sierra Club?" in *No Land Is an Island: Individual Rights and Government Control of Land Use*, San Francisco: Institute for Contemporary Studies, 1975.

66. Robert G. Healy, *Land Use and the States*, Washington, D.C.: Resources for the Future, 1976, pp. 89-90.

67. Daniel K. Richardson, *The Cost of Environmental Protection: Regulating Housing Development in the Coastal Zone*, New Brunswick, N.J.: Center for Urban Policy Research, 1976, pp. 130-31.

68. In 1975, the year in which Richardson had performed the research, the total development/construction cost for such a unit was roughly $16,000. See George Sternlieb, "The Private Sector's Role in the Provision of Reasonably Priced Housing," in *Resources for Housing*, Proceedings of the First Annual Conference of the Federal Home Loan Bank Board of San Francisco, December 9-10, 1975, San Francisco: Federal Home Loan Bank of San Francisco, 1976, p. 220.

69. Thomas Muller and Franklin J. James, *Environmental Impact Evaluation and Housing Costs*, Washington, D.C.: Urban Institute, 1975. While not examining the impact upon garden apartments, had the authors done so, they would have likely derived even smaller percentages, given the comparison of results for SFUs and garden apartments in Richardson, *The Cost of Environmental Protection*.

70. Environmental Analysis Systems, Inc., *The California Environmental Quality Act: An Evaluation Emphasizing Its Impact Upon California Cities and Counties with Recommendations for Improving Its Effectiveness*, San Diego: Environmental Analysis Systems, Inc., November 1975.

71. James C. Nicholas, Mary C. Olsen, Joyce Costomiris, and Adele Levesque, *State Regulation/Housing Prices*, New Brunswick, N.J.: Center for Urban Policy Research, 1982.

72. See Robert W. Burchell and David Listokin, *Practitioner's Guide to Fiscal Impact Analysis*, New Brunswick, N.J.: Center for Urban Policy Research, 1980, Appendix.

73. See Richard Stone and D. A. Rowe, "The Durability of Consumers' Durable Goods," *Econometrica*, Vol. XXVII 1960, pp. 407-16; J. B. Kau and D. Keenan, "On the Theory of Interest Rates, Consumer Durables, and the Demand for Housing," paper presented to the Mid-Year Meeting of the American Real Estate and Urban Economics Association, May 1979.

74. Many popular household durables, such as television sets and stereos, were not available prior to the late-1940s, and some not even until well after. The array of goods created by the revolution in communications and electronics technology may have itself increased the demand for dwelling space, though no empirical study has been undertaken on the possible substitution effect (in a context of rising real incomes) between such goods and dwelling space.

Appendix A

Methodology

Overview of Data Sources

The surveys in this book are grouped into two categories: 1) Public Use Samples of the U.S. Census of Housing and the Annual Housing Survey; and 2) a questionnaire developed by the author and administered to residents of garden apartment developments. The Census data identify nationwide trends occurring in the garden apartment market since 1970. Though neither the Decennial Census nor the Annual Housing Survey explicitly set aside a category of "garden apartment," several variables contained in their user programs, when used in tandem, isolate such a housing type with a high degree of accuracy. Inclusion of data on other types of housing are necessary to affirm or negate the uniqueness of shifts occurring within the garden apartment market. The resident survey consists of interviews with households in thirty-six garden apartment complexes in various New Jersey communities.

Census Public Use Samples

Description of Data Base

The Census data consist of Public Use Samples for the 1970 Decennial Census of Housing and the national sample of the Annual Housing Survey

(AHS) in 1973, 1977, and 1978. The 1970 data, conducted as separate 5 and 15 percent samples, describe housing and household characteristics of one ten-thousandth of the nation's dwelling units.[1] The Annual Housing Survey, initiated in 1973, is a cluster sample of approximately one-thousandth of the nation's units. The details of these survey instruments are more than adequately described elsewhere[2] and need not be further elaborated upon. Of greater concern are the merits of each in providing an adequate data base for this particular study.

Strengths and Limitations of Data Base

Census Public Use Samples are superior for researching aggregate housing market conditions and trends. They provide data on a nationwide scale that no non-Census survey can approach, and they afford flexibility in data analysis lacking in published counts. Despite representing only a fraction of the universe, the samples are based on the individual unit, rather than on the block or the tract. This feature facilitates cross tabulation between variables.

The 1970 Census of Housing Public Use Sample contains a sizeable number of structural, financial, and household characteristics. Yet despite its apparent flexibility, it is beset with limitations for applied research. First, given that the one-in-ten thousand sample was used for this book, this left the 1960 sample unusable. Given that the principal share of garden apartment growth occurred after that year, it is not surprising that the "grand" total of suburban garden apartments came to fourteen, obviously far too low a figure for statistical analysis of any kind. Second, it does not distinguish either public or privately-owned subsidized dwellings from the rest of the sample. Third, the sample covers a limited range of considerations; there are few questions that address structural condition and none that address resident perceptions. Finally, the questionnaire forms in the 5 and 15 percent samples are not identical. Most damaging is the fact that although the 5 percent sample inquires into the number of stories in a structure, it does not do so into the length of time in which a household lived in its present unit. For the 15 percent sample, the situation is reversed. Since data on garden apartments would be of little value without knowledge of the number of stories, the 5 percent sample had to be used, and consequently all potential information on moving behavior in 1970 had to be foregone.

The Annual Housing Survey obtains housing-related data that the Decennial Census does not. In addition to identifying all household characteristics addressed in the Census, the AHS examines a wide range of information on potential structural problems. The AHS inquires into resident satisfaction toward dwelling and neighborhood, moving plans, and reason(s) for any anticipated move. As its name implies, it is conducted annually, sampling (with the exception of losses from and additions to the existing inventory) identical units, and thus providing the researcher with an ability to predict short-term changes in inventory characteristics. It distinguishes between public, privately-owned subsidized, and privately-owned nonsubsidized dwellings. Finally, for present purposes there are no major inconsistencies between survey forms for different years.

Field Procedure

All analysis of data was completely contingent upon the development of a statistical definition of a garden apartment. The nine limiting variables in the 1978 AHS that were employed, with specifications, are indicated in Exhibit 3-1. These variables were also applied to earlier Annual Housing Surveys and the 1970 data files. Once working definitions of other housing types were established—and the task here was considerably easier—the frequency distributions and cross tabulations could be conducted.

Resident Survey

Description of Data Base

The resident survey actually consisted of two surveys employing an identical questionnaire. The first was a re-survey of dwelling units located in apartment complexes in various towns and suburbs throughout New Jersey. These developments had provided much of the data base for the Center for Urban Policy Research's 1972 study, *Housing Development and Municipal Costs.*[3] In that study, interviewers contacted almost 7,500 households living in four predominant forms of post-World War II housing development—single-family detached, townhouse, high-rise apartment, and garden apartment—successfully completing approximately 4,100 questionnaire forms, of which over 1,800 reflected responses from garden apartments. The sample universe consisted of: 1) recently-built developments, the selection of which was defined by county cluster and community type; and 2) the same developments (although not necessarily the same units) included in a 1963 garden apartment survey and published as *The Garden Apartment Development: A Municipal Cost-Revenue Analysis.*[4] The eight developments in that particular survey were resurveyed in 1972 to provide a basis for historical comparison.

The 1972 questionnaire examined the respondents' characteristics, moving patterns, and attitudes toward their housing and local public services. The researchers sought to develop a procedure for assessing the probable impact of the previously listed housing forms on the capacity of municipalities to provide services. Once developed, local officials would presumably be better able to separate fact from fancy in evaluating the likelihood of new housing in their respective communities to "pay their own way."

The 1980 survey consisted of 794 questionnaire forms conducted primarily by the author. It both narrows and expands the focus of its predecessor. On one hand, it examines dwelling and household characteristics only of garden apartments. While this housing type is hardly studied in isolation from others, it is the central point of reference. Within that limitation, this book examines a broader range of market and policy issues. The previous survey was subsumed under an overriding theme: fiscal impact analysis. For the 1980 survey, the garden apartment is examined in the context of the web of economic, social, and demographic factors affecting housing preferences.

Only those addresses that had yielded successful interviews eight years earlier were contacted again. The names of the developments are in Exhibit A-1. That an unsurveyed unit had the same number of bedrooms as an unsurveyed unit did not render it sufficient for inclusion in the current sample. There are a number of reasons for this decision, despite the potential time-saving factor that might have resulted from contacting any unit in that complex, whether or not previously surveyed. Each reason flows from the necessity for reducing bias in changes that may account for differences in responses. First, as a practical matter, the bedroom interchangeability approach requires the interviewer to view a building from the exterior, and count the number of bedrooms in each potentially surveyable unit in advance. This is not always easy to do. Second, in several developments, ground floor units rented for less than upper floor units because the former did not provide wall-to-wall carpeting. Finally, resident perceptions of neighbors and neighborhood could have been affected by the relative location of the dwelling within the development; e.g. traffic noise levels, abundance of trees or shrubbery.

Several problems prevented a complete replication of each observation (address) from the 1972 sample. First, as a result of an on-site field canvass, several developments were found to contain at least one characteristic that warranted their exclusion from the updated survey, given the focus on the unsubsidized, non-urban portion of the market. One development was located in Newark and consisted of garden cooperatives, most of which were federally-subsidized under Section 236 or Section 8 Existing Housing. Another development also principally consisted of rent-subsidized cooperatives. Two others consisted of rent-subsidized apartments, one of them of townhouse rather than garden design. Second, addresses on approximately 10 percent of the 1972 questionnaire cover sheets were left blank by the interviewers. In developments where this had occurred, the only recourse was to sample any unit in the complex, but in as close to the same bedroom distribution as the original survey. Third, almost two percent of the responses in 1972 had the same addresses indicated for two different households. To compensate, the number of duplicates was noted, and one interview from each pair was eliminated from the current working universe. Finally, five questionnaires from the 1972 survey indicated a nonexistent address. As with duplicates, these cases were eliminated.

The second portion of the 1980 survey examined the possibility of significant differences occurring due as a result of a complex having been built either before or after the beginning of 1972. The development of this data base required eliminating the target number of completed surveys, eliminating from the sample complexes not fitting structural, tenure, and financial criteria, and selecting the particular units to be contacted within each sample development.

A maximum sample size of approximately 250 was deemed to be adequate; it is a figure large enough to account for potentially significant differences between newer and older complexes, yet small enough to fit within practical time limitations. Since this represented approximately one-third of the responses of the repeat survey, ten developments would then be sufficient to provide a diversity of responses.

Three counties in New Jersey—Middlesex, Morris, and Mercer—accounted for a much larger portion of successful observations in 1972 than the others, together comprising about 80 percent of all responses. The sample would thus be best served by concentrating fully upon these counties. For each of their municipalities, the planning office or equivalent agency was contacted and requested to provide information on any garden apartment complexes that had been constructed in their jurisdiction since early-1972. In this way, a working universe was generated. Ten sample complexes were selected through the use of a random number table; each county had to contain at least one complex.

As with the larger sample, a field canvass proved to be useful. A few of the selected apartment complexes turned out to consist solely of townhouses, while others had been completed for occupancy prior to 1972. These developments were randomly replaced by others, which, in turn, were also canvassed, with no similar problems occurring. The developments selected are denoted by an asterisk in Exhibit A-1.

In order to acquire a desired distribution of successful interviews among the ten developments, a percentage weight was assigned to each on the basis of total dwelling units, and then multiplied by the ceiling number of observations in the sub-sample. One particular complex, for example, contained 12 percent of all units; thus, it would contain a maximum of 12 percent (or 31 units) of the 250 targeted.

The final issue was the selection of dwelling units to be contacted within

EXHIBIT A-1

Developments Sampled in Statewide (New Jersey) Survey: 1980
(in alphabetical order)

Name of Development	*Municipality*	*County*
Adelaide Gardens	Highland Park	Middlesex
Beverwyck Gardens	Parsippany-Troy Hills	Morris
Chestnut Willow	East Windsor	Mercer
Clearview Gardens	Parsippany-Troy Hills	Morris
Colonial Gardens*	Woodbridge	Middlesex
Colonial House*	Woodbridge	Middlesex
Cuthbert Manor	Haddon	Camden
Edison Village*	Edison	Middlesex
Emerald Gardens	Dover	Ocean
Flemington Arms	Flemington	Hunterdon
Hampton Arms	East Windsor	Mercer
Hensyn Village*	Mount Olive	Morris
Hillside Apartments	Edison	Middlesex
King's Village*	Mount Olive	Morris
Knoll Manor	Parsippany-Troy Hills	Morris
Lincoln Gardens	Parsippany-Troy Hills	Morris
Madison Arms	Flemington	Hunterdon
Marina Park Gardens	Collingswood	Camden
Meadowbrook Gardens	Parsippany-Troy Hills	Morris
Montgomery Apartments	Highland Park	Middlesex
Netcong Village*	Netcong	Morris
Old Forge East*	Morristown	Morris
Olde Queens Apartments	Highland Park	Middlesex
Orchard Gardens	Highland Park	Middlesex
Park-Lake Village	Parsippany-Troy Hills	Morris
Partridge Run	Parsippany-Troy Hills	Morris
Penn & Ovington	Edison	Middlesex
Redstone Apartments	Parsippany-Troy Hills	Morris
Ridgedale Gardens*	Piscataway	Middlesex
Riverview Apartments	Highland Park	Middlesex
Sharon Arms*	Washington	Mercer
Thornberry Apartments	Vineland	Cumberland
Toms River Apartments	Dover	Ocean
Wayne Gardens	Collingswood	Camden
Windsor Castle	East Windsor	Mercer
Woodbridge Terrace*	Woodbridge	Middlesex

Note: Asterisk (*) denotes development opened for occupancy during or after 1972.

each sample development. The objective was to make the survey "tight," while allowing sufficient slack to take into account potential refusals and nonresponses. As a result, every third unit was contacted. The sample ultimately yielded 227 responses.

Strengths and Limitations of Data Base

The data base has a number of advantages. First, the sample consists clearly and verifiably of garden apartments, and not other types of low-rise rentals. Second, it is ideal for longitudinal research. Because the complexes previously surveyed are not merely similar to those currently surveyed, but are in fact the very same ones, sampling bias is reduced. Finally, the large size of the previous survey produces a strong likelihood of cross tabulations yielding significant results.

The most prominent shortcoming of the sample is its lack of geographic scope. The results describe the characteristics, attitudes, and moving behavior only of garden apartment residents in New Jersey. A second limitation is that, being a non-Census survey, there is apt to be a sizeable number of people who refuse to answer either the entire questionnaire or certain parts of it.

Field Procedure

Immediately following a brief pre-test to uncover problems with the questionnaire that might later occur with more damaging consequences, the sampling process began, extending over the Summer and Fall of 1980. Apartment managers had already been contacted by a form letter indicating that interviewing would soon be taking place. If no negative response was forthcoming, it was interpreted as an approval.

Whether or not a contact yielded a successful interview, the following information was copied onto each survey cover sheet: date of initial contact, name of apartment complex, apartment number or address, and wherever possible, household surname(s), the latter acquired through examining mailboxes and front doors. Where households displayed no interest in granting an interview, the surname was not particularly important to acquire.

For those households who were not at home, would not answer the door, or would not grant an interview for the present, but did indicate an interest in being interviewed at a later time it was extremely important that the surname be acquired for the purpose of making telephone callbacks.

NOTES

1. Because of the enormous cost involved, the actual sample used here was the one-in-ten thousand, or one percent of the one-in-one hundred.

2. See U.S. Bureau of the Census, *Public Use Samples of Basic Records from the 1970 Census: Description and Documentations*, Washington, D.C.: U.S. Government Printing Office, 1972; John Goering, *Housing in America: The Characteristics and Uses of the Annual Housing Survey*, Washington, D.C.: U.S. Department of Housing and Urban Development, Office of Policy Development and Research, February 1980.

3. George Sternlieb, W. Patrick Beaton, Robert W. Burchell, James W. Hughes, Franklin J. James, David Listokin, and Duane Windsor, *Housing Development and Municipal Costs*, New Brunswick, N.J.: Center for Urban Policy Research, 1974.

4. George Sternlieb, *The Garden Apartment Development: A Municipal Cost-Revenue Analysis*, New Brunswick, N.J.: Rutgers University, Bureau of Economic Research, 1964. Data from this study, however, were not used here because: 1) the addresses or apartment numbers for each case were unknown; and 2) the questionnaire form was so brief that the instances in which comparisons could have been performed were rare.

Selected Bibliography On Garden Apartments

"A Leisure-Oriented Apartment Project Draws Upper-Income Tenants." *House and Home*, Vol. 38, No. 3, September 1970, p. 44.

American Society of Planning Officials. *Apartments in the Suburbs*. Chicago: American Society of Planning Officials, PAS Information Report No. 187, 1964.

"An Apartment Community for Married College Students." *House and Home*, Vol. 40, No. 4, October 1971, p. 42.

"An Apartment Project Planned and Run for Together-Minded People." *House and Home*, Vol. 41, No. 5, May 1972, pp. 90–93.

"A New Look in Low-Income Rental Housing." *House and Home*, Vol. 34, No. 3, September 1968, pp. 102–07.

"Apartments in Suburbia: Local Responsibility and Judicial Restraint." *Northwestern Law Review*, July/August 1964, pp. 334–42.

"Apartments: Is It Time to Rethink the Product?" *Housing* (formerly *House and Home*), Vol. 55, No. 4, April 1979, pp. 60–66.

"Apartments: They're Marching Again—But Not by the Numbers." *House and Home*, Vol. 52, No. 2, August 1977.

"A Shortcut to Estimating Garden Apartment Feasibility." *House and Home*, Vol. 28, No. 3, September 1965, pp. 84–85.

"A Western-Style Rental Project in an Eastern State Capital." *House and Home*, Vol. 42, No. 3, September 1972, pp. 90–93.

Babcock, Richard F. and Fred P. Bosselman. "Suburban Zoning and the Apartment Boom." *University of Pennsylvania Law Review*, Vol. 111, June 1963, pp. 1040–91.

Bair, Frederick H., Jr. *Intensity Zoning: Regulating Townhouses, Apartments, and Planned Developments*. PAS Information Report No. 314, Chicago: American Society of Planning Officials, 1964, pp. 232–35.

Bosselman, Fred P. "Apartments for Whom?" in *Planning 1964*, Selected Papers from the ASPO National Planning Conference, Boston, April 5–9, 1964, Chicago: American Society of Planning Officials, 1964, pp. 232–35.

Brooks, Mary E. *Lower-Income Housing: The Planners' Response*. PAS Information Report No. 282, Chicago: American Society of Planning Officials, July/August 1972.

Bucks County Planning Commission. *Multiple-Family Housing*. Doylestown, Pa.: County of Bucks, Planning Commission, 1959.

Bucks County Planning Commission. *Apartments: Analysis of Issues and Standards*. Doylestown, Pa.: County of Bucks, Planning Commission, June 1967.

Burchell, Robert W. and Listokin, David. *The Fiscal Impact Handbook: Estimating Local Costs and Revenues of Land Development*. New Brunswick, N.J.: Center for Urban Policy Research, 1978.

"Central Heating and Cooling in a Garden Apartment Project." *House and Home*, Vol. 34, No. 3, September 1968, pp. 130–31.

Clark, William H. "Apartments and Taxes." *New Jersey Municipalities*, July 1963, pp. 17–21.

Davidoff, Linda and Paul. "The Suburbs Have to Open Their Gates." in *Suburbia in Transition*, Louis Masotti and Jeffery K. Hadden, eds., New York: New Viewpoints, 1974, pp. 134–50.

"Development Plan Separates Traffic." *Architectural Record*, April 1965, pp. 218–20.

Fairfax County Planning Commission. *Student Contribution from Apartments and Mobile Homes*. Fairfax, Va.: County of Fairfax, Planning Commission, 1966.

Fall's Church Planning Office. *Apartments: Analysis of Multiple Family Dwellings, the Prospects and Recommendations*. Fall's Church, Va.: Township of Fall's Church, Planning Office, 1962.

"Family Apartments: There's a Huge Demand for Them. . .But It's a Tough Market to Build For." *House and Home*, Vol. 38, No. 5, November 1970, pp. 68–72.

"Findley Place Housing, Minneapolis." *Architectural Record*, March 1980, pp. 110–11.

"Five Rental Projects that Have Made It." *House and Home*, Vol. 45, No. 1, January 1973, pp. 78–93.

"For a Market that Needed Apartments: Amenities and a Park-Like Environment." *House and Home*, Vol. 41, No. 5, May 1972, pp. 82–85.

Freeman, Carl M. "Needed: New Planning Approaches for Suburban Communities." in *Planning 1964*, Selected Papers from the ASPO National Planning Conference, Boston, April 5–9, 1964, Chicago: American Society of Planning Officials, 1964, pp. 235–38.

Fullerton Development Services Department. *Apartment Survey*. Fullerton, Cal.: City of Fullerton, Development Services Department, 1972.

"Garden Apartments and Townhouses." *House and Home*, Vol. 23, No. 2, February 1963, pp. 85–109.

"Garden Apartments for Apartment Living." *Architectural Record*, September 1969, pp. 85–109.

"Garden Apartments for Tight Sites." *House and Home*, Vol. 35, No. 3, March 1969, pp. 92–101.

Green Brook Garden Apartment Committee. *Should Green Brook Permit Garden Apartments?* Green Brook, N.J.: Green Brook Garden Apartment Committee, December 1964.

Grossman, Howard, J. *Survey and Analysis of New Apartment Construction in a Suburban County*. Norristown, Pa.: County of Montgomery, Planning Commission, 1965.

Grossman, Howard J. "Apartments in Community Planning: A Suburban Area Case Study." *Urban Land*, January 1966, pp. 3–6.

Haar, Charles M. and Iatridis, Demetrius. *Housing the Poor in Suburbia: Public Policy at the Grass Roots*. Cambridge, Mass.: Ballinger, 1974.

"Heritage Gardens, Winthrop: Housing for the Elderly," *Architectural Record*, March 1980, pp. 114–17.

Holley, Paul N. *School Enrollment by Housing Type*. Chicago: American Society of Planning Officials, PAS Information Report No. 210, May 1966.

"Housing: One Government Agency Reaches for Good Architecture." *Architectural Record*, September 1972, pp. 145–53.

"How an Apartment Builder Taps the Young-Singles Market." *House and Home*, Vol. 36, No. 3, September 1969, pp. 98–101.

"How to Attract—and Keep—High-Rent Tenants." *House and Home*, Vol. 35, No. 6, June 1969, pp. 76–87.

"How to Make the Numbers Work in Apartments." *Professional Builder*, April 1978, pp. 92–103.

"How to Put Life Into Flat Apartment Sites." *House and Home*, Vol. 37, No. 6, June 1970, pp. 76–83.

"It's Time to Try Rentals." *Professional Builder*, February 1979, pp. 132–35.

"Landscaping: It's the Key Ingredient in Today's Better Apartment Projects." *House and Home*, Vol. 36, No. 4, October 1969, pp. 68–75.

Lauber, Daniel. *Recent Cases in Exclusionary Zoning*. PAS Information Report No. 292, Chicago: American Society of Planning Officials, June 1973.

"Low Income Housing with Amenities." *AIA Journal*, August 1972, p. 50.

"Low-Rise Lives." *Progressive Architecture*, October 1979, pp. 49–53.

Maryland-National Capital Park and Planning Commission. *Dwelling Unit Density, Population, and Potential Public School Enrollment Yield by Existing Zoning Classification: Montgomery County*, Silver Spring, Md.: Maryland-National Capital Park and Planning Commission, 1965.

Melamed, Anshel. "High-Rent Apartments in the Suburbs." *Urban Land*, October 1961, pp. 1–10.

Miami Valley Regional Planning Commission. *Apartments in the Region*. Dayton, Ohio: Miami Valley Regional Planning Commission, 1969.

Monmouth County Planning Board. *Multi-Family Housing in Monmouth County*. Freehold, N.J.: County of Monmouth, Planning Board, January 1973.

"Much More than Garden-Type Apartments." *Business Week*, March 14, 1970, pp. 46–47.

Nassau County Planning Commission. *Apartments: Their Past and Future Impact on Suburban Living Patterns*. Mineola, L.I., N.Y.: County of Nassau, Planning Commission, 1963.

New Jersey County and Local Government Study Commission. *Housing and Suburbs: Fiscal and Social Impact of Multifamily Development*. Trenton, N.J.: State of New Jersey, County and Municipal Government Study Commission, October 1974.

Neutze, Max. *The Suburban Apartment Boom*. Baltimore: Johns Hopkins University Press, 1968.

Newton Planning Department. *Apartment Study*. Newton, Mass.: Town of Newton, Planning Department, April 1971.

"No Profit in Rentals? These Do Just Fine." *House and Home*, Vol. 47, No. 9, September 1975, pp. 46–51.

Norcross, Carl and Hysom, John. *Apartment Communities: The Next Big Market*. Washington, D.C.: Urban Land Institute, Technical Bulletin #61, 1968.

O'Mara, W. Paul, et al. *Residential Development Handbook*, Washington, D.C.: Urban Land Institute, 1978, pp. 126–28.

Orange County Planning Commission. *Residential Uses, Students, and School Taxes in Orange County: A Cost-Benefit Analysis*. Goshen, N.Y.: County of Orange, Planning Commission, April 1975.

Parkins, John A., Jr. "Judicial Attitudes Toward Multiple-Family Dwellings: A Reappraisal." *Washington and Lee Law Review*, Spring 1971, pp. 220–30.

"Reed-Roberts Streets Housing, Pittsburgh." *Architectural Record*, October 1971, pp. 134–35.

"Rental Housing's Swing to Quality." *House and Home*, Vol. 25, No. 5, May 1964, pp. 89–117.

"Rezoning Suburbia." *Progressive Architecture*, May 1971, pp. 92–94.

Rhode Island Department of Community Affairs. *Apartment Occupant Survey: An Analysis and Review*. Providence, R.I.: State of Rhode Island, Department of Community Affairs, July 1972.

Rolde Company. *Garden Apartments and School Age Children*. Washington, D.C.: National Association of Home Builders, 1962.

Rose, Jerome G. and Rothman, Robert. *After Mount Laurel: The New Suburban Zoning*. New Brunswick, N.J.: Center for Urban Policy Research, 1977.

Rosenthal, Jack. "The Suburban Apartment Boom." in *Suburbia in Transition*, Louis Masotti and Jefferey K. Hadden, eds., New York: New Viewpoints, 1974.

Rubinowitz, Leonard S. *Low-Income Housing: Suburban Strategies*. Cambridge, Mass.: Ballinger, 1974.

St. Louis County Department of Planning. *Multi-Family Housing in St. Louis County: A Survey and Evaluation*. Clayton, Mo.: County of St. Louis, Department of Planning, 1965.

St. Louis County Department of Planning. *Apartments in St. Louis County: A Study of the Growth and Impact of Suburban Apartments in St. Louis County Prepared at the Request of the St. Louis County Council*. Clayton, Mo.: County of St. Louis, Department of Planning, February 1972.

Schafer, Robert. *The Suburbanization of Multifamily Housing*. Lexington, Mass.: Lexington Books, 1974.

Sternlieb, George. *The Garden Apartment Development: A Municipal Cost-Revenue Analysis*. New Brunswick, N.J.: Rutgers University, Bureau of Economic Research, 1964.

Sternlieb, George and Burchell, Robert W. "The Numbers Game: Forecasting Household Size." *Urban Land*, January 1974, pp. 3–20.

Sternlieb, George et al. *Housing Development and Municipal Costs*. New Brunswick, N.J.: Center for Urban Policy Research, 1974.

"Surprise: Luxury Housing for Empty Nesters Uncovers a Broader Market." *House and Home*, Vol. 38, No. 5, November 1970, pp. 30–32.

Sussna, Stephen. "What the Courts Say About Anti-Apartment Zoning." *Buildings*, March 1972, pp. 64–65.

Syracuse, Lee A. *Arguments for Apartment Zoning*. Washington, D.C.: National Association of Home Builders, 1968.

"The Case for Investing in a Good Apartment Environment." *House and Home*, Vol. 34, No. 3, September 1968, pp. 92–101.

"The Demand for Good New Apartments." *House and Home*, Vol. 18, No. 4, October 1960, pp. 90–102.

"The Multifamily Boom in Suburbia." *House and Home*, Vol. 33, No. 2, February 1968, p. 71.

"The New Mix: Garden Apartments and the Recreation Bit." *House and Home*, Vol. 39, No. 2, February 1971, pp. 50–57.

"The Tenants' Point of View: A Survey of Garden Apartment Residents' Attitudes in Five Cities." *Urban Land*, February 1970, pp. 3–8.

"Top-of-the-Line Apartments for a Forgotten Market." *Housing*, Vol. 57, No. 2, February 1980, pp. 68–72.

Westchester County Department of Planning. *School Taxes and Residential Development*. White Plains, N.Y.: County of Westchester, Department of Planning, November 1971.

"What Grabs the Typical Garden Apartment Tenant?" *House and Home*, Vol. 34, No. 5, November 1968, pp. 94–95.

Woodbridge Department of Planning and Development. *Garden Apartment Evaluation*. Woodbridge, N.J.: Township of Woodbridge, Planning Department, August 1968.

"Woodlake: A Small Community Complete Within Itself." *Architectural Record*, January 1966, pp. 164–65.

"You Won't Even Consider Apartment? First, Consider This Advice." *Housing*, Vol. 59, No. 4, April 1981, p. 18.

Index